Praise for *The iPhone Developer's Cookbook*

"This book would be a bargain at ten times its price! If you are writing iPhone software, it will save you weeks of development time. Erica has included dozens of crisp and clear examples illustrating essential iPhone development techniques and many others that show special effects going way beyond Apple's official documentation."
—Tim Burks, iPhone Software Developer, TootSweet Software

"Erica Sadun's technical expertise lives up to the Addison-Wesley name. *The iPhone Developer's Cookbook* is a comprehensive walkthrough of iPhone development that will help anyone out, from beginners to more experienced developers. Code samples and screenshots help punctuate the numerous tips and tricks in this book."
—Jacqui Cheng, Associate Editor, *Ars Technica*

"We make our living writing this stuff and yet I am humbled by Erica's command of her subject matter and the way she presents the material: pleasantly informal, then very appropriately detailed technically. This is a going to be the Petzold book for iPhone developers."
—Daniel Pasco, Lead Developer and CEO, Black Pixel Luminance

"*The iPhone Developer's Cookbook: Building Applications with the iPhone SDK* should be the first resource for the beginning iPhone programmer, and is the best supplemental material to Apple's own documentation."
—Alex C. Schaefer, Lead Programmer, ApolloIM, iPhone Application Development Specialist, MeLLmo, Inc

"Erica's book is a truly great resource for Cocoa Touch developers. This book goes far beyond the documentation on Apple's Web site, and she includes methods that give the developer a deeper understanding of the iPhone OS, by letting them glimpse at what's going on behind the scenes on this incredible mobile platform."
—John Zorko, Sr. Software Engineer, Mobile Devices

The iPhone™ Developer's Cookbook

The iPhone™ Developer's Cookbook

Building Applications with the iPhone SDK

Erica Sadun

✦✦ Addison-Wesley

Upper Saddle River, NJ • Boston • Indianapolis • San Francisco
New York • Toronto • Montreal • London • Munich • Paris • Madrid
Cape Town • Sydney • Tokyo • Singapore • Mexico City

The publisher offers excellent discounts on this book when ordered in quantity for bulk purchases or special sales, which may include electronic versions and/or custom covers and content particular to your business, training goals, marketing focus, and branding interests. For more information, please contact:

U.S. Corporate and Government Sales
(800) 382-3419
corpsales@pearsontechgroup.com

For sales outside the United States please contact:

International Sales
international@pearsoned.com

Visit us on the Web: informit.com/aw

Library of Congress Cataloging-in-Publication Data:

Sadun, Erica.
  The iPhone developer's cookbook : building mobile applications with the iPhone SDK / Erica Sadun.
      p. cm.
  ISBN-10: 0-321-55545-7 (pbk. : alk. paper)
  ISBN-13: 978-0-321-55545-8 (pbk. : alk. paper) 1. iPhone (Smartphone)–Programming. 2. Computer software–Development. 3. Mobile computing. I. Title.
  QA76.8.I64S33 2009
  005.26—dc22

2008030294

ISBN-13: 978-0-321-55545-8
ISBN-10: 0-321-55545-7

Text printed in the United States on recycled paper at RR Donnelley in Crawfordsville, Indiana.
First printing October 2008

Editor-in-Chief
Karen Gettman

Senior Acquisitions Editor
Chuck Toporek

Senior Development Editor
Chris Zahn

Managing Editor
Kristy Hart

Project Editor
Chelsey Marti

Copy Editor
Keith Cline

Indexers
Cheryl Lenser, Erika Millen

Proofreader
San Dee Phillips

Technical Reviewers
Tim Burks, Daniel Pasco, Alex C. Schaefer

Publishing Coordinator
Romny French

Cover Designer
Gary Adair

Composition
Nonie Ratcliff

❖

I dedicate this book with love to my husband, Alberto, who has put up with too many gadgets and too many SDKs over the years while remaining both kind and patient at the end of the day.

❖

Contents

Preface

Few platforms match the iPhone's unique developer technologies. It combines OS X-based mobile computing with an innovative multitouch screen, location awareness, an onboard accelerometer, and more. When Apple introduced the iPhone Cocoa Touch SDK beta in early March 2008, developers responded in numbers that brought Apple's servers to its knees. Apple delivered more than one hundred thousand SDK downloads in less than one week. The *iPhone Developer's Cookbook* was written to address this demand, providing an accessible resource for those new to iPhone programming.

Who This Book Is For

This book is written for new iPhone developers with projects to get done and a new unfamiliar SDK in their hands. Although each programmer brings different goals and experiences to the table, most developers end up solving similar tasks in their development work: "How do I build a table?"; "How do I create a secure keychain entry?"; "How do I search the Address Book?"; "How do I move between views?"; and "How do I use Core Location?"

The *iPhone Developer's Cookbook* is aimed squarely at anyone just getting started with iPhone programming. With its clear, fully documented examples, it will get you up to speed and working productively. It presents already tested ready-to-use solutions, letting programmers focus on the specifics of their application rather than on boilerplate tasks.

How This Book Is Structured

This book offers single-task recipes for the most common issues new iPhone developers face: laying out interface elements, responding to users, accessing local data sources, and connecting to the Internet. The cookbook approach delivers cut-and-paste convenience. Programmers can add source recipes into their projects and then customize them to their needs. Each chapter groups related tasks together. Readers can jump directly to the kind of solution they're looking for without having to decide which class or framework best matches that problem.

Here's a rundown of what you'll find in this book's chapters:

- **Chapter 1: Getting Started with the iPhone SDK**

  Chapter 1 introduces the iPhone SDK and explores the iPhone as a delivery platform, limitations and all. It explains the breakdown of the standard iPhone application and enables you to build your first Hello World style samples.

- **Chapter 2: Views**

  Chapter 2 introduces iPhone views, objects that live on your screen. You see how to lay out, create, and order your views to create backbones for your iPhone applications. You read about view hierarchies, geometries, and animations as well as how users can interact with views through touch.

- **Chapter 3: View Controllers**

  The iPhone paradigm in a nutshell is this: small screen, big virtual worlds. In Chapter 3, you discover the various UIViewController classes that enable you to enlarge and order the virtual spaces your users interact with. You learn how to let these powerful objects perform all the heavy lifting when navigating between iPhone application screens.

- **Chapter 4: Alerting Users**

  The iPhone offers many ways to provide users with a heads up, from pop-up dialogs and progress bars to audio pings and status bar updates. Chapter 4 shows how to build these indications into your applications and expand your user-alert vocabulary.

- **Chapter 5: Basic Tables**

  Tables provide an interaction class that works particularly well on a small, cramped device. Many, if not most, apps that ship with the iPhone and iPod touch center on tables, including Settings, YouTube, Stocks, and Weather. Chapter 5 shows how iPhone tables work, what kinds of tables are available to you as a developer, and how you can use table features in your own programs.

- **Chapter 6: Advanced Tables**

  iPhone tables do not begin and end with simple scrolling lists. You can build tables with titled sections, with multiple scrolling columns, and more. You can add controls such as switches, create translucent cell backgrounds, and include custom fonts. Chapter 6 starts from where "Basic Tables" left off. It introduces advanced table recipes for you to use in your iPhone programs.

- **Chapter 7: Media**

  As you'd expect, the iPhone can load and display media from a wide variety of formats. It does music; it does movies. It handles images and Web pages. You can present PDF documents and photo albums and more. Chapter 7 shows way after way that you can import or download data into your program and display that data using the iPhone's multitouch interface.

- **Chapter 8: Control**

  The UIControl class provides the basis for many iPhones interactive elements, including buttons, text fields, sliders, and switches. Chapter 8 introduces controls and their use, both through well-documented SDK calls and through less-documented ones.

- **Chapter 9: People, Places, and Things**

  In addition to standard user interface controls and media components that you'd see on any computer, the iPhone SDK provides a number of tightly focused developer solutions specific to iPhone and iPod touch delivery. Chapter 9 introduces the most useful of these, including Address Book access ("people"), core location ("places"), and sensors ("things").

- **Chapter 10: Connecting to Services**

  As an Internet-connected device, the iPhone is particularly suited to subscribing to Web-based services. Apple has lavished the platform with a solid grounding in all kinds of network computing services and their supporting technologies. The iPhone SDK handles sockets, password keychains, SQL access, XML processing, and more. Chapter 10 surveys common techniques for network computing and offering recipes that simplify day-to-day tasks.

- **Chapter 11: One More Thing: Programming Cover Flow**

  Although Cover Flow is not officially included in the iPhone SDK, it offers one of the nicest and most beautiful features of the iPhone experience. With Cover Flow, you can offer your users a gorgeously intense visual selection experience that puts standard scrolling lists to shame. Chapter 11 introduces Cover Flow and shows how you can use it in your applications.

Prerequisites

Here are basics you need on hand to begin programming for the iPhone or iPod touch:

- **A copy of Apple's iPhone SDK**. Download your copy of the iPhone SDK from Apple's iPhone Dev Center (http://developer.apple.com/iphone/). You must join Apple's (free) developer program before you download.

- **An iPhone or iPod touch.** Although Apple supplies a simulator as part of its SDK, you really do need to have an actual unit to test on if you're going to develop any serious software. You'll be able to use the cable that shipped with your iPhone or iPod touch to tether your unit to the computer and install the software you've built.

- **An Apple iPhone Developer License.** You will not be able to test your software on an actual iPhone or iPod touch until you join Apple's iPhone Developer program (http://developer.apple.com/iphone/program). Members receive a certificate that allows them to sign their applications and download them to the platforms in question for testing and debugging. The program costs $99/year for individuals and companies, $299/year for in-house enterprise development.

- **An Intel-based Macintosh running Leopard.** The SDK requires a Macintosh running Leopard OS X 10.5.3 or later. Apple requires an Intel-based computer in 32-bit mode. Many features do not work properly on PPC-based Macs or Intel Macs in 64-bit mode. Reserve plenty of disk space and at least 1GB of RAM.

- **At least one available USB 2.0 port.** This enables you to tether your development iPhone or iPod touch to your computer for file transfer and testing.

- **An Internet connection.** This connection enables you to test your programs with a live WiFi connection as well as with EDGE.

- **Familiarity with Objective-C.** The SDK is built around Objective-C 2.0. The language is based on standard C with object-oriented extensions. If you have any object-oriented and C background, making the move to Objective-C is both quick and simple. Consult any Objective-C/Cocoa reference book to get up to speed.

Note

Although the SDK supports development for the iPhone and iPod touch, as well as possible yet-to-be-announced platforms, this book refers to the target platform as iPhone for the sake of simplicity. When developing for the touch, most material is applicable. This excludes certain obvious features such as telephony and onboard speakers. This book attempts to note such exceptions in the manuscript.

Contacting the Author

If you have any comments or questions about this book, please drop me an e-mail message at erica@ericasadun.com or stop by www.ericasadun.com. My Web site hosts many of the applications discussed in this book. Please feel free to visit, download software, read documentation, and leave your comments.

Acknowledgments

This book would not exist without the efforts of Chuck Toporek, Romny French, Chris Zahn, and the entire AW production team (specifically Gary Adair, Keith Cline, Kristy Hart, Cheryl Lenser, Chelsey Marti, Jake McFarland, and Erika Millen).

Thanks go as well to Neil Salkind, my agent of many years, to the tech reviewers who helped keep this book in the realm of sanity rather than wishful thinking, and to all my colleagues at TUAW and the Digital Media/Inside iPhone blog.

I am deeply indebted to the wide community of iPhone developers, including Alex Schaefer, Nick Penree, James Cuff, Jay Freeman, Mark Montecalvo, August Joki, Max Weisel, Optimo, Kevin Brosius, Planetbeing, Pytey, Roxfan, UnterPerro, Youssef Francis, Bryan Henry, Daniel Peebles, ChronicProductions, Greg Hartstein, Emanuele Vulcano, np101137, and Sean Heber, among many others too numerous to name individually. Their techniques, suggestions, and feedback helped make this book possible.

Special thanks go out to my family and friends, who supported me through month after month of new beta releases and who patiently put up with my unexplained absences and frequent howls of despair. I appreciate you all hanging in there with me. And thanks to my children for their steadfastness, even as they learned that a hunched back and the sound of clicking keys is a pale substitute for a proper mother.

About the Author

Erica Sadun has written, coauthored, and contributed to about three dozen books about technology, particularly in the areas of programming, digital video, and digital photography. An unrepentant geek, Sadun has never met a gadget she didn't need. Her checkered past includes run-ins with NeXT, Newton, iPhone, and myriad successful and unsuccessful technologies. When not writing, she and her geek husband parent three adorable geeks-in-training, who regard their parents with restrained bemusement.

Introducing the iPhone SDK

The iPhone and iPod touch introduce innovative mobile platforms that are a joy to program. They are the first members of Apple's new family of pocket-based computing devices. Despite their diminutive proportions, they run a first-class version of OS X with a rich and varied SDK that enables you to design, implement, and realize a wide range of applications. For your projects, you can take advantage of the iPhone's multitouch interface and fabulous onboard features using Xcode. In this chapter, you discover how the SDK is put together and learn to build your first iPhone-based Hello World applications.

Apple's iPhone SDK

Are you ready to start programming for the iPhone? You'll need Apple's iPhone Software Developer Kit (SDK), which is free and available to members of Apple's online (free) developer program. Download your copy of the iPhone SDK from Apple's site at http://developer.apple.com/iphone. It consists of several components that form the basis of the iPhone development environment. These components include the following software:

- **Xcode.** Xcode is the most important tool in the iPhone development arsenal. It provides a comprehensive project development and management environment, complete with source editing, comprehensive documentation, and a graphical debugger. Xcode is built around several open source GNU tools, namely gcc (compiler) and gdb (debugger).

- **Instruments.** Instruments profiles how iPhone applications work under the hood. It samples memory usage and monitors performance. This lets you identify and target problem areas in your applications and work on their efficiency. Instruments offers graphical time-based performance plots that show where your applications are using the most resources. Instruments is build around the open source DTrace package developed by Sun Microsystems. Instruments plays a critical role in tracking down memory leaks and making sure your applications run efficiently on the iPhone platform.

- **Dashcode.** Dashcode creates stand-alone Web-based applications that run outside of a traditional browser environment. Conceptually, the iPhone version works just like the desktop version, complete with layout and debugging tools. Dashboard provides a Web-based development approach rather than native application compilation and is not covered in this book.

- **Simulator.** The iPhone Simulator runs on the Macintosh and enables you to create and test applications on your desktop. You can do this without connecting to an actual iPhone or iPod touch. The Simulator offers the same API used on the iPhone and provides a preview of how your concept designs will look. When working with the Simulator, Xcode compiles Intel x86 code that runs natively on the Macintosh rather than ARM-based code used on the iPhone.

- **Interface Builder.** Interface Builder (IB) provides a rapid prototyping tool that enables you to lay out user interfaces graphically and link to those prebuilt interfaces from your Xcode source code. With IB, you draw out your interface using visual design tools and then connect those onscreen elements to objects and method calls in your application.

Together, the components of this iPhone SDK suite enable you to develop both traditional and Web-based applications. From a native application developer's point of view, the most important components are Xcode and the Simulator, with Instruments providing an essential tuning tool. In addition to these tools, there's an important piece not on this list. This piece ships with the SDK but is easy to overlook. I refer to Cocoa Touch.

Cocoa Touch is the library of classes provided by Apple for rapid iPhone application development. This library, which takes the form of a number of framework libraries, enables you to build graphical event-driven applications using user interface elements such as windows, text, and tables. Cocoa Touch on the iPhone is analogous to AppKit on Mac OS X and supports creating rich, reusable interfaces on the iPhone.

Many developers are surprised by the size of iPhone applications; they're tiny. Cocoa Touch's library support is the big reason for this. By letting Cocoa Touch handle all the heavy UI lifting, your applications can focus on getting their individual tasks done. The result is compact, focused code that does a single job at a time.

Assembling iPhone Projects

iPhone Xcode projects contain varied standard and custom components. Figure 1-1 shows a typical project. Project elements include source code, linked frameworks, and media such as image and audio files. Xcode compiles your source, links it to the frameworks, and builds an application bundle suitable for iPhone installation. It adds your media to this application bundle, enabling your program to access that media as the application runs on the iPhone.

iPhone code is normally written in Objective-C 2.0. This is an object-oriented superset of ANSI C, which was developed from a mix of C and Smalltalk. If you're unfamiliar with the language, Apple provides several excellent online tutorials at its iPhone developer site. Among these are an introduction to object-oriented programming with Objective-C and an Objective-C 2.0 reference. These will quickly get you up to speed with the language.

Frameworks are software libraries provided by Apple that supply the reusable class definitions for Cocoa Touch. Add frameworks to Xcode by dragging them onto your project's Frameworks folder. After including the appropriate header files (such as UIKit/UIKit.h or QuartzCore/QuartzCore.h), you call their routines from your program.

Associated media might include audio, image, and video files to be bundled with the package as well as text-based files that help define your application to the iPhone operating system. Drop media files into your project and reference them from your code.

The project shown in Figure 1-1 is an especially simple one. It consists of a single source file (main.m) along with the default iPhone project frameworks (UIKit, Foundation, and Core Graphics) and a few supporting files (helloworld.png, Default.png, Icon.png, Info.plist). Together these items form all the materials needed to create a basic Hello World–style application.

Note

The HelloWorld_Prefix.pch file is created automatically by Xcode. It contains precompiled header files. NIB and XIB files (.nib, .xib) refer to files created in Interface Builder. These user interface definition files are linked to your application and called by your app at runtime.

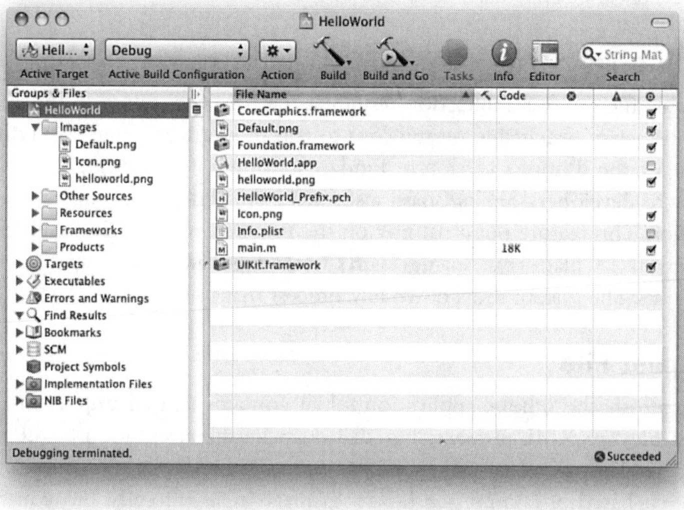

Figure 1-1   Xcode projects bring source code, frameworks, and media together to form the basis for iPhone applications.

iPhone Application Components

Like their Macintosh cousins, iPhone applications live in application bundles. Application bundles are just folders named with an .app extension. Your program's contents and resources reside in this folder, including the compiled executable, supporting media (such as images and audio), and a few special files that describe the application to the OS. The folder is treated by the operating system as a single bundle.

Application Folder Hierarchy

Unlike the Mac, iPhone bundles do not use Contents and Resources folders to store data or a MacOS folder for the executable. All materials appear at the top level of the folder. For example, instead of putting a language support .lproj folder into Contents/Resources/, Xcode places it directly into the top .app folder. You can still use subfolders to organize your project, but these are ad hoc user-defined folders and do not follow any standard.

The iPhone SDK's core OS support includes the NSBundle class. This class makes it easy to locate your application's root folder and to navigate down to your custom sub-folders to point to and load resources.

> **Note**
>
> As on a Macintosh, user domains mirror system ones. Official Apple-distributed applications reside in the primary /Applications folder. Third-party applications live in /var/mobile/Applications instead. For the most part, the underlying UNIX file system is obscured by the iPhone's sandbox, which is discussed later in this section.

The Executable

The executable file of your application resides at the top-level folder of the application bundle. It must carry executable permissions to run properly and must be authenticated by SpringBoard, the iPhone's version of Finder. Starting with firmware 1.2, which was released only to developers, SpringBoard instituted a watchdog feature to prevent arbitrary code execution. This feature put a damper on the use of command-line utilities that you find on other UNIX platforms. SpringBoard's watchdog feature also added memory utilization limits. The system shuts down any process that uses too many system resources.

The Info.plist File

As on a Macintosh, the iPhone application folder contains that all-important Info.plist file. Info.plist files are XML property lists that describe the application to the operating system. Property lists store key-value pairs for many different purposes and can be saved in readable text-based or compressed binary formats. In an Info.plist file, you specify the application's executable (CFBundleExecutable) and identifier (CFBundleIdentifier). This identifier is critical to proper behavior and execution.

Use the standard Apple domain naming formats (for example, com.sadun.appname) in your applications by editing your project's settings in Xcode (see Figure 1-2). Specify your personal domain and let Xcode append the product identifier. To change identifiers, right-click your project file in Xcode and choose Get Info from the pop-up. Use the Search field to find `Product_Name` and then edit that value as needed.

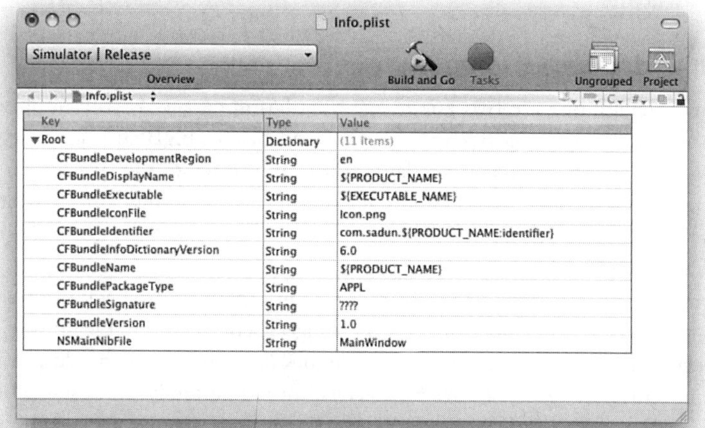

Figure 1-2   Customize your application's bundle identifier by editing the Info.plist file. The PRODUCT_NAME identifier is specified in your project's settings.

The product identifier enables you to communicate with other applications and to properly register your application with SpringBoard, the "Finder" of the iPhone. SpringBoard runs the home screen from which you launch your applications. The product identifier also forms the basis for the built-in preferences system, the user defaults.

Applications preferences are automatically stored in the user Library (in /var/mobile/ Library/Preferences) using the application's identifier. This identifier is appended with the .plist extension (for example, com.sadun.appname.plist), and the preferences are stored using a binary plist format. You can read a binary plist by transferring it to a Macintosh. Use Apple's plutil utility to convert from binary to a text-based XML format: `plutil -convert xml1 plistfile`. Apple uses binary plists to lower storage requirements and increase system performance.

As with the Macintosh, Info.plist files offer further flexibility and are highly customizable. With them, you can set SpringBoard variables (for example, `SBUsesNetwork`) or specify how your icon should display (for example, `UIPrerenderedIcon`). Some SpringBoard variables enable you to define multiple roles for a single application. For example, the Photos and Camera utilities are actually the same application, MobileSlideShow, playing separate "roles." You can also specify whether the application is hidden from view.

Other standard Info.plist keys include `UIStatusBarStyle` for setting the look and color of the status bar and `UIStatusBarHidden` for hiding it altogether. `UIInterfaceOrientation` lets you override the accelerometer to create a landscape-only (`UIInterfaceOrientationLandscapeRight`) presentation. Register your custom application URL schemes (for example, myCustomApp://) by setting `CFBundleURLTypes`. See Chapter 10, "Connecting to Services," for more information about URL schemes.

The Icon and Default Images

Icon.png and Default.png are two key image files. Icon.png acts as your application's icon, the image used to represent the application on the SpringBoard home screen. Default.png (officially known as your "launch image") provides the splash screen displayed during application launch. Unlike Default.png, the icon filename is arbitrary. If you'd rather not use "icon.png," set the `CFBundleIconFile` key in your Info.plist file to whatever filename you want to use.

Apple recommends matching Default.png to your application's background. Many developers use Default.png launch images for a logo splash or for a "Please wait" message. These go against Apple's human interface guidelines (launch images should provide visual continuity, not advertising or excuses for delays) but are perfectly understandable uses.

The "official" application icon size is 57-by-57 pixels. SpringBoard automatically scales larger art. Provide flat (not glossy) art with squared corners. SpringBoard smoothes and rounds those corners and adds an automatic gloss and shine effect. If for some compelling reason you need to use prerendered art, set `UIPrerenderedIcon` to <true/> in your Info.plist file.

> **Note**
>
> If you plan to submit your application to App Store, you need to create a high-resolution (512-by-512 pixel) version of your icon. Although you can up sample your 57-by-57 icon.png art, it won't look good. Going the other way allows you to maintain high-quality art that you can compress to your icon as needed.

XIB (NIB) files

Interface Builder creates XIB (also called NIB on the Macintosh) files that store precooked addressable user interface classes. These files appear at the top level of your application bundle and are called directly from your program. At the time of this writing, the Interface Builder filename has not yet stabilized, although the .xib (Xcode Interface Builder) extension seems to be winning out for iPhone.

> **Note**
>
> When you develop programs that do not use XIB or NIB Interface-Builder bundles, remove the `NSMainNibFile` key from Info.plist and discard the automatically generated MainWindow.xib file from to your project.

Files Not Found in the Application Bundle

As with the Macintosh, things you do not find inside the application bundle include preferences files (generally stored in the application sandbox in Library/Preferences), application plug-ins (stored in /System/Library at this time and not available for general development), and documents (stored in the sandbox in Documents).

Another thing that seems to be missing (at least from the Macintosh programmer point of view) is Application Support folders. Copy support data, which more rightfully would be placed into an Application Support structure, to your Documents or Library folders.

Sandboxes

The iPhone OS restricts all SDK development to application "sandboxes" for the sake of security. The iPhone sandbox limits your application's access to the file system to a minimal set of folders, network resources, and hardware. It's like attending an overly restrictive school with a paranoid principal:

- Your application can play in its own sandbox, but it can't visit anyone else's sandbox.

- You cannot share toys. You cannot share data. You cannot mess in the administrative offices. Your files must stay in the folders provided to you by the sandbox, and you cannot copy files to or from other application folders.

- Your application owns its own Library, Documents, and /tmp folders. These mimic the standard folders you'd use on a less-restrictive platform but specifically limits your ability to write and access this data.

In addition to these limitations, your application must be signed digitally and authenticate itself to the operating system with a coded application identifier, which you must create at Apple's developer program site. On the bright side, sandboxing ensures that all program data gets synced whenever your device is plugged into its home computer. On the downside, at this time Apple has not clarified how that synced data can be accessed from a Windows- or Macintosh-based desktop application. (Chapter 7, "Media," discusses recovering data from the mdbackup files created by iTunes and its Mobile Devices framework.)

Note

Sandbox specification files (using the .sb extension) are stored in /var/mobile/Applications along with the actual sandbox folders. These files control privileges such as read-and-write access to various bits of the file system. If such a possibility should present itself, do not edit this file directly. You will render your application unusable. An exemplar sandbox file usually appears in /usr/share/sandbox.

Platform Limitations

When talking about mobile platforms like the iPhone, several concerns always arise, such as storage, interaction limits, and battery life. Mobile platforms can't offer the same disk space their desktop counterparts do. And along with storage limits, constrained interfaces and energy consumption place very real restrictions on what you as a developer can accomplish.

With the iPhone, you can't design for a big screen, for a mouse, for a physical keyboard, or even for a physical always-on A/C power supply. Instead, platform realities must shape and guide your development. Fortunately, Apple has done an incredible job designing a new platform that somehow leverages flexibility from its set of limited storage, limited interaction controls, and limited battery life.

Storage Limits

The iPhone hosts a powerful yet compact OS X installation. Although the entire iPhone OS fills no more than a few hundred megabytes of space—almost nothing in today's culture of large operating system installations—it provides an extensive framework library. These frameworks of precompiled routines enable iPhone users to run a diverse range of compact applications, from telephony to audio playback, from e-mail to Web browsing. The iPhone provides just enough programming support to create flexible interfaces while keeping system files trimmed down to fit neatly within tight storage limits.

Data Access Limits

Every iPhone application is sandboxed. That is, it lives in strictly regulated portion of the file system. Your program cannot access from other applications and from certain cordoned-off folders including the onboard iTunes library. It can, however, access any data that is freely available over the Internet when the iPhone is connected to a network.

Memory Limits

On the iPhone, memory management is critical. The iPhone does not support disk-swap-based virtual memory. When your run out of memory, the iPhone reboots—as Apple puts it, random reboots are probably not the user experience you were hoping for. With no swap file, you must carefully manage your memory demands and be prepared for the iPhone OS to terminate your application if it starts swallowing too much memory at once. You must also take care as to what resources your applications use. Too many high-resolution images or audio files can bring your application into the autoterminate zone.

> **Note**
>
> Xcode automatically optimizes your PNG images using the pngcrush utility shipped with the SDK. (You'll find the program in the iPhoneOS platform folders in /Developer. Run it from the command line with the `-iphone` switch to convert standard PNG files to iPhone-formatted ones.) For this reason, use PNG images in your iPhone apps where possible as your preferred image format.

Interaction Limits

Losing physical input devices and working with a tiny screen doesn't mean you lose interaction flexibility. With multitouch, you can build user interfaces that defy the rules. The iPhone's touch technology means you can design applications complete with text input and pointer control using a virtual screen that's much larger than the actual physical reality held in your palm.

A smart autocorrecting onscreen keyboard and an accelerometer that detects orientation provide just two of the key technologies that separate the iPhone from the rest of the mobile computing pack. What this means, however, is that you need to cut back on things such as text input and scrolling windows.

Focus your design efforts on easy-to-tap interfaces rather than on desktop-like mimicry. Remember, you can use just one window at a time—unlike desktop applications that are free to use multiwindow displays.

Note

The iPhone screen supports up to five touches at a time, although it's rare to find any application that uses more than two at once.

Energy Limits

For mobile platforms, you cannot ignore energy limitations. That being said, Apple's SDK features help to design your applications to limit CPU use and avoid running down the battery. A smart use of technology (for example, like properly suspending programs) lets your applications play nicely on the iPhone and keeps your software from burning holes in users' pockets (sometimes almost literally). Some programs when left running produce such high levels of waste heat that the phone becomes hot to the touch and the battery quickly runs down. The Camera application is one notable example.

Application Limits

Apple has instituted a strong "one-application-at-a-time" policy. That means as a third-party developer you cannot develop applications that run in the background like Apple's Mail and Phone utilities. Each time your program runs, it must clean up and metaphorically get out of Dodge before passing control on to the next application selected by the user. You can't leave a daemon running that checks for new messages or that sends out periodic updates. An "Open SDK" created by hobbyists exists that bypasses this limitation, but applications built with those tools cannot be added to and sold through the iPhone App Store.

On the other hand, Apple does support push data from Web services. Registered services can push badge numbers and messages to users, letting them know that data is waiting on those servers.

> **Note**
>
> According to the iPhone Terms of Service, you may not create external frameworks for your iPhone application or use Cocoa's plug-in architecture for applications submitted to the App Store.

User Behavior Limits

Although it's not a physical device-based limitation, get used to the fact that iPhone users approach phone-based applications sporadically. They enter a program, use it quickly, and then leave just as quickly. The handheld nature of the device means you must design your applications around short interaction periods and prepare for your application to be cut off as a user sticks the phone back into a pocket. Save your application state between sessions and relaunch quickly to approximate the same task your user was performing the last time the program was run.

SDK Limitations

As you might expect, building applications for the iPhone is similar to building applications for the Macintosh. You use Objective-C 2.0. You compile by linking to an assortment of frameworks. In other ways, the iPhone SDK is limited. Here are some key points to keep in mind:

- **Garbage Collection is MIA and probably always will be.** Apple insiders suggest that platform limitations simply do not allow for garbage collection to be implemented in any sane and useful manner. You are responsible for retaining and releasing objects in memory.

- **Many libraries are only partly implemented.** Core Animation is partially available through the Quartz Core framework, but many classes and methods remain missing in action. The lesson here is that you're working in early-release software. Work around the missing pieces and make sure to submit your bug reports to Apple so that it (we hope) fixes the parts that need to be used. Be aware that Apple has deliberately cut access to some proprietary classes.

- **The public SDK frameworks are not as varied as the private ones.** In the original iPhone open SDK jailbreak world, you used to be able to call on the iTunes Store frameworks to search the mobile store and the Celestial framework for easy QuickTime-like audio/video playback. With the debut of the official SDK, these are no longer publicly available, and Apple has limited third-party development strictly to a public framework subset.

Programming Paradigms

iPhone programming centers on two important paradigms: objected-oriented programming and the Model-View-Controller (MVC) design pattern. The iPhone SDK is designed around supporting these concepts in the programs you build. To do this, it has introduced delegation (**controller**) and data source methods (**model**) and customized view classes (**view**). Here is a quick rundown of some important iPhone/Cocoa Touch design vocabulary used through this book.

Object-Oriented Programming

Objective-C is heavily based on Smalltalk, one of the most historically important object-oriented languages. Object-oriented programming uses the concepts of encapsulation and inheritance to build reusable classes with published external interfaces and private internal implementation. You build your applications out of concrete classes that can be stacked together like Lego toys, because it's always made clear which pieces fit together through class declarations.

Multiple inheritance is an important feature of Objective-C's approach to object-oriented programming. iPhone classes can inherit behaviors and data types from more than one parent. Take the class UITextView, for example. It's both text *and* a view. Like other view classes, it can appear onscreen. It has set boundaries and a given opacity. At the same time, it inherits text-specific behavior. You can easily change its display font, color, or text size. Objective-C and Cocoa Touch combine these behaviors into a single easy-to-use class.

Model-View-Controller

MVC separates the way an onscreen object looks from the way it behaves. An onscreen button (the view) has no intrinsic meaning. It's just a button that users can push. That view's controller acts as an intermediary. It connects user interactions such as button taps to targeted methods in your application, which is the model. The application supplies and stores meaningful data and responds to interactions such as these button taps by producing some sort of useful result.

Each MVC element works separately. You might swap out a push button with, for example, a toggle switch without changing your model or controller. The program continues to work as before, but the GUI now has a different look. Alternatively, you might leave the interface as is and change your application where a button triggers a different kind of response in your model. Separating these elements enables you to build maintainable program components that can be updated independently.

The MVC paradigm on the iPhone breaks down into the following categories:

- **View.** View components are provided by children of the UIView class and by its associated (and somewhat misnamed) UIViewController class.

- **Controller.** The controller behavior is implemented through three key technologies: delegation, target-action, and notification.
- **Model.** Model methods supply data through protocols such as data sourcing and meaning by implementing callback methods triggered by the controller.

Together these three elements form the backbone of the MVC programming paradigm. Let's look at each of these elements of the iPhone MVC design pattern in a bit more detail. The following sections introduce each element and its supporting classes.

View Classes

The iPhone builds its views based on two important classes: `UIView` and `UIViewController`. These two classes are responsible for defining and placing all onscreen elements.

As views draw things on your screen, `UIView` represents the most abstract view class. Nearly all user interface classes descend from `UIView` and its parent `UIResponder`. Views provide all the visual application elements that make up your application. Important `UIView` classes include `UITextViews`, `UIImageViews`, `UIAlertViews`, and so forth. The `UIWindow` class, a kind of `UIView`, provides a viewport into your application and provides the root for your display.

Because of their onscreen nature, all views establish a frame of some sort. This is an onscreen rectangle that defines the space each view occupies. The rectangle is established by the view's origin and extent.

Views are hierarchical and are built with trees of subviews. You can display a view by setting it as your main window's content view, or you can add it to another view by using the `addSubview` method to assign a child to a parent. You can think about views as attaching bits of transparent film to a screen, each of which has some kind of drawing on it. Views added last are the ones you see right away. Views added earlier may be obscured by other views sitting on top of them.

Despite the name, the `UIViewController` class does not act strictly as controllers in the MVC sense. They're responsible for laying items out on the screen and obscuring many of the more intricate layout details. Apple terminology does not always match the MVC paradigm taught in computer science classes.

First and foremost, view controllers are there to make your life easier. They take responsibility for rotating the display when a user reorients his or her iPhone. They resize views to fit within the boundaries when using a navigation bar or a toolbar. They handle all the interface's fussy bits and hide the complexity involved in directly managing interaction elements. You can design and build iPhone applications without ever using a `UIViewController` or one of its subclasses, but why bother? The class offers so much convenience it's hardly worth writing an application without them.

In addition to the base controller's orientation and view resizing support, two special controllers, the `UINavigationController` and `UITabBarController`, magically handle view shifting for you. The navigation version enables you to drill down between views, smoothly sliding your display between one view and the next. Navigation controllers remember which views came first and provide a full breadcrumb trail of "back" buttons to return to previous views without any additional programming.

The tabbed view controller lets you easily switch between view controller instances using a tabbed display. So if your application has a top ten list, a game play window, and a help sheet, you can add a three-buttoned tab bar that instantly switches between these views without any additional programming to speak of.

Every UIViewController subclass implements its own loadView method. This is the method that lays out the controller's subviews and sets up all the triggers, callbacks, and delegates. So in that sense alone, the UIViewController does act as a controller by providing these links between the way things look and how interactions are interpreted. And, because you almost always send the callbacks to the UIViewController itself, it often acts as your model in addition to its primary role as a controller for whatever views you create and want to display. It's not especially MVC, but it is convenient and easy to program.

Controller

When Apple designs interactive elements such as sliders and tables, they have no idea how you'll use them. The classes are deliberately general. With MVC, there's no programmatic meaning associated with row selection or button presses. It's up to you as a developer to provide the model that adds meaning. The iPhone provides several ways in which prebuilt Cocoa Touch classes can talk to your custom ones. Here are the three most important: delegation, target-action, and notifications.

Delegation

Many UIKit classes use **delegation** to hand off responsibility for responding to user interactions. When you set an object's delegate, you tell it to pass along any interaction messages and let that delegate take responsibility for them. UITableViews are a good example of this. When a user taps on a table row, the UITableView has no built-in way of responding to that tap. Instead, it consults its delegate—usually a view controller class or your main application delegate—and passes along the selection change through a delegate method.

The UITableView delegate method tableView: didSelectRowAtIndexPath: is a typical example. Your model takes control of this method and implements how it should react to the row change. You might display a menu or navigate to a subview or place a check mark next to the current selection. The response depends entirely on how you implement the delegated selection change method.

To set an object's delegate, use some variation on the setDelegate: method. This instructs your application to redirect interaction callbacks to the delegate. You let Xcode know that your object implements delegate calls by adding a mention of the delegate protocol it implements in the class declaration. This appears in angle brackets, to the right of the class inheritance. Listing 1-1 shows a kind of UIViewController that implements delegate methods for UITableView views. The MergedTableController class is, therefore, responsible for implementing all required table delegate methods.

Delegation isn't limited to Apple's classes. It's simple to add your own protocol declarations to your classes and use them to define callback vocabularies. Listing 1-1 creates the `FTPHostDelegate` protocol, which declares the `ftpHost` instance variable. When used, that object must implement all three methods declared in the protocol.

> **Note**
>
> If your application is built around a central table view, use `UITableViewController` instances to simplify table creation and use.

Listing 1-1   Defining and Adding Delegate Protocols Declarations to a Class Definition

```
@protocol FTPHostDelegate <NSObject>
- (void) percentDone: (NSString *) percent;
- (void) downloadDone: (id) sender;
- (void) uploadDone: (id) sender;
@end

@interface MergedTableController : UIViewController <UITableViewDelegate,
UITableViewDataSource>
{
    UIView                  *contentView;
    UITableView             *subView;
    UIButton                *button;
    id <FTPHostDelegate>    *ftpHost;
    SEL                     finishedAction;
}
@end
```

Target-Action

Target-actions are a lower-level way of redirecting user interactions. You'll encounter these almost exclusively for children of the `UIControl` class. With target-action, you tell the control to contact a given object when a specific user event takes place. For example, you'd specify which object to contact when users press a button.

Listing 1-2 shows a typical example. This snippet defines a `UIBarButtonItem` instance, a typical button-like control used in iPhone toolbars. It sets the item's target to `self` and the action to `@selector(setHelvetica:)`. When tapped, it triggers a call to the defining object sending the `setHelvetica:` message.

Listing 1-2   Using Target-Actions for Adding Responses to Controls

```
UIBarButtonItem *helvItem = [[[UIBarButtonItem alloc]
    initWithTitle:@"Helvetica" style:UIBarButtonItemStyleBordered
    target:self action:@selector(setHelvetica:)] autorelease];
```

As you can see, the name of the method (`setHelvetica:`) is completely arbitrary. Target-actions do not rely on an established method vocabulary the way delegates do. In use, however, they work exactly the same way. The user does something, in this case presses a button, and the target implements the selector to provide a meaningful response.

Whichever object defines this `UIBarButtonItem` instance must implement a `setHelvetica:` method. If it does not, the program will crash at runtime with an undefined method call error.

Standard target-action pairs always pass a single argument, the interaction object. In this case, this is the `UIBarButtonItem` instance that was pressed. This self-reference, where the triggered object is included with the call, enables you to build more general action code. Instead of building separate methods for `setHelvetica:`, `setGeneva:`, and `setCourier:`, you could create a single `setFontFace:` method to update a font based on which button the user pressed.

To build target-action into your own classes, add a target variable of type `id` (any object class) and an action variable of type `SEL` (method selector).

Notifications

In addition to delegates and target-actions, the iPhone uses yet another way to communicate about user interactions between your model and your view—and about other events, for that matter. **Notifications** enable objects in your application to talk among themselves, as well as to talk to other applications on your system. By broadcasting information, notifications enable objects to send state messages: "I've changed," "I've started doing something," or "I've finished."

Other objects might be listening to these broadcasts, or they might not. For your objects to "hear" a notification, they must register with a notification center and start listening for messages. The iPhone implements at least four kinds of notification centers:

- **NSNotificationCenter.** This is the gold standard for in-application notification. You can subscribe to any or all notifications with this kind of notification center and listen as your objects talk to each other. The notifications are fully implemented and can carry data as well as the notification name. This name + data implementation offers great flexibility, and you can use this center to perform complex messaging.

- **NSDistributedNotificationCenter.** This center is meant for interapplication notification. It is not fully implemented on the iPhone and should be avoided.

- **DarwinNotificationCenter.** The iPhone relies on Darwin notification centers for interapplication messaging. It's limited in that it enables you to only broadcast announcements and will not let you send data with those announcements. So you can announce that something has changed, but you can't send along information about which item has changed. Despite this limitation, Darwin notification is reliable and robust. Messages arrive dependably. Darwin notification is built using standard BSD notification (for example, `notify_post()`, `notify_register_mach_port()`, and so on).

- **TelephonyNotificationCenter.** Telephony notifications are private and unpublished. Unfortunately, Apple did not open up this center, but if you sneak your way into listening to this special-purpose center, you'll know when phone calls and SMS messages arrive.

It's easy to subscribe to a notification center. Add your application delegate or, more typically, your `UIViewController` as a registered observer. You supply an arbitrary selector to be called when a notification arrives, in this case `trackNotifications:`. The method takes one argument, an `NSNotification`. Ensure that your callback method will hear all application notifications by setting the name and object arguments to `nil`.

All notifications contain three data elements: the notification name, an associated object, and a user information dictionary. If you're unsure what notifications `UIKit` objects in your application produce, have your callback print out the name from all the notifications it receives—for example, `NSLog(@"%@", [notification name])`. Apple does not document notification protocols with the same love and care that it documents delegate and data source protocols.

The kinds of notification vary by the task you are performing. For example, notifications when rotating an application include `UIApplicationWillChangeStatusBarOrientation Notification` and `UIDeviceOrientationDidChangeNotification`. In some cases, these correspond strongly with existing delegate methods. In other cases, they don't, so you'd be wise to monitor notifications while writing programs to find any gaps in Apple's delegate protocol implementations. Here's how you listen:

```
[[NSNotificationCenter defaultCenter] addObserver:self
    selector:@selector(trackNotifications:) name:nil object:nil];
```

> **Note**
>
> The recipes in this book generally use `printf` rather than `NSLog()` as the former worked more reliably during the SDK beta period.

Model

You're responsible for building all application semantics—the model portion of any MVC app. You create the callback methods triggered by your application's controller and provide the required implementation of any delegate protocol. There's one place, however, that the iPhone SDK gives you a hand with meaning, and that's with data sources. Data sources enable you to fill `UIKit` objects with custom content.

Data Sources

A data source refers to any object that supplies another object with on demand data. Some UI objects are containers without any native content. When you set another object as its data source, usually via a call like `[uiobject setDataSource:applicationobject]`, you enable the UI object (the view) to query the data source (the model) for data such as table cells for a given `UITableView`. Usually the data source pulls its data in from a file such as a local database, from a Web service such as an XML feed, or from a scanned source such as locally detected WiFi hotspots. `UITableView` and `UIPickerView` are two of the few Cocoa Touch classes that support or require data sources.

Data sources are like delegates in that you must implement their methods in another object, typically the `UITableViewController` that owns the table. They differ in that they create/supply objects rather than react to user interactions.

Listing 1-3 shows a typical data source methods method that returns a table cell for a given row. Like other data source methods, it enables you to separate implementation semantics that fill a given view from the Apple-supplied functionality that builds the view container.

Objects that implement data source protocols must declare themselves just as they would with delegate protocols. Listing 1-1 showed a class declaration that supports both delegate and data source protocols for `UITableViews`. Apple thoroughly documents data source protocols.

Listing 1-3 Data Source Methods Supply Information That Fills a View with Meaningful Content

```
// Return a cell for the ith row, labeled with its number
- (UITableViewCell *)tableView:(UITableView *)tableView
cellForRowAtIndexPath:(NSIndexPath *)indexPath
{
    UITableViewCell *cell = [tableView dequeueReusableCellWithIdentifier:
@"any-cell"];
    if (cell == nil) {
        cell = [[[UITableViewCell alloc] initWithFrame:CGRectZero
reuseIdentifier:@"any-cell"] autorelease];
    }
    // Set up the cell
    cell.text = [tableTitles objectAtIndex:[indexPath row]];
    cell.editingStyle = UITableViewCellEditingStyleDelete;
    return cell;
}
```

The `UIApplication` Object

In theory, you'd imagine that the iPhone "model" component would center on the `UIApplication` class. In practice, it does not, at least not in any MVC sense of the word *model*. In the world of the Apple SDK, each program contains precisely one `UIApplication` instance, which you can refer to via `[UIApplication sharedInstance]`.

For the most part, unless you need to open a URL in Safari, recover the key window, or adjust the look of the status bar, you can completely ignore `UIApplication`. Build your program around a custom application delegate class that is responsible for setting things up when the application launches and closing things down when the application terminates. Otherwise, hand off the remaining model duties to methods in your custom `UIViewController` classes or to custom model classes.

> **Note**
>
> Use `[[UIApplication sharedInstance] keyWindow]` to locate your application's main window object.

Uncovering Data Source and Delegate Methods

In addition to monitoring notifications, message tracking can prove to be an invaluable tool. Add the following snippet to your class definitions to expose all the methods—both documented and undocumented, data source and delegate—that your class responds to:

```
-(BOOL) respondsToSelector:(SEL)aSelector {
    printf("SELECTOR: %s\n", [NSStringFromSelector(aSelector) UTF8String]);
    return [super respondsToSelector:aSelector];
}
```

Building an iPhone Application Skeleton

Nearly every iPhone application you build will contain a few key components. Here is a quick rundown of those components, how often you'll use them, and what they do:

- **The `main()` function (always use).** Every C-based program centers around a `main()` function. For the iPhone, this function primes memory management and starts the application event loop.

- **The `applicationDidFinishLaunching:` method (always use).** This method is the first thing triggered in your program. This is where you create a basic window, set its contents, and tell it to become the key responder for your application.

- **The `applicationWillTerminate:` method (usually use).** This method enables you to handle any status finalization before handing control back to SpringBoard. Use this to save defaults, update data, and close files.

- **The `loadView` method (always use).** Assuming you've built your application around a `UIViewController`—and there's usually no reason not to do so—the mandatory `loadView` method sets up the screen and lays out any subviews. Make sure to call `[super loadView]` whenever you inherit from a specialized subclass such as `UITableViewController` or `UITabBarController`.

- **The `shouldAutorotateToInterfaceOrientation:` method (usually use).** Unless you have pressing reasons to force your user to remain in portrait orientation, add the should-autorotate method to allow the `UIViewController` method to automatically match your screen to the iPhone's orientation.

There are many other methods you'll use over and over again. These five provide important touch points that you should consider every time you create a new application.

The Hello World Application

Listing 1-4 provides a basic image-based Hello World application. This application is built using a `UINavigationController` and a custom `UIViewController` (called `HelloController` here) that displays a picture. As the name suggests, the application does little more than open itself and present itself onscreen. What you get here, therefore, are all the essentials. These are the skeletal features on which you can hang the body of your application when you're ready to start writing more meaningful code.

The Classes

A navigation controller is responsible for creating that blue-gray header with the title you see in Figure 1-3. Although the header does little in this simple demonstration, in real-world apps it's a critical player. You'll see navigation bars in action when looking at the iPhone Mail and Safari applications. The `UINavigationController` class simplifies adding these features to your application.

Figure 1-3   `UIViewController` controllers can automatically handle view orientation changes by scaling their subviews. When working with images, you'll probably want to catch orientation changes and swap out a landscape-friendly version rather than accept the squeezed aspect shown here.

Here, the view controller loads an image and handles reshaping it for orientation changes. Figure 1-3 shows the interface built by this source in both portrait and landscape orientation. Clearly, when dealing with images, you'll probably want to catch orientation changes and swap out landscape image versions for portrait ones and vice versa. I chose not to in this sample for two reasons. First, so you would get a clear visual of how the automatic reshaping takes place. Second, to understand how powerful this reshaping is—with almost no code, the application handles reorientation all by itself.

The Code

This program contains definitions for two classes (`HelloController` and `SampleAppDelegate`) plus the `main()` function. This code, like all code in this book, appears together as a single file. Rather than provide the five separate files this code would normally entail, a combined listing makes this far more readable in book form. I strongly encourage you to use the standard multifile system for your real applications.

The `main()` function was generated automatically by Xcode and remains essentially untouched by human hands. It calls `UIApplicationMain()`, passing it the name of the main application delegate, which in this case is called `SampleAppDelegate`—for no other reason than I call all the sample-code application delegates in this book that. Feel free to name your own delegates as desired.

The `applicationDidFinishLaunching[colon]` method is called next. Here, the code creates a new window using the standard `mainScreen` geometry. It builds a navigation controller and assigns a new `HelloController`—my `UIViewController` subclass—as its root view controller. That assigns the `HelloController` view as the navigation controller's primary subview. Doing just this enables this program to support the full range of navigation bar features.

To finish setting up the window, this program sets `nav.view` (the entire view headed by that navigation bar) as the window's subview and orders the window out.

In the `HelloController` class, `loadView` creates the main application view, which in this case is nothing more than a `UIImageView` loaded with the contents of helloworld.png. Using `self.view = contentView` assigns the image view to the controller.

Setting a few flags for autorotation and adding `shouldAutorotateToInterfaceOrientation:` ensures the application responds to iPhone orientation changes.

A Note About Sample Code and Memory Management

The Hello World code that follows is the first of many samples throughout this *iPhone Developer's Cookbook*. This book was written during the public SDK beta period starting in March 2008. During that time, Apple released several iterations of the SDK, which constantly underwent changes in terms of class definitions and, more important, memory management. All the sample code has been written and rewritten, tested and retested to make sure that it continues to work with each SDK revision.

I have loosened memory management in the code throughout this book to ensure that the samples remain robust and working. If you wonder, while reading through code, about seemingly extraneous retains and a lack of matching releases, it is all to that end, to ensure that the sample code continues to operate. Feel free to tighten things where desired.

All samples in this book use the same base project (for example, Hello World). This ensures that the samples will not overwhelm your device with a hundred odd stray icons and names. You can find up-to-date sample code, Xcode projects, and video at my site, ericasadun.com.

Listing 1-4   **Hello World**

```objc
#import <UIKit/UIKit.h>
@class UIImageView;

// Custom UIViewController displays a simple image
@interface HelloController : UIViewController
{
    UIImageView *contentView;
}
@end

@implementation HelloController
- (id)init
{
    if (self = [super init])
    {
        self.title = [[[NSBundle mainBundle] infoDictionary]
objectForKey:@"CFBundleName"];
        // place any further initialization here
    }
    return self;
}

- (void)loadView
{
    // Load an application image and set it as the primary view
    contentView = [[UIImageView alloc] initWithFrame:[[UIScreen mainScreen]
    ➥applicationFrame]];
    [contentView setImage:[UIImage imageNamed:@"helloworld.png"]];
    self.view = contentView;
    [contentView release]; // reduce retain count by one

    // Provide support for auto-rotation and resizing
    contentView.autoresizesSubviews = YES;
    contentView.autoresizingMask = (UIViewAutoresizingFlexibleWidth |
    ➥UIViewAutoresizingFlexibleHeight);
}

// Allow the view to respond to iPhone Orientation changes
```

Listing 1-4   **Continued**

```
- (BOOL) shouldAutorotateToInterfaceOrientation:
(UIInterfaceOrientation) interfaceOrientation
{
     return YES;
}

- (void) dealloc
{
     // add any further clean-up here
     [contentView release];
     [super dealloc];
}
@end

// Application Delegate handles application start-up and shut-down
@interface SampleAppDelegate : NSObject <UIApplicationDelegate> {
}
@end

@implementation SampleAppDelegate

// On launch, create a basic window
- (void)applicationDidFinishLaunching:(UIApplication *)application {
     UIWindow *window = [[UIWindow alloc] initWithFrame:[[UIScreen mainScreen]
     ➥bounds]];
     UINavigationController *nav = [[UINavigationController alloc]
     ➥initWithRootViewController:[[HelloController alloc] init]];
     [window addSubview:nav.view];
     [window makeKeyAndVisible];
}

- (void)applicationWillTerminate:(UIApplication *)application {
     // handle any final state matters here
}

- (void)dealloc {
     [super dealloc];
}

@end

int main(int argc, char *argv[])
{
     NSAutoreleasePool * pool = [[NSAutoreleasePool alloc] init];
     int retVal = UIApplicationMain(argc, argv, nil, @"SampleAppDelegate");
     [pool release];
     return retVal;
}
```

Building Hello World

The following sections create the Hello World iPhone application using Xcode and the iPhone SDK. You'll create a new iPhone project, customize it a bit, and swap in the Hello World sample code from Listing 1-4.

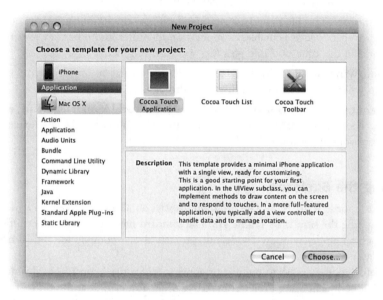

Figure 1-4   The New Project window contains three iPhone application templates that you can use to build your programs.

Create an iPhone Project

To create Hello World, you need a fresh, new project in Xcode. Select File, New Project (Command-Shift-N). The New Project window (see Figure 1-4) opens. Select iPhone, Application, Cocoa Touch Application (View Based Application in newer versions of Xcode), and click Choose. Use the standard Leopard controls to navigate to where you want to save your new application, enter a name (**Hello World**), and click Save. Xcode opens a new iPhone project window and populates it with all the basic elements and frameworks you need to build your first iPhone application. Items you will see in this project include the following:

- **Foundation and Core Graphics frameworks.** These essential frameworks enable you to build your iPhone applications using the same fundamental classes and calls you are familiar with from the Macintosh.

- **UIKit framework.** This framework provides iPhone-specific user interface elements and is key to developing applications that can be seen and interacted with on the iPhone screen.
- **HelloWorld.app.** Displayed in red, this placeholder will be used to store your finished application. Like on the Macintosh, iPhone applications are bundles and consist of many items stored in a central folder.
- **Info.plist.** This file describes your application to the iPhone's system and enables you to specify its executable, its application identifier, and other key features. It works in the same way Info.plist files work on the Mac.
- **mainWindow.xib.** This Interface Builder file creates an unpopulated window. You will not use this for this first walk-through.
- **main.m, HelloWorldAppDelegate.h, HelloWorldAppDelegate.m, and so on.** These files contain a rough skeleton that you can customize and expand to create your application.

Running the Skeleton

If you like, choose Run, Run. The program displays an all-black screen, and you can exit by tapping the simulated Home key. The standard project skeleton does little more than launch an empty window. By default, projects always compile for and launch in the simulator.

You tell Xcode whether to build your application for the Leopard-based simulator or for the iPhone by choosing Project, Set Active SDK. You cannot at the time of writing load your software onto an iPhone without a developer certificate. The iPhone Developer Program starts at $99/year and offers access to the on-iPhone App Store. To apply for the program, visit http://developer.apple.com/iphone/program.

Customize the iPhone Project

The following steps convert the standard skeleton into your Hello World project:

1. **Remove classes.** Select the Classes folder in the Groups & Files column on the left and press Delete. Xcode asks you to confirm. Click Also Move to Trash.
2. **Remove the .xib file.** You won't want to use it for this project.
3. **Remove two lines from the Info.plist file.** These are the lines with the NSMainNibFile key and the line that immediately follows after, the MainWindow string.
4. **Add an Images folder.** Right-click Hello World in the Groups & Files column and choose Add, New Group. Name the new folder **Pictures**.
5. **Add images to the project.** Drag the three images from the Chapter One project folder provided with this book onto the Pictures folder: Icon.png, Default.png, and helloworld.png. Check Copy Items into Destination Group's Folder (if needed) and click Add.

6. **Replace main.m.** Open main.m and replace all the text in that file with the text from the main.m file provided in the Chapter One project folder. Save your changes with File, Save (Command-S) and close the main.m window.

7. **Select the iPhone Simulator.** Choose Project, Set Active SDK, iPhone Simulator.

8. **Run it.** Choose Build, Build & Run (Command-R). The program will compile and launch in the iPhone simulation window.

Here are a few how-tos you'll want to know about while running a simulated iPhone application the first time:

- **Reorienting the screen.** With the Hello World application running, you can reorient the Simulator using Command-Left arrow and Command-Right arrow.

- **Going home.** Tap the Home button (Command-Shift-H) to leave the application and return to the SpringBoard home screen.

- **Locking the "phone."** Hardware, Lock (Command-L) simulates locking the phone.

- **Viewing the console.** In Xcode, choose Run, Console (Command-Shift-R) to view the Xcode console window. This window is where your `printf`, `NSLog`, and `CFShow` messages are sent by default. In the unlikely case where `NSLog` messages do not appear, use the Xcode organizer (Window, Organizer, Console) or open /Applications/Utilities/Console to view `NSLog` messages instead.

- **Running Instruments.** Use Run, Start with Performance Tool to select an Instruments template (such as Object Allocations or CPU Sampler) to use with the Simulator. Instruments monitors memory and CPU use as your application runs.

> **Note**
>
> Although the Organizer window offers direct access to crash logs, you'll probably want to enable Developer Mode for Crash Reporter, too. This enables you to see trace backs immediately, without having to click Report all the time. To do this, open /Developer/Applications/Utilities/CrashReporterPrefs, select Developer, and quit. (Tip is courtesy of Emanuele Vulcano of infinite-labs.net.)

Editing Identification Information

The default Info.plist file enables you to create a working program but won't, in its default state, properly handle iPhone provisioning, a necessary precondition for on-phone application testing and distribution, which is discussed later in this chapter. The iPhone requires a signed identity, which you generate on Apple's iPhone developer program site (http://developer.apple.com/iphone/program). For Simulator use only, you can double-click the Info.plist file to open it in a new window. Here, you'll see the application identifier for your program, and you can edit just the company name entry.

Customization does not end with the Info.plist file. Close the Info and double-click InfoPlist.strings. This file is listed among your other project files. Edit "©
__MyCompanyName__, 2008" to match the actual copyright you want to use for your program. Again choose File, Save (Command-S) to save your changes.

Using the Debugger

Xcode's integrated debugger provides a valuable tool for iPhone application development. The following walk-through shows you where the debugger is and provides a few basic ways to use it with your program. In these steps, you'll discover how to set breakpoints and use the debugger console to inspect program details.

Set a Breakpoint

Locate the `loadView` method in your Hello World program. Click in the leftmost Xcode window column, just to the left of the closing bracket. A blue breakpoint indicator appears (see Figure 1-5). The dark blue color means the breakpoint is active. Tap once to deactivate—the breakpoint turns light blue—and once more to reactivate. You can remove breakpoints by dragging them offscreen and add them by clicking in the column, next to any line of code.

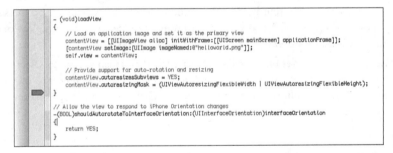

Figure 1-5   Blue breakpoint indicators appear in the leftmost Xcode window column.

Run the Program

Make sure the breakpoint is dark blue and that the button at the top of the Xcode screen says "Deactivate" (which means that the breakpoint is active) and run the program. The program will automatically stop when it hits the breakpoint and a red arrow point appears on top of the blue arrow.

Open the Debugger Windows

Choose Run, Debugger (Command-Shift-Y) to open the main debugger and Run, Console (Command-Shift-R) to open the console window. Figure 1-6 shows both windows. The debugger provides a graphical front end for inspecting program objects. The console offers a standard Gnu Debugger (gdb) command line.

Figure 1-6   Xcode's graphical debugger enables you to interactively inspect program state. A command-line version of gdb runs concurrently in the console window, as shown by the (gdb) prompt. A red arrow appears at the active breakpoint.

Inspect

Once stopped at the breakpoint, you can use the interactive debugger or the gdb command line to inspect objects in your program. For this example, navigate down the variable chain through Arguments, self, contentView, UIView,_viewFlags to confirm that the autoresizeMask has been properly set. Assuming Apple has not changed its constants, this mask should be 18, corresponding to 2 for flexible width and 16 for flexible height.

Consider Other Breakpoint Options

The breakpoint menu at the top of the Xcode window enables you to add customized breakpoint actions rather than use a generic break in execution. Figure 1-7 shows these options. To learn more about the Xcode debugger and its features, consult Apple's *Xcode User Guide: Debugging Programs.*

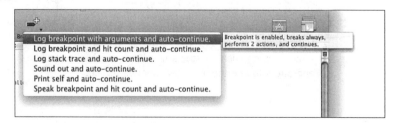

Figure 1-7   Use predefined breakpoint actions to automatically execute debugger actions.

Apple's iPhone Developer Program

You cannot run programs directly on the iPhone until you've entered Apple's (paid) iPhone developer program. The program starts at $99 and allows you to develop iPhone applications as an individual ($99/year), a company ($99/year), or for in-house enterprise ($299/year). Apply at http://developer.apple.com/iphone/program.

The iPhone uses code signing. Only properly signed applications are allowed to run on the iPhone. Once accepted into this program, you'll be able to create a signing certificate that authenticates you as a developer and provision iPhones or iPod touch units for testing. The details for this program, for ad hoc distribution (for small controlled audiences of users), for the general provisioning process, and for access to Apple's iPhone App Store remain in flux. Check with Apple for up-to-date information.

Development Phones

Development phones and iPods must be registered with Apple and provisioned through Xcode. When you've successfully joined the developer program and paid for your access, you'll be able to use Apple's program portal to obtain your certificates and register your units. The process is fussy. I urge you to follow Apple's instructions exactly as you create development and distribution certificates and build provisioning profiles for your applications.

When you first tether your iPhone to your computer using a standard USB cable, Xcode detects your unit (see Figure 1-8). If you want to use your device for development, confirm that; otherwise click Ignore. A development unit needs to be devoted exclusively to development. Using a device as a development unit means that it is subject to onboard data changes and might no longer work reliably as a field unit.

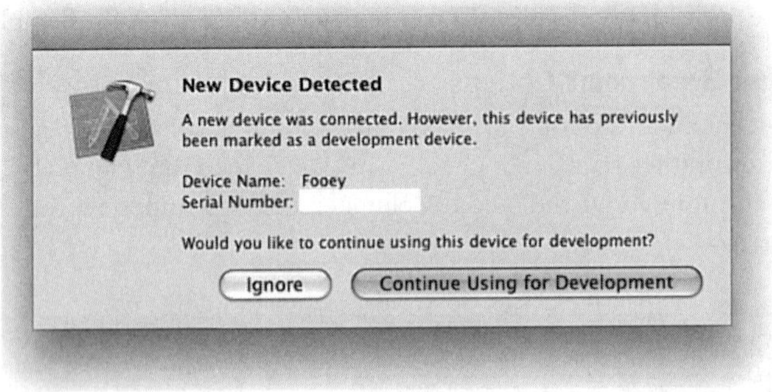

New Device Detected

A new device was connected. However, this device has previously been marked as a development device.

Device Name: Fooey
Serial Number:

Would you like to continue using this device for development?

(Ignore)   (Continue Using for Development)

Figure 1-8   Xcode automatically detects new iPhones and iPod touches and offers to add them as development devices.

Application Identifiers

Apple uses two kinds of provisions: development provisions and distribution ones. Development provisioning allows you to download software to your iPhone for testing. Distribution provisions create applications suitable for App Store or ad hoc distribution. The iPhone lists its active provisions in Settings, General, Profile.

To distribute applications on the iPhone, Apple requires that you register Application IDs at their site. To do this, you must be a registered team administrator. Use the Developer Program portal at Apple's iPhone Dev Center. Use Program Portal, App IDs to enter the new ID, and then create a provisioning profile at Program, Provisioning.

To develop applications, you can use specific application identifiers for on-phone testing or, better, create a single reverse domain wildcard `com.mydomain.*` application identifier that provisions all your applications for testing. This wildcard provision must match each application ID in your Info.plist file. I personally use `com.sadun.*`. Pick a reverse domain that describes your business or individual identity.

After creating the wildcard provision at the program portal, download the new development provisioning profile. Back in Xcode, do the following:

1. Drag the `mobileprovision` file into your organizer. Alternatively, you can drag it onto the Xcode application icon.

2. Select Debug or Release from your project window.

3. In your project window's Groups & Files list, open Targets and double-click your application name. A Target Info dialog opens.

4. Select Debug or Release in the Target Info window, matching whatever you selected in the project window.

5. Click the Properties tab. Enter your new application ID into the Identifier field. If you provisioned with a wildcard, enter the actual application name, not the wildcard (for example, `com.mydomain.myapplication` and *not* `com.mydomain.*`).

6. Click the Build tab. Set your Code Signing Identity to Any iPhone OS Device and iPhone Developer. This phrase is used to match the development certificate in your keychain. To check your keychain, open /Applications/Utilities/Keychain Access. The category My Certificates should contain at least one certificate containing iPhone Developer in its name. If you've signed up for distribution, you'll likely have an iPhone distribution certificate, too.

7. Set your Code Signing Provision Profile to Any iPhone OS Device, and the name of the provision you just created for your application ID from the pop-up menu. (Do not select Default Provisioning Profile for Code Signing Identity. Your application will neither load to nor run on the iPhone.)

After following these steps, you should be able to compile your application for the iPhone (Project, Set Active SDK, Device—iPhone OS), install it, and run it from the device itself. If you run into problems, consult Apple's documentation and Developer Technical Support.

From Xcode to Your iPhone: The Organizer Interface

Once added to Xcode, manage your development units using Xcode's Organizer tool (Window, Organizer; Control-Command-O). This window (shown in Figure 1-9) forms the control hub for access between your development computer and your iPhone or iPod testbed. This window allows you to add and remove applications, view midtest console results, examine crash logs, and snap screenshots of your unit while testing your code. Here's a quick rundown of the major features available to you through the Organizer console.

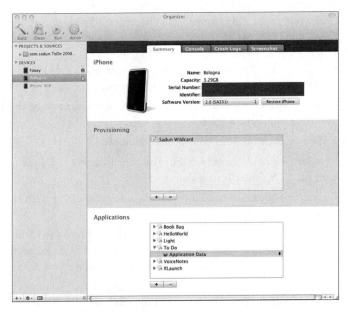

Figure 1-9   The Xcode-based iPhone Organizer window (Window, Organizer) provides a single control hub for most of your application testing needs. Here, you can load firmware, install and remove applications, read through crash logs, snap device-based screenshots, and more.

Projects and Sources List

Keep your current projects in easy reach by dragging them onto the Organizer console. Once added, double-click the project name to open that project. You can add individual source files as well as complete projects. Use the Build, Clean, Run, and Action options at the top of the Organizer window, to perform even more development tasks directly from the Organizer.

Devices List

The Devices list shows the name and status of those devices you've authorized as development platforms. The indicators to the right of each name show if the device is attached (green light) or not (red light).

Summary Tab

The Summary tab tells you the name, capacity, serial number, and identifier of your iPhone or iPod touch. Here is where you can provision your unit (that is, authorize it to work with the projects you build in Xcode), add and remove applications, and load the latest firmware.

Each developer license allows you to provision up to five iPhones/iPod touches at a time for testing. The Provisioning list shows a list of application provisions available to your unit. Add a check to each provision you want to use. The provision determines which applications may or may not be run on the device. As a rule, distribution provisions are listed here (as are the development ones, but they are grayed out).

A list of installed applications appears at the bottom of the Summary tab. Use the + and − buttons to add or remove applications. Open the disclosure triangle next to each application name to disclose the application data (the Documents and Library folders) associated with that application.

Note

Apple offers full instructions on how to provision your iPhone and create your personal signing certificates on its iPhone program portal pages. See http://developer.apple.com/iphone/program.

Console Tab

Use the console to view system messages from your connected units. This screen shows `NSLog()` calls as you're running software on the tethered iPhone. In addition to the debugging messages you add to your iPhone applications, you'll also see system notices, device information, and debugging calls from Apple's system software. It's basically a text-based mess. Logged data also appears on the Xcode debugging console (Run, Console) along with any `printf` output.

Crash Logs Tab

Get direct access to your crash logs by selecting a particular crash (labeled with the iPhone application name and the date and time of the crash) from the screen's leftmost column. The crash details, including thread information, exception types, and so forth, appear in the text view to the right of that column.

Screenshot Tab

Snap your tethered iPhone's screen by clicking the Capture button on the Screenshot tab. The screenshot feature takes a picture of whatever is running on the iPhone, whether your applications are open. So you can access shots of Apple's built-in software and any other applications running on the iPhone.

Once snapped, you can drag snapped images onto the desktop or save them as an open project's new Default.png image. Archival shots appear in a library on the left side of the window. Select one and press the Delete key to permanently remove it.

> **Note**
>
> Screenshots are stored in your Application Support folder in Developer/Shared/Xcode/Screenshots.

About Tethering

At this time, Apple provides no way to transfer, debug, or monitor applications wirelessly. That means you'll do nearly all your work tethered over a standard iPhone USB cable. The physical reality of tethered debugging can be problematic. Reasons for this include the following points:

- When you unplug the cable, you unplug all the interactive debugging, console, and screenshot features. So you need to keep that cable plugged in all the time.
- You cannot reasonably use the iPhone with a dock. Sure, the dock is stable, but touching the screen while testing interfaces is extremely awkward when the iPhone is seated at a 75-degree angle.
- The tether comes to the bottom not the top of the unit, meaning it's very easy to catch that cable and knock your iPhone to the floor.

Obviously, untethered testing would vastly improve many of these issues. Unfortunately, Apple has not yet introduced that option. If you like, you can Rube Goldberg-ize your iPhone to get around these problems. One solution is to attach Velcro to the back of an iPhone case—a case that leaves the bottom port connector open—and use that to stabilize your iPhone on your desk. It's ugly, but it keeps your iPhone from getting knocked to the floor all the time.

Testing Applications on Your iPhone

Before you can test your application on the iPhone, you must first compile your source for the iPhone's ARM processor and get that bundle copied over to your unit. Fortunately, Xcode allows you to easily choose whether to compile your iPhone application for the simulator or for a tethered device. Here are the steps to take:

1. Tether a provisioned iPhone to your Macintosh.

2. Choose Project, Set Active SDK, Device, and compile just as you did for the Simulator. Make sure you've provisioned the application (Target, Build, Code Signing Identity and Target, Build, Code Signing Provisioning Profile and have added a matching project identifier to Target, Properties, Identifier.

3. Compile your project and run it via Run, Go or Run, Run. These menu choices compile your program, preparing the application for the iPhone. Then they install and run it.

4. Wait. It takes a little time to compile, sign, sandbox, and install your application on an iPhone, especially with bigger project files and especially when you have several applications on your iPhone. It's often a good chance to take a quick break as your program loads.

After you've installed the application, it automatically launches, and if you've compiled with the debugger (Project, Set Active Build Configuration, Debug), the Gnu Debugger (gdb) opens in the Xcode debugging console window. The debugging functionality remains available to you until you quit the application. You can quit either through Xcode (typically by compiling a new version of the program and preparing to install it) or by pressing Home on the iPhone.

Testing on the iPhone is vital. As simple and convenient as the Simulator is, it falls far short of the mark when it comes to a complete iPhone testing experience. At the time of writing, you cannot use the Simulator to test the onboard camera (see Chapter 7), keychain access (see Chapter 10), or accelerometer feedback (see Chapter 9, "People, Places, and Things"). And, of course, given that the iPhone is the target platform, it's important that your software runs its best on its native system rather than on the Simulator. The iPhone itself offers the fully leaded un-watered-down testing platform, at least as far as a fully leaded sandboxed application with limited system read-and-write access will allow.

Note

SpringBoard learns about new and removed applications through two system notifications: `com.apple.mobile.application_installed` and `com.apple.mobile.application_uninstalled`. Xcode sends these notifications to a Darwin notification center, and SpringBoard listens in.

Compiling for Distribution

Submitting applications to App Store requires that you compile your program for distribution rather than development. Here's a quick rundown of the steps you need to take:

1. Create a distribution certificate at the iPhone program portal. Download it to your Macintosh and add it to your keychain. You need do this only once. After creating a development or distribution certificate, it stays in your keychain regardless of the number of applications you build.

2. If you haven't done so already, register a wildcard application identifier at the program portal.

3. Create a distribution provisioning profile for that wildcard application identifier. Name it with an easy-to-identify name (for example, My Wildcard Distribution Profile). Download it and add it to Xcode by dropping it onto the Xcode application icon or into the Organizer window.

4. Open the Project Info window (Command-I). In the Configurations tab, select Release. Click Duplicate and rename the new copy to **Distribution**. This new distribution configuration will store all the information you need for creating an App Store–compatible build. Once created, you can switch between the Debug, Release, and Distribution profiles, and they'll remember their settings. Just be aware that you need to set the configuration in two places: on the main project window and in the Target Info window, as you're about to see.

5. Close the Project Info window. Select Distribution from the Active Build Configuration pop-up in the main project window (Figure 1-1). This is the first of two places that you'll set the build configuration.

6. Open the Target Info window (double-click Targets, *Project Name* in the main project window) and select the Build tab.

7. In the Target Info, Build window, select Distribution from the Configuration pop-up. This is the second required configuration setting.

8. Under Code Signing Identity, change iPhone Developer to iPhone Distribution.

9. Select the new wildcard distribution profile from the Code Signing Provisioning Profile pop-up.

10. Build your project. Then, choose Groups & Files, *Project Name,* Products, *Application Name,* Reveal in Finder to find the newly created application bundle.

These steps enable you to build a distribution version of your program. After building your project, you can then zip up the new bundle and submit it to App Store.

Using Undocumented API Calls

Officially, Apple prohibits the use of undocumented API calls. If you want your application to conform to the App Store restrictions, restrain from using any unpublished items. Unofficially, Apple's policy has always been that you can use any API call in public frameworks as long as you accept the risk that your program may stop working when Apple releases new operating system updates. This unofficial policy currently crosses over to the iPhone. If an item appears in a public framework, you may use it at your own risk.

That spirit of open access informs this book. Undocumented calls appear throughout, particularly in Chapter 4, "Alerting Users." Every use is marked. You will not find a recipe that uses an undocumented call without it being stated explicitly.

At the same time, this book does not cross certain lines. The rules for book samples are as follows:

- **Private frameworks are private.** You may link to and access only those public items that appear in the Apple-sanctioned Frameworks folder.

- **You don't run daemons.** All code executes in the primary application.

- **You must quit when the iPhone says so.** The code respects Apple's one application at a time policy.

- **You cannot use plug-ins or execute arbitrary code.** Apple and App Store approve all code.

- **The sandbox is the sandbox.** Nothing in this book shows you how to access private areas such as the onboard iTunes Media folder.

Courteous computing doesn't mean limited computing. If you'd rather avoid undocumented API calls—and I know a large number of readers will—the remaining majority of tricks and tips throughout this book will still allow you to add excitement and novelty into your iPhone development experience.

Ad Hoc Distribution

Apple allows you to distribute your applications outside the App Store via Ad Hoc distribution. With Ad Hoc, you can send your applications to up to 100 registered devices and run those applications using a special kind of mobile provision that allows the applications to execute under the iPhone's FairPlay restrictions. Ad Hoc distribution is especially useful for beta testing and for submitting review applications to news sites and magazines.

Start by registering your device. Use the iPhone Developer Program Portal to register device identifiers (Program Portal, Devices). Recover these identifiers from the iPhone directly (use the `UIDevice` calls from Chapter 9), from iTunes (click on the word Serial Number in the iPhone's summary tab), or from System Profiler (select USB, iPhone, Serial Number). Enter the identifier and a unique username.

Next, build your provision. To build a mobile provision, select Program Portal, Provisioning, Distribution. Click Add Profile. Select Ad Hoc, enter a profile name, your standard wildcard Application identifier (for example, `com.yourname.*`), and select the device or devices to deploy on. Click Submit and wait for Apple to build the new mobile provision. Download the provision file. Drop it onto Xcode. You will use it to build your application.

You need to include a special entitlement file in Ad Hoc projects. In Xcode, choose File, New File, Code Signing, Entitlements. Click Next. Create a new entitlement called dist.plist. Click Finish. The entitlement property list appears in the Products folder. Double-click it to open and uncheck `get-task-allow`. (That is, set it to a Boolean value of FALSE.)

After setting up your entitlement, you need to add it to your target settings. Select your Distribution configuration from the project window. Double-click the project target, (Targets > Your Project Name). The Target Info window opens. In the Build tab, set your configuration again to Distribution if it is not already set. Double-click Code Signing Entitlements. Add the filename dist.plist to the Code Signing Entitlement and click OK.

Now you're ready to build your application. Make sure your Code Signing Identity is set to iPhone Distribution. Select your new ad-hoc mobile provision from the Any iPhone OS Device pop-up. Select Build, Clean (Command-Shift-K) and then Build, Build (Command-B) your project. Select the newly compiled product from the Products folder in the project window. Right-click it and choose Reveal in Finder. A Finder window opens, showing the compiled item.

Distribute a copy of this application, which you just compiled with the mobile ad hoc provision, along with the provision itself that you downloaded from Apple. Your user can drop the provision and the application into iTunes before syncing your application to his or her iPhone. The application will run only on those phones you registered, providing a secure way to distribute these apps directly to your user.

Summary

This chapter has introduced you to the iPhone application, how it is built, and how you can build your own basic Hello World utility using just a few steps. Here are some things you may want to take away with you before leaving this chapter:

- Downloading and installing the SDK and building and testing your first application shouldn't take you more than a few hours to do based on your download speed. The SDK is over a gigabyte in size, but once downloaded it's really easy to create your first application.

- The iPhone application bundle is much simpler and less structured than its Macintosh brother, although it shares many common features, including Info.plist and lproj folders.

- Unfortunately, the iPhone SDK requires you to test only on a tethered device. WiFi testing is not yet available. Despite that, the Organizer in Xcode provides a superb organizer for testing your applications with its console, crash logs, and screenshots.

- If you come from a Cocoa background, you'll be prepared if not overprepared to create iPhone applications. Familiarity with Objective-C and Cocoa best practices will put you on a firm development footing.

2

Views

Pretty much everything that appears on the iPhone's screen is a view. Views act like little canvases that you can draw on with colors, pictures, and buttons. You can drag them around the screen. You can resize them. You can layer them. In this chapter, you discover how to design and build screen content using Cocoa Touch and UIViews. You learn about view hierarchy, geometry, and animation, and find out how to combine event feedback from UITouches into meaningful UIView responses. There's so much that UIViews can do that a single chapter has no hope of covering the entire class with the thoroughness it deserves. Instead, this chapter introduces essential functionality and recipes that you can use as a starting point for your own UIView exploration.

UIView **and** UIWindow

The iPhone rule goes like this: one window, many views. If you keep that idea in mind, the iPhone interface design scenario simplifies. Metaphorically speaking, UIWindow is the TV set, and UIViews are the actors on your favorite show. They can move around the screen, appear, and disappear, and may change the way they look and behave over time.

The TV set, on the other hand, normally stays still. It has a set screen size that doesn't change even if the virtual world you see through it is practically unlimited. You may even own several TVs in the same household (just like you can create several UIWindow instances in the same application), but you can watch just one at a time.

UIViews are GUI building blocks. They provide visual elements that are shown onscreen and invite user interaction. Every iPhone user interface is built from UIViews displayed within one UIWindow, which is itself a specialized kind of UIView. The window acts a container; it is the root of the display hierarchy. It holds all the visible application components within itself. The following sections will give you just a taste of the kind of ways you can control and manipulate views, their hierarchy, and their geometry.

Hierarchy

A tree-based hierarchy orders what you see on your iPhone screen. Starting with the main window, views are laid out in a specifically hierarchical way. All views may have children, called subviews. Each view, including the root window, owns an ordered list of these subviews. Views might own many subviews; they might own none. Your application determines how views are laid out and who owns whom.

Subviews display onscreen in order, always from back to front. And because the iPhone supports view transparency, this works exactly like a stack of animation cells—those transparent sheets used to create cartoons. Only the parts of the sheets that have been painted are shown. The clear parts allow any visual elements behind that sheet to be seen.

Figure 2-1 shows a little of the layering used in a typical window. Here you see the window that owns a `UINavigationController`-based window. The window (represented by the clear, rightmost element) owns a Navigation subview, which in turn owns two subview buttons (one left and one right) and a table. These items stack together to build the GUI.

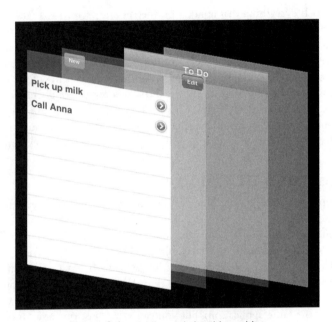

Figure 2-1   Adding subview hierarchies
allows you to build complex GUIs.

Notice how the buttons appear over the navigation bar and how the table is sized so that it won't obscure either the buttons or bar. The button frames are small, taking up very little space onscreen. The table frame is large, occupying the majority of screen space. Here are some ways you can manage subviews in your programs:

- To add a subview, use a call to `[parentView addSubview:child]`. Newly added subviews are always frontmost on your screen.

- Query any view for its children by asking it for `[parentView subviews]`. This returns an array of views, ordered from back to front.

- Remove a subview from its parent with `[childView removeFromSuperview]`.

- Reorder subviews using `[parentView exchangeSubviewAtIndex:i withSubviewAtIndex:j]`. Move subviews to the front or back using `bringSubviewToFront:` or `sendSubviewToBack:`.

- Tag your subviews using `setTag:`. This identifies views by tagging them with a number. Retrieve that view from the child hierarchy by calling `viewWithTag:` on the parent.

Note

You can tag any instance that is a child of `UIView`, including windows and controls. So if you have many onscreen buttons and switches, for example, add tags so that you can tell them apart when users trigger them.

Geometry and Traits

Every view uses a frame to define its boundaries. The frame specifies the outline of the view: its location, width, and height. You define the frame rectangle using Core Graphics structures. For frames, this usually means a `CGRect` rectangle made up of an origin (a `CGPoint`, x and y) and a size (a `CGSize`, width and height). Here are some quick facts about these types.

CGRect

The `CGRect` structure defines an onscreen rectangle. It contains an origin (rect.origin) and a size (rect.size). These are `CGRect` functions you'll want to be aware of:

- `CGRectMake() method()(origin.x, origin.y, size.width, size.height)` Defines rectangles in your code.

- `NSStringFromCGRect()converts() method()` A `CGRect` structure to a formatted string.

- `CGRectFromString()recovers() method()` A rectangle from its string representation.

- `CGRectInset() enables() method()` You to create a smaller or larger a rectangle that's centered on the same point. Use a positive inset for smaller rectangles, negative for larger ones.

- `CGRectIntersectsRect() lets() method()` You know whether rectangle structures intersect. Use this function to know when two rectangular onscreen objects overlap.

- `CGRectZero is() method()` A rectangle constant located at (0,0) whose width and height are zero. You can use this constant when you're required to create a frame but you're still unsure what that frame size or location will be at the time of creatione.

CGPoint and CGSize

Points refer to locations defined with x and y coordinates; sizes have width and height. Use `CGPointMake() method (x, y)` to create points. `CGSizeMake(width, height)` creates sizes. Although these two structures appear to be the same (two floating-point values), the iPhone SDK differentiates between them. Points refer to locations. Sizes refer to extents. You cannot set `myFrame.origin` to a size.

As with rectangles, you can convert them to and from strings: `NSStringFromCGPoint()`, `NSStringFromCGSize()`, `CGSizeFromString()`, and `CGPointFromString()` perform these functions.

Defining Locations

You can define a view's location by setting its center (which is a `CGPoint`) or bounds (`CGRect`). Unlike the frame, a view's bounds reflect the view's frame in its *own* coordinate system. In practical terms, that means the origin of the bounds is (0.0, 0.0), and its size is its width and height.

When you want to move or resize a view, update its frame's origin, center, or size. You don't need to worry about things such as rectangular sections that have been exposed or hidden. The iPhone takes care of the redrawing. This lets you treat your views like tangible objects and delegate the rendering issues to Cocoa Touch. For example

```
[myView setFrame:CGRectMake(0.0f, 50.0f, mywidth, myheight)];
```

Transforms

Standard Core Graphics calls transform views in real time. For example, you can apply clipping, rotation, or other 2D geometric effects. Cocoa Touch supports an entire suite of affine transforms (translate, rotate, scale, skew, and so on). The `drawRect:` method for any `UIView` subclass provides the entry point for drawing views through low-level Core Graphics calls.

Note

When calling Core Graphics functions, keep in mind that Quartz lays out its coordinate system from the bottom left, whereas `UIViews` have their origin at the top left.

Other View Traits

In addition to the physical screen layout, you can set the following view traits among others:

- Every view has a translucency factor (alpha) that ranges between opaque and transparent. Adjust this by issuing `[myView setAlpha:value]`, where the alpha values falls between 0.0 (fully transparent) and 1.0 (fully opaque).

- You can assign a color to the background of your view. `[myView setBackgroundColor:[UIColor redColor]]` colors your view red.

View Layout

Figure 2-2 shows the layout of a typical iPhone application screen. For current releases of the iPhone, the screen size is 320x480 pixels in portrait mode, 480x320 pixels in landscape. At the top of the screen, whether in landscape or portrait mode, a standard status bar occupies 20 pixels of height. To query the status bar frame, call `[[UIApplication sharedApplication] statusBarFrame]`.

If you'd rather free up those 20 pixels of screen space for other use, you can hide the status bar entirely. Use this `UIApplication` call: `[UIApplication sharedApplication] setStatusBarHidden:YES animated:NO]`. Alternatively, set the `UIStatusBarHidden` key to `<true/>` in your application Info.plist file.

To run your application in landscape-only mode, set the status bar orientation to landscape. Do this even if you plan to hide the status bar (that is, `[[UIApplication sharedApplication] setStatusBarOrientation: UIInterfaceOrientationLandscapeRight]`). This forces windows to display side to side and produces a proper landscape keyboard.

The `UIScreen` object acts as a stand in for the iPhone's physical screen (`[UIScreen mainScreen]`). The screen object maps view layout boundaries into pixel space. It returns either the full screen size (`bounds`) or just the rectangle that applies to your application (`applicationFrame`). This latter takes the size of your status bar and, if used, any toolbars/navigation bars into account.

By default, `UINavigationBar`, `UIToolbar`, and `UITabBar` objects are 44 pixels in height each. Use these numbers to calculate the available space on your iPhone screen and lay out your application views when not using Interface Builder's layout tools.

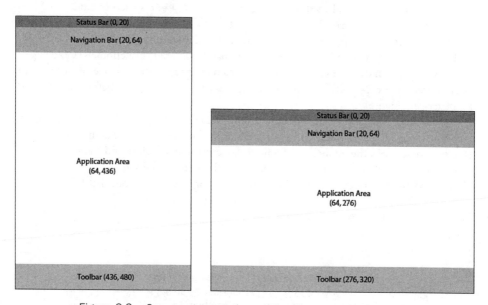

Figure 2-2   On current generations of the iPhone, the status bar is 20 pixels high, often followed below by a 44-pixel-high navigation bar. If you use a toolbar at the bottom of your screen, that will also occupy 44 pixels. It helps to use Photoshop or some other image layout program to design your screens taking these geometries into account.

Gestures

Views intercept user touches. This integration between the way things look and the way things react enables you to add a meaningful response to taps, drags, and what have you. Adding touch handlers like touchesBegan: withEvent: to your views allows you to intercept user touches, determine the phase of the touch (the equivalent of mouse down, mouse dragged, mouse up), and produce feedback based on those touches.

The UITouch class tells you where the event took place (locationInView:) and the tap count (tapCount), which is vital for distinguishing between single- and double-taps. Several recipes in this chapter demonstrate how to use these gesture responses and how to integrate view geometry and hierarchy into your applications for enticing, layered, direct-manipulation interfaces.

Recipe: Adding Stepwise Subviews

Expand your view hierarchy by calling addSubview:. This adds a subview to some other view. Recipe 2-1 shows a simple UIViewController's loadView method that defines a series of stepped subviews. It demonstrates the basics of allocating, framing, and adding views.

These subviews are not nested, in that they all belong to the same parent. They're indented so that you can see them all at once. The indentation uses the handy CGRectInset() function. Pass it a rectangle (using the CGRect structure) and two insets—horizontal and vertical—and it returns the inset, centered rectangle. Here, each subview is inset from its parent or sibling's frame by 32 pixels on each side.

In their simplest form, views are little more than transparent placeholders. Coloring the view backgrounds distinguishes one view from another in the absence of meaningful content (see Figure 2-3). It's a useful trick when trying to test layouts before committing to an actual design.

Always keep your coordinate system in mind. When working with view hierarchy, you must define a view's frame in its parent's coordinate system. The example in Recipe 2-1 requests the application frame to lay out the main view and then resets its origin to (0, 0). Resetting the origin updates the frame from the screen's to the main view's coordinate system. This reset forms the basis for the view layout that follows.

Recipe 2-1   **Adding Nested Subviews**

```
- (void) loadView
{
    // Create the main view
    CGRect appRect = [[UIScreen mainScreen] applicationFrame];
    contentView = [[UIView alloc] initWithFrame:appRect];
    contentView.backgroundColor = [UIColor whiteColor];

    // Provide support for autorotation and resizing
    contentView.autoresizesSubviews = YES;
    contentView.autoresizingMask = (UIViewAutoresizingFlexibleWidth |
    ➥UIViewAutoresizingFlexibleHeight);
```

Recipe 2-1   **Continued**

```
self.view = contentView;
[contentView release];

// reset the origin point for subviews. The new origin is 0,0
appRect.origin = CGPointMake(0.0f, 0.0f);

// Add the subviews, each stepped by 32 pixels on each side
UIView *subview = [[UIView alloc] initWithFrame:CGRectInset(appRect, 32.0f,
➥32.0f)];
subview.backgroundColor = [UIColor lightGrayColor];
[contentView addSubview:subview];
[subview release];

subview = [[UIView alloc] initWithFrame:CGRectInset(appRect, 64.0f, 64.0f)];
subview.backgroundColor = [UIColor darkGrayColor];
[contentView addSubview:subview];
[subview release];

subview = [[UIView alloc] initWithFrame:CGRectInset(appRect, 96.0f, 96.0f)];
subview.backgroundColor = [UIColor blackColor];
[contentView addSubview:subview];
[subview release];
}
```

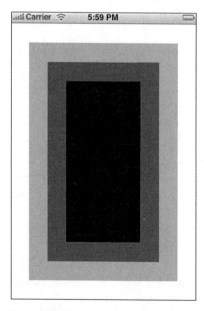

Figure 2-3   The code in Recipe 2-1 defines a UIView controller's
main view with three colored, nested subviews.

Reorienting

Extending Recipe 2-1 to enable orientation changes takes thought. You cannot just swap each subview's heights and widths as you might assume. That's because the shapes of horizontal and vertical applications on the iPhone use different aspect ratios. Assuming a 20-pixel status bar, portrait view areas are 320 pixels wide by 460 pixels high; landscapes are 480 pixels wide by 300 pixels high (refer to Figure 2-2). This difference throws off interfaces that depend solely on rotation to reorient.

To rotate this example, add code that distinguishes landscape orientations from portrait ones and adjust the frames accordingly. This is shown in Recipe 2-2.

Avoid reorientation schemes that rely on toggling (for example, "I was just in portrait mode so, if the orientation changed, I must be in landscape mode.") It's entirely possible to switch from left-landscape to right-landscape without hitting a portrait state in-between. Orientation is all about sensors and feedback, and the iPhone is not guaranteed to catch any middle state between two orientations. Fortunately, UIKit provides a UIViewController callback that alerts you to new orientations and that specifies what that orientation will be.

Recipe 2-2   **Adding Reorientation Support to the Preceding Subview Example**

```
- (void)willRotateToInterfaceOrientation:
    (UIInterfaceOrientation)orientation
        duration:(NSTimeInterval)duration  {

    CGRect apprect;
    apprect.origin = CGPointMake(0.0f, 0.0f);

    // adjust the frame size based on actual orientation
    if ((orientation == UIInterfaceOrientationLandscapeLeft) ||
    ➥(orientation == UIInterfaceOrientationLandscapeRight))
        apprect.size = CGSizeMake(480.0f, 300.0f);
    else
        apprect.size = CGSizeMake(320.0f, 460.0f);

    // resize each subview accordingly
    float offset = 32.0f;
    for (UIView *subview in [contentView subviews])    {
        CGRect frame = CGRectInset(apprect, offset, offset);
        [subview setFrame:frame];
        offset += 32.0f;
    }
}

// Allow the view to respond to iPhone Orientation changes
- (BOOL)shouldAutorotateToInterfaceOrientation:
    (UIInterfaceOrientation)interfaceOrientation
```

```
{
    return YES;
}
```

Recipe: Dragging Views

Cocoa Touch simplifies direct view manipulation. When dealing with many onscreen views, the iPhone takes charge of deciding which view the user touched and passes any touch events to the proper view for you. This helps you write concrete direct-manipulation interfaces where users touch, drag, and interact with onscreen objects.

Recipe 2-3 centers on touches in action. This example creates a child of UIImageView called DragView that enables users to drag the view around the iPhone screen. Being an image view, it's important to enable its user interaction, via [dragger setUserInteractionEnabled:YES]. This holds true for backdrops as well as direct-interaction views. Whenever working with UIImageView in direct-manipulation interfaces, make sure to enable interaction, no matter what role in the view hierarchy. With image views, the user interaction toggle affects all the view's children as well as the view itself.

When a user first touches any DragView (see the flowers in Figure 2-4), the object stores the start location as an offset from the view's origin. As the user drags, the view moves along with the finger—always maintaining the same origin offset so that the movement feels natural.

Figure 2-4   The code in Recipe 2-3 creates an interface with 16 flowers that can be dragged around the iPhone screen.

> **Note**
>
> The way the example in Figure 2-4 is built, you can use multiple fingers to drag more than one flower around the screen at once. It's not multitouch per se because each flower (UIView) responds to only one touch at a time. A discussion of true multitouch interaction follows later in this chapter.

Touching an object also does one more thing in this code: It pops that object to the front of the parent view. This means any dragged object always floats *over* any other object onscreen. Do this by telling the view's parent (its superview) to bring the view to its front.

UITouch

The UITouch class defines how fingers move across the iPhone screen. Touches are sent while invoking the standard began, moved, and ended handlers. You can also query user events (of the UIEvent class) to return touches affecting a given view through touchesForView: and touchesForWindow:. These calls return an unordered set (NSSet) of touches.

> **Note**
>
> Send allObjects to any NSSet to return an array of those objects.

A touch tells you several things: where the touch took place (both the current and most recent previous location), what stage of the touch was used (essentially mouse down, mouse moved, mouse up), a tap count (for example, single-tap/double-tap), when the touch took place (through a time stamp), and so forth.

For nonmultitouch interaction styles, assume that you're dealing with a single touch at any time. The code in Recipe 2-3 recovers the first available touch for each event by calling anyObject on the returned touch set.

Recipe 2-3   Building Multiple Draggable Views

```
/*
 *   DragView: Draggable views
 */

@interface DragView : UIImageView
{
    CGPoint startLocation;
}
@end

@implementation DragView

// Note the touch point and bring the touched view to the front
- (void) touchesBegan:(NSSet*)touches withEvent:(UIEvent*)event
```

Recipe 2-3   **Continued**
```
{
    CGPoint pt = [[touches anyObject] locationInView:self];
    ↪startLocation = pt;
    [[self superview] bringSubviewToFront:self];
}

// As the user drags, move the flower with the touch
- (void) touchesMoved:(NSSet*)touches withEvent:(UIEvent*)event
{
    CGPoint pt = [[touches anyObject] locationInView:self];
    CGRect frame = [self frame];

    frame.origin.x += pt.x - startLocation.x;
    frame.origin.y += pt.y - startLocation.y;
    [self setFrame:frame];
}
@end

/*
 *  Hello Controller: The primary view controller
 */

@interface HelloController : UIViewController
{
    UIView *contentView;
}
@end

@implementation HelloController

#define MAXFLOWERS 16

CGPoint randomPoint() {return CGPointMake(random() % 256, random() % 396);}

- (void)loadView
{
    // Create the main view with a black background
    CGRect apprect = [[UIScreen mainScreen] applicationFrame];
    contentView = [[UIView alloc] initWithFrame:apprect];
    contentView.backgroundColor = [UIColor blackColor];
    self.view = contentView;
    [contentView release];

    // Add the flowers to random points on the screen
    for (int i = 0; i < MAXFLOWERS; i++)
    {
```

```
        CGRect dragRect = CGRectMake(0.0f, 0.0f, 64.0f, 64.0f);
        dragRect.origin = randomPoint();
        DragView *dragger = [[DragView alloc] initWithFrame:dragRect];
        [dragger setUserInteractionEnabled:YES];

        // select random flower color
        NSString *whichFlower = [[NSArray arrayWithObjects:@"blueFlower.png",
        ➥@"pinkFlower.png", @"orangeFlower.png", nil] objectAtIndex:(random() %
        ➥3)];
        [dragger setImage:[UIImage imageNamed:whichFlower]];

        // add the new subview
        [contentView addSubview:dragger];
        [dragger release];
    }
}

-(void) dealloc
{
    [contentView release];
    [super dealloc];
}
@end
```

Adding Persistence

Persistence represents a key iPhone design touch point. After users leave a program, Apple strongly recommends that they return to a state that matches as closely to where they left off as possible. Adding persistence to this sample code involves several steps:

1. Storing the data

2. Resuming from a saved session

3. Providing a startup image that matches the last session

Storing State

Every view knows its position because you can query its `frame`. This enables you to recover and store positions for each onscreen flower. The flower type (green, pink, or blue) is another matter. For each view to report its current flower, the `DragView` class must store that value, too. Adding a string instance variable enables the view to return the image name used. Listing 2-1 shows the extended `DragView` class definition.

Listing 2-1   **The Updated `DragView` Class Includes a String to Store the Flower Type**

```
@interface DragView : UIImageView
{
    CGPoint startLocation;
```

Listing 2-1   **Continued**

```
    NSString *whichFlower;
}
@property (nonatomic, retain) NSString *whichFlower;
@end
```

Adding this extra variable enables the HelloController class to store both a list of colors and a list of locations to its defaults file. A simple loop collects both values from each draggable view and then stores them. Listing 2-2 presents an updateDefaults method, as defined in HelloController. This method saves the current state to disk. It should be called in the application delegate's applicationWillTerminate: method, just before the program ends.

Notice the use here of NSStringFromCGRect(). It provides a tight way to store frame information as a string. To recover the rectangle, issue CGRectFromString(). Each call takes one argument: a CGRect in the first case, an NSString * in the second. The UIKit framework provides calls that translate points and sizes as well as rectangles to and from strings.

Defaults, as you can see, work like a dictionary. Just assign an object to a key and the iPhone "automagically" updates the preferences file associated with your application ID. Your application ID is defined in Info.plist. Defaults are stored in Library/Preferences inside your application's sandbox. Calling the synchronize function updates those defaults immediately instead of waiting for the program to terminate.

Listing 2-2   **Storing Flower Locations via User Defaults**

```
// Collect all the colors and locations and save them for the next use
- (void) updateDefaults
{
    NSMutableArray *colors = [[NSMutableArray alloc] init];
    NSMutableArray *locs = [[NSMutableArray alloc] init];

    for (DragView *dv in [contentView subviews]) {
        [colors addObject:[dv whichFlower]];
        [locs addObject:NSStringFromCGRect([dv frame])];
    }

    [[NSUserDefaults standardUserDefaults] setObject:colors forKey:@"colors"];
    [[NSUserDefaults standardUserDefaults] setObject:locs forKey:@"locs"];
    [[NSUserDefaults standardUserDefaults] synchronize];
    [colors release];
    [locs release];
}
```

Recovering State

Persistence awareness generally resides in the view controller's init or loadView (for example, before the view actually appears). These methods should find any previous state information and, for this example, match the flowers to that state. When querying user defaults, this code checks whether state data is unavailable (for example, the value returned is nil). When state data goes missing, the method creates random flowers at random points. Listing 2-3 shows a state-aware version of loadView.

Note

When working with large data sources, you may want to initialize and populate your saved object array in the UIViewController's init method, and then draw them in loadView. Where possible, use threading when working with many objects to avoid blocking.

Listing 2-3   **Checking for Previous State**

```
- (void)loadView
{
    // Create the main view
    CGRect apprect = [[UIScreen mainScreen] applicationFrame];
    contentView = [[UIView alloc] initWithFrame:apprect];
    contentView.backgroundColor = [UIColor blackColor];
    self.view = contentView;

    // Attempt to read in previous colors and locations
    NSMutableArray *colors, *locs;
    colors = [[NSUserDefaults standardUserDefaults] objectForKey:@"colors"];
    locs = [[NSUserDefaults standardUserDefaults] objectForKey:@"locs"];

    for (int i = 0; i < MAXFLOWERS; i++)
    {
        // Use a random point unless there's a previous location
        CGRect dragRect = CGRectMake(0.0f, 0.0f, 64.0f, 64.0f);
        dragRect.origin = randomPoint();
        if (locs && ([locs count] == MAXFLOWERS))
            ➡dragRect = CGRectFromString([locs objectAtIndex:i]);
        DragView *dragger = [[DragView alloc] initWithFrame:dragRect];
        [dragger setUserInteractionEnabled:YES];

        // Use a random color unless there's a previous color
        NSString *whichFlower = [[NSArray arrayWithObjects:@"blueFlower.png",
        ➡@"pinkFlower.png", @"orangeFlower.png", nil] objectAtIndex:(random()
        ➡% 3)];
        if (colors && ([colors count] == MAXFLOWERS))
            ➡whichFlower = [colors objectAtIndex:i];
        [dragger setWhichFlower:whichFlower];
        [dragger setImage:[UIImage imageNamed:whichFlower]];
```

Listing 2-3   **Continued**

```
            // Add the subview
            [contentView addSubview:dragger];
            [dragger release];
        }

}
```

Startup Image

Apple has not yet included persistence screenshot capabilities into its official SDK release, although the functionality is partially available in the UIKit framework as an undocumented call. To access the _writeApplicationSnapshot feature shown in Listing 2-4, you must add it by hand to the UIApplicationClass interface. Once added, you can build a cached shot of your screen before ending the application.

Note

See Chapter 1, "Introducing the iPhone SDK," for further discussion about using undocumented calls and features in your programs.

The idea is this: When you leave the application, you snap a picture of the screen. Then when your application starts up (presumably returning you to the same state you left with), the cached image acts as the Default.png image, giving the illusion that you're jumping directly back without any startup sequence.

Apple has yet to enable this feature with the iPhone SDK, and at the time of writing, applications cannot check in to find updated snapshots. Hopefully, Apple will provide this functionality in a future firmware release.

Listing 2-4   **Screenshotting Before Application Termination**

```
@interface UIApplication (Extended)
-(void) _writeApplicationSnapshot;
@end


[[UIApplication sharedApplication] _writeApplicationSnapshot];
```

Recipe: Clipped Views

When working with direct-manipulation interfaces, it's unlikely that you'll want to deal solely with rectangular views. Soft borders, rounded corners, and other visual enhancements are easily added to UIView instances.

Clipping creates view shapes that fill only part of a view's frame. You can produce clipping with Core Graphics using the drawRect: method of a UIView object, just as you would on a Macintosh. Core Graphics enables you to build paths from sources including points, lines, standard shapes (such as ellipses), and Bézier curves. Clipping your views to these paths creates the illusion of nonrectangular onscreen objects. Figure 2-5 shows a number of onscreen circular clipped views, clearly overlapping with each other. These views were created by the code shown in Listing 2-5. This code creates a path, performs the clipping, and then draws into the clipped view.

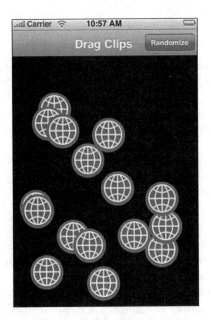

Figure 2-5   Clipping enables you to create
nonrectangular views onscreen from rectangular source
material, using rectangular UIView frames.

Listing 2-5   **Clipping a View to a Circular Path**

```
- (void) drawRect: (CGRect) aRect
{

    CGRect bounds = CGRectMake(0.0f, 0.0f, SIDELENGTH, SIDELENGTH);

    // Create a new path
    CGContextRef context = UIGraphicsGetCurrentContext();
    CGMutablePathRef path = CGPathCreateMutable();

    // Add circle to path
    CGPathAddEllipseInRect(path, NULL, bounds);
    CGContextAddPath(context, path);
```

Listing 2-5   **Continued**

```
    // Clip to the circle and draw the logo
    CGContextClip(context);
    [logo drawInRect:bounds];
    CFRelease(path);
}
```

Balancing Touches with Clipping

Visual clipping does not affect how UIViews respond to touches. The iPhone senses user taps throughout the entire view frame. This includes the undrawn area such as the corners of the frame outside the actual circles of Figure 2-5 just as much as the clipped presentation. That means that unless you add some sort of hit test, users may attempt to tap through to a view that's "obscured" by the clear portion of the UIView frame.

Listing 2-6 adds a simple hit test to the clipped views, determining whether touches fall within the clipping path. I implemented circular clipping and circular hit tests to provide the simplest example. Use any computable test method you like to determine whether a user touch intersects the view. Add pointInside:withEvent: to your UIView subclass and return YES when the touch has properly hit your view or NO when it does not.

Listing 2-6   **Checking Circular Views against Touches**

```
- (BOOL) pointInside:(CGPoint)point withEvent:(UIEvent *)event
{
    CGPoint pt;
    float HALFSIDE = SIDELENGTH / 2.0f;

    // normalize with centered origin
    pt.x = (point.x - HALFSIDE) / HALFSIDE;
    pt.y = (point.y - HALFSIDE) / HALFSIDE;

    // x^2 + y^2 = hypoteneus length
    float xsquared = pt.x * pt.x;
    float ysquared = pt.y * pt.y;

    // If the length < 1, the point is within the clipped circle
    if ((xsquared + ysquared) < 1.0) return YES;
    return NO;
}
```

Accessing Pixel-by-Pixel Values

There are many ways to test user touches against views. Listing 2-6 computed whether a touch fell within a circle's radius. With hit masks and variable transparency images, you can test against a point's alpha value. Translucency controls whether you trigger a response. Listing 2-7 extends the `UIImageView` class to add an image's bitmap representation. It tests touches against alpha values in the bitmap, point by point. Pixels whose alpha levels fall below 0.5 will not respond to touches using this code.

Note
The code in this listing returns a bitmap context, and its bitmap data is based on Apple sample code.

Listing 2-7   **Testing Touch Hits Against a Bitmap**

```
// Return a bitmap context using alpha/red/green/blue byte values
CGContextRef CreateARGBBitmapContext (CGImageRef inImage)
{
    CGContextRef    context = NULL;
    CGColorSpaceRef colorSpace;
    void *          bitmapData;
    int             bitmapByteCount;
    int             bitmapBytesPerRow;

    size_t pixelsWide = CGImageGetWidth(inImage);
    size_t pixelsHigh = CGImageGetHeight(inImage);
    bitmapBytesPerRow   = (pixelsWide * 4);
    bitmapByteCount     = (bitmapBytesPerRow * pixelsHigh);
    colorSpace = CGColorSpaceCreateDeviceRGB();

    if (colorSpace == NULL)
    {
        fprintf(stderr, "Error allocating color space\n");
        return NULL;
    }

    // allocate the bitmap & create context
    bitmapData = malloc( bitmapByteCount );
    if (bitmapData == NULL)
    {
        fprintf (stderr, "Memory not allocated!");
        CGColorSpaceRelease( colorSpace );
        return NULL;
    }
```

Listing 2-7   **Continued**

```
    context = CGBitmapContextCreate (bitmapData, pixelsWide, pixelsHigh, 8,
➥bitmapBytesPerRow, colorSpace, kCGImageAlphaPremultipliedFirst);
    if (context == NULL)
    {
        free (bitmapData);
        fprintf (stderr, "Context not created!");
    }
    CGColorSpaceRelease( colorSpace );
    return context;
}


// Return Image Pixel data as an ARGB bitmap
unsigned char *RequestImagePixelData(UIImage *inImage)
{
    CGImageRef img = [inImage CGImage];
    CGSize size = [inImage size];

    CGContextRef cgctx = CreateARGBBitmapContext(img, size);
    if (cgctx == NULL) return NULL;

    CGRect rect = {{0,0},{size.width, size.height}};
    CGContextDrawImage(cgctx, rect, img);
    unsigned char *data = CGBitmapContextGetData (cgctx);
    CGContextRelease(cgctx);

    return data;
}


// Create an Image View that stores a copy of its image as an addressable bitmap
@interface BitMapView : UIImageView
{
    unsigned char *bitmap;
    CGSize size;
    UIView *colorView;
}
@end
@implementation BitMapView

// Hit test relies on the alpha level of the touched pixel
- (BOOL) pointInside:(CGPoint)point withEvent:(UIEvent *)event
{
    long startByte = (int)((point.y * size.width) + point.x) * 4;
    int alpha = (unsigned char) bitmap[startByte];
    return (alpha > 0.5);
}
```

Listing 2-7   **Continued**

```
-(void) setImage:(UIImage *) anImage
{
    [super setImage:anImage];
    bitmap = RequestImagePixelData(anImage);
    size = [anImage size];
}
@end
```

Recipe: Detecting Multitouch

By enabling multitouch interaction in your `UIViews`, the iPhone enables you to recover and respond to multifinger interaction. This recipe, shown in Recipe 2-4, demonstrates how to add multitouch to your iPhone applications.

To begin, set `multipleTouchEnabled` to `YES` or override `isMultipleTouchEnabled` for your view. This tells your application to poll for more than one `UITouch` at a time. Now when you call `touchesForView:`, the returned set may contain several touches. Use `NSSet`'s `allObjects` method to convert that set into an addressable `NSArray`. When the array's count exceeds one, you know you're dealing with multitouch.

In theory, the iPhone could support an arbitrary number of touches. In practice, multitouch is limited to five finger touches at a time. Even five at a time goes beyond what most developers need. There aren't many meaningful gestures you can make with five fingers at once. This particularly holds true when you grasp the iPhone with one hand and touch with the other. Perhaps it's a comfort to know that if you need to, the extra finger support has been built in. Unfortunately, when you are using three or more touches at a time, the screen has a tendency to lose track of one or more of those fingers. It's hard to programmatically track smooth gestures when you go beyond two finger touches.

Touches are not grouped. If, for example, you touch the screen with two fingers from each hand, there's no way to determine which touches belong to which hand. The touch order is arbitrary. Although grouped touches retain the same finger order for the lifetime of a single touch event (down, move, up), the order may change the next time your user touches the screen. When you need to distinguish touches from each other, build a touch dictionary indexed by the touch objects.

> **Note**
>
> The `drawRect:` routine in Recipe 2-4 clears its context each time it is called. This removes previous circles and lines from the display. Comment out this line if you want to see an event trail.

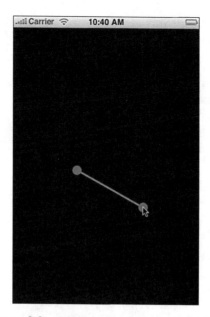

Figure 2-6   The iPhone enables you to capture
multitouch events as well as single-touch ones.
In this example, two circles mark the points at
which the user has touched the screen.

Recipe 2-4   **Visualizing Multitouch**

```
@interface MultiTouchView : UIView
{
    CGPoint loc1, loc2;
}
@property (nonatomic) CGPoint loc1;
@property (nonatomic) CGPoint loc2;
@end

@implementation MultiTouchView
@synthesize loc1;
@synthesize loc2;

- (BOOL) isMultipleTouchEnabled {return YES;}

- (void) touchesBegan:(NSSet*)touches withEvent:(UIEvent*)event
{
    NSArray *allTouches = [touches allObjects];
    int count = [allTouches count];
    if (count > 0) loc1 = [[allTouches objectAtIndex:0] locationInView:self];
    if (count > 1) loc2 = [[allTouches objectAtIndex:1] locationInView:self];
```

Recipe 2-4 **Continued**

```
    [self setNeedsDisplay];
}

// React to moved touches the same as to "began"
- (void) touchesMoved:(NSSet*)touches withEvent:(UIEvent*)event
{
    [self touchesBegan:touches withEvent:event];
}

- (void) drawRect: (CGRect) aRect
{
    // Get the current context
    CGContextRef context = UIGraphicsGetCurrentContext();
    CGContextClearRect(context, aRect);

    // Set up the stroke and fill characteristics
    CGContextSetLineWidth(context, 3.0f);
    CGFloat gray[4] = {0.5f, 0.5f, 0.5f, 1.0f};
    CGContextSetStrokeColor(context, gray);
    CGFloat red[4] = {0.75f, 0.25f, 0.25f, 1.0f};
    CGContextSetFillColor(context, red);

    // Draw a line between the two location points
    CGContextMoveToPoint(context, loc1.x, loc1.y);
    CGContextAddLineToPoint(context, loc2.x, loc2.y);
    CGContextStrokePath(context);

    CGRect p1box = CGRectMake(loc1.x, loc1.y, 0.0f, 0.0f);
    CGRect p2box = CGRectMake(loc2.x, loc2.y, 0.0f, 0.0f);
    float offset = -8.0f;

    // circle point 1
    CGMutablePathRef path = CGPathCreateMutable();
    CGPathAddEllipseInRect(path, NULL, CGRectInset(p1box, offset, offset));
    CGContextAddPath(context, path);
    CGContextFillPath(context);
    CFRelease(path);

    // circle point 2
    path = CGPathCreateMutable();
    CGPathAddEllipseInRect(path, NULL, CGRectInset(p2box, offset, offset));
    CGContextAddPath(context, path);
    CGContextFillPath(context);
    CFRelease(path);
}
@end
```

> **Note**
>
> Apple provides many Core Graphics/Quartz 2D resources on its developer Web site. Although these forums, mailing lists, and source code samples are not iPhone specific, they offer an invaluable resource for expanding your iPhone Core Graphics knowledge.

`UIView` **Animations**

`UIView` animation provides one of the odd but lovely perks of working with the iPhone as a development platform. It enables you to slow down changes when updating views, producing smooth animated results that enhance the user experience. Best of all, this all occurs without you having to do much work.

`UIView` animations are perfect for building a visual bridge between a view's current and changed states. With them, you emphasize visual change and create an animation that links those changes together. Animatable changes include the following:

- Changes in location—moving a view around the screen
- Changes in size—updating the view's frame
- Changes in transparency—altering the view's alpha value
- Changes in rotation or any other affine transforms that you apply to a view

Building `UIView` **Animation Blocks**

`UIView` animations work as blocks, a complete transaction that progresses at once. Start the block by issuing `beginAnimations:context:`. End the block with `commitAnimations`. These class methods are sent to `UIView` and not to individual views. In the block between these two calls, you define the way the animation works and perform the actual view updates. The animation controls you'll use are as follows:

- **`beginAnimations:context.`** Marks the start of the animation block.
- **`setAnimationCurve.`** Defines the way the animation accelerates and decelerates. Use ease-in/ease-out (`UIViewAnimationCurveEaseInOut`) unless you have some compelling reason to select another curve. The other curve types are ease in (accelerate into the animation), linear (no animation acceleration), and ease out (accelerate out of the animation). Ease-in/ease-out provides the most natural-feeling animation style.
- **`setAnimationDuration.`** Specifies the length of the animation, in seconds. This is really the cool bit. You can stretch out the animation for as long as you need it to run. Be aware of straining your user's patience and keep your animations below a second or two in length.
- **`commitAnimations.`** Marks the end of the animation block.

Sandwich your actual view change commands after setting up the animation details and before ending the animation. Listing 2-8 shows `UIView` animations in action by setting an animation curve and the animation duration (here, one second). The actual change being animated is a transparency update. The alpha value of the content view goes to zero, making it invisible. Instead of the view simply disappearing, this animation block slows down the change and fades it out of sight.

> **Note**
>
> Apple often uses two animation blocks one after another to add bounce to their animations. For example, they might zoom into a view a bit more than needed and then use a second animation to bring that enlarged view down to its final size. Use "bounces" to add a little more life to your animation blocks. Be sure that the animations do not overlap. Either add a delay so that the second animation does not start until the first ends (`performSelector: withObject: afterDelay:`) or assign an animation delegate callback (`animationDidStop: finished:`) to catch the end of the first animation and start the second.

Listing 2-8 Using `UIView` Animation Calls

```
[UIView beginAnimations:nil context:context];
[UIView setAnimationCurve:UIViewAnimationCurveEaseInOut];
[UIView setAnimationDuration:1.0];
[contentView setAlpha:0.0f];
[UIView commitAnimations];
```

Recipe: Fading a View In and Out

There are times you'll want to add information to your screen that overlays your view but does not of itself do anything. For example, you might show a top scores list or some instructions or provide a context-sensitive tool tip. Recipe 2-5 demonstrates how to use a `UIView` animation block to slowly fade a noninteractive overlay view into and out of sight.

This is done by creating a custom `ToggleView`. As defined by this code, `ToggleViews` are `UIViews` with one child, an image view. When tapped, the animation block toggles the alpha setting from off to on or on to off. The key bits for making this happen well and reliably are as follows:

- Make sure the child does not look for interaction events. Cocoa Touch does not allow transparent views to catch touches. So you must allow the parent, the `ToggleView`, to handle all user interactions instead. When creating the child, the method sets the child's property `userInteractionEnabled` to NO.

- Make sure to catch only mouse down events. For simple on-off-on-off toggles, catch and respond only to presses for the most natural user feedback. Otherwise, user taps will hide and then immediately show your image view again.

- Pick a reasonable animation time. If you lengthen the animation beyond what your user is willing to handle, you'll end up handling new taps before the first animation has completed. The one-second animation shown here is just about the longest time you'll want to use. Half- or quarter-second animations are better for common interface changes.

Recipe 2-5   Using `UIView` Animations with Transparency Changes

```
@interface ToggleView: UIView
{
    BOOL isVisible;
    UIImageView *imgView;
}
@end

@implementation ToggleView
- (id) initWithFrame: (CGRect) aFrame;
{
    self = [super initWithFrame:aFrame];
    isVisible = YES;
    imgView = [[UIImageView alloc] initWithFrame:[[UIScreen mainScreen]
    ➥applicationFrame]];
    [imgView setImage:[UIImage imageNamed:@"alphablend.png"]];
    imgView.userInteractionEnabled = NO;
    [self addSubview:imgView];
    [imgView release];
    return self;
}

- (void) touchesBegan:(NSSet*)touches withEvent:(UIEvent*)event
{
    // only respond to mouse down events
    UITouch *touch = [touches anyObject];
    if ([touch phase] != UITouchPhaseBegan) return;

    isVisible = !isVisible;

    CGContextRef context = UIGraphicsGetCurrentContext();
    [UIView beginAnimations:nil context:context];
    [UIView setAnimationCurve:UIViewAnimationCurveEaseInOut];
    [UIView setAnimationDuration:1.0];
    [imgView setAlpha:(float)isVisible];
```

```
    [UIView commitAnimations];
}
- (void) dealloc
{
    [imgView release];
    [super dealloc];
}
@end
```

Recipe: Swapping Views

The UIView animation block doesn't limit you to a single change. Recipe 2-6 combines frame size updates with transparency changes to create a more compelling animation. You do this by adding several directives at once to the animation block. Recipe 2-6 performs four actions at a time. It zooms and fades one view into place, while zooming out and fading away another. Figure 2-7 provides a preview of this animation in action.

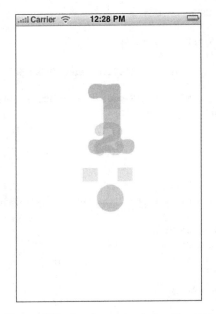

Figure 2-7   Issuing several view changes
within a single UIView animation block can
create complex visual effects.

Recipe 2-6   **Combining Multiple View Changes in Animation Blocks**

```
@interface ToggleView: UIView
{
     BOOL isOne;
     UIImageView *imgView1, *imgView2;
}
@end

@implementation ToggleView

#define BIGRECT CGRectMake(0.0f, 0.0f, 320.0f, 435.0f)
#define SMALLRECT CGRectMake(130.0f, 187.0f, 60.0f, 60.0f)

- (id) initWithFrame: (CGRect) aFrame;
{
    self = [super initWithFrame:aFrame];

    // Load both views, make them noninteractive
    imgView1 = [[UIImageView alloc] initWithFrame:BIGRECT];
    imgView2 = [[UIImageView alloc] initWithFrame:SMALLRECT];
    [imgView1 setImage:[UIImage imageNamed:@"one.png"]];
    [imgView2 setImage:[UIImage imageNamed:@"two.png"]];
    imgView1.userInteractionEnabled = NO;
    imgView2.userInteractionEnabled = NO;

    // image 1 is in front of image 2 to begin
    [self addSubview:imgView2];
    [self addSubview:imgView1];
    isOne = YES;
    [imgView1 release];
    [imgView2 release];
    return self;
}
- (void) touchesBegan:(NSSet*)touches withEvent:(UIEvent*)event
{
    // Determine which view occupies which role
    UIImageView *big = isOne ? imgView1 : imgView2;
    UIImageView *little = isOne ? imgView2 : imgView1;
    isOne = !isOne;

    // Pack all the changes into the animation block
    CGContextRef context = UIGraphicsGetCurrentContext();
    [UIView beginAnimations:nil context:context];
    [UIView setAnimationCurve:UIViewAnimationCurveEaseInOut];
    [UIView setAnimationDuration:1.0];

    [big setFrame:SMALLRECT];
```

Recipe 2-6   **Continued**

```
    [big setAlpha:0.5];
    [little setFrame:BIGRECT];
    [little setAlpha:1.0];

    [UIView commitAnimations];

    // Hide the shrunken "big" image.
    [big setAlpha:0.0f];
    [[big superview] bringSubviewToFront:big];
}
-(void) dealloc
{
    [imgView1 release];
    [imgView2 release];
    [super dealloc];
}
@end
```

Recipe: Flipping Views

Transitions enable you to extend your UIView animation blocks to add even more visual flair. Two transitions—UIViewAnimationTransitionFlipFromLeft and UIViewAnimationTransitionFlipFromRight—enable you to do just what their names suggest. At this time, you can flip views left or flip views right. These are the only two official transitions available for UIViews.

Note

During the SDK beta period, Apple promised additional animations that were never realized, specifically UIViewAnimationTransitionCurlUp and UIViewAnimationTransitionCurlDown. These extra animations may appear at some future time.

To use transitions in UIView animation blocks, you need to do two things. First, you must add the transition as a block parameter. Use setAnimationTransition: to assign the transition to the enclosing UIView animation block. Second, you should rearrange the view order while inside the block. This is best done with exchangeSubviewAtIndex: withSubviewAtIndex:. Recipe 2-7 demonstrates how to create a simple flip view using these techniques. When tapped, the views use the animation to flip from one side to the next, as shown in Figure 2-8.

Do not confuse the UIView animation blocks with the Core Animation CATransition class. Unfortunately, you cannot assign a CATransition to your UIView animation. To use a CATransition, you must apply it to a UIView's layer, which is shown in the next recipe.

Figure 2-8   Use `UIView`'s built-in
transition animations to flip your
way from one view to the next.

Recipe 2-7   **Using Transitions with `UIView` Animation Blocks**

```
@interface FlipView : UIImageView
@end

@implementation FlipView
- (void) touchesEnded:(NSSet*)touches withEvent:(UIEvent*)event
{
    // Start Animation Block
    CGContextRef context = UIGraphicsGetCurrentContext();
    [UIView beginAnimations:nil context:context];
    [UIView setAnimationTransition: UIViewAnimationTransitionFlipFromLeft
    ➥forView:[self superview] cache:YES];
    [UIView setAnimationCurve:UIViewAnimationCurveEaseInOut];
    [UIView setAnimationDuration:1.0];

    // Animations
    [[self superview] exchangeSubviewAtIndex:0 withSubviewAtIndex:1];

    // Commit Animation Block
    [UIView commitAnimations];
}
@end
```

Recipe: Applying `CATransitions` to Layers

Core Animation Transitions expand your UIView animation vocabulary with just a few small differences in implementation. CATransitions work on layers rather than on views. Layers are the Core Animation rendering surfaces associated with each UIView. When working with Core Animation, you apply CATransitions to a view's default layer ([myView layer]) rather than the view itself.

You don't set your parameters through UIView the way you do with UIView animation. You create a Core Animation object, set *its* parameters, and then add the parameterized transition to the layer. Listing 2-9 shows a simple pushFromLeft method that you might swap out for the flip method shown in Recipe 2-7.

Animations use both a *type* and a *subtype*. The type specifies the kind of transition used. The subtype sets its direction. Together the type and subtype tell how the views should act when you apply the animation to them.

Core Animation Transitions are distinct from the two UIView flips discussed in the previous recipe. Cocoa Touch offers four types of Core Animation. These available types include cross fades, pushes (used in Listing 2-9), reveals (where one view slides off another), and covers (where one view slides onto another). The last three types enable you to specify the direction of motion for the transition through subtypes. For obvious reasons, cross fades do not have a direction and they do not use subtypes.

Core Animation is part of the Quartz Core framework. To use this sample code, you must add the Quartz Core framework to your project and import <QuartzCore/QuartzCore.h> into your code.

Note

Apple's Core Animation features 2D and 3D routines built around Objective-C classes. These classes provide graphics rendering and animation for your iPhone and Macintosh applications. Core Animation avoids many low-level development details associated with, for example, direct OpenGL while retaining the simplicity of working with hierarchical views.

Listing 2-9   **Adding a Core Animation Transition to a** UIView **Layer**

```
@implementation PushView
- (void) touchesEnded:(NSSet*)touches withEvent:(UIEvent*)event
{

    CATransition *animation = [CATransition animation];
    [animation setDelegate:self];
    [animation setDuration:1.0f];
    [animation setTimingFunction:UIViewAnimationCurveEaseInOut];
    [animation setType: kCATransitionPush];
    [animation setSubtype: kCATransitionFromLeft];

    [[self superview] exchangeSubviewAtIndex:0 withSubviewAtIndex:1];
```

Listing 2-9   **Continued**

```
    [[[self superview] layer] addAnimation:animation
    ➥forKey:@"transitionViewAnimation"];
}
@end
```

Undocumented Animation Types

The iPhone actually implements more animation types than official documents would suggest. As Listing 2-10 shows, the iPhone is perfectly capable of handling map curls à la the Google Maps application. This code, which works on the iPhone but not the Simulator, relies on extracting animation names from the UIKit binary framework file.

Like all undocumented calls, this is not without risk. Apple may change or delete these animations at any time. Other animation types include pageCurl, pageUnCurl, suckEffect, spewEffect, cameraIris (from the Photos application), cameraIrisHollowOpen, cameraIrisHollowClose, genieEffect (typically used for deleting garbage), unGenieEffect, rippleEffect, twist, tubey, swirl, charminUltra, zoomyIn, zoomyOut, and oglFlip.

Note the use of setRemovedOnCompletion: NO. This freezes the animation at its end, allowing the curled map to remain visible, as shown in Figure 2-9.

Figure 2-9   This eye-catching effect uses an
undocumented Core Animation type called mapCurl.

Listing 2-10   Calling Undocumented Animation Types

```
- (void) performCurl
{
    // Curl the image up or down
    CATransition *animation = [CATransition animation];
    [animation setDelegate:self];
    [animation setDuration:1.0f];
    [animation setTimingFunction:UIViewAnimationCurveEaseInOut];
    [animation setType:(notCurled ? @"mapCurl" : @"mapUnCurl")];
    [animation setRemovedOnCompletion:NO];
    [animation setFillMode: @"extended"];
    [animation setRemovedOnCompletion: NO];
    notCurled = !notCurled;

    [[topView layer] addAnimation:animation forKey:@"pageFlipAnimation"];
}
```

General Core Animation Calls

The iPhone provides partial support for Core Animation calls. By *partial,* I mean that many standard classes are missing in action. CIFilter is one such class. It's not included in Cocoa Touch, although the CALayer and CATransition classes are both filter-aware. If you're willing to work through these limits, you can freely use standard Core Animation calls in your programs.

Listing 2-11 shows iPhone native Core Animation code based on a sample from Lucas Newman (http://lucasnewman.com). When run, this method scales down and fades away the contents of a UIImageView. The source adds a translucent reflection layer, which follows the view.

This code remains virtually unchanged from the Mac OS X sample it was based on. More complex Core Animation samples may offer porting challenges, but for simple reflections, shadows, and transforms, all the functionality you need can be had at the native iPhone level.

Listing 2-11   Native iPhone Core Animation Calls

```
// Adapted from http://lucasnewman.com/animationsamples.zip
- (void) scaleAndFade
{
    // create the reflection layer
    CALayer *reflectionLayer = [CALayer layer];

    // share the contents image with the screen layer
    reflectionLayer.contents = [contentView layer].contents;
    reflectionLayer.opacity = 0.4;
    reflectionLayer.frame = CGRectOffset([contentView layer].frame, 0.5,
    ➥416.0f + 0.5);
```

Listing 2-11   **Continued**

```
// flip the y-axis
reflectionLayer.transform = CATransform3DMakeScale(1.0, -1.0, 1.0);
reflectionLayer.sublayerTransform = reflectionLayer.transform;
[[contentView layer] addSublayer:reflectionLayer];

#define ANIMATION_DURATION (4.0)

    [CATransaction begin];
    [CATransaction setValue:[NSNumber numberWithFloat:ANIMATION_DURATION]
➥forKey:kCATransactionAnimationDuration];

    // scale it down
    CABasicAnimation *shrinkAnimation = [CABasicAnimation
➥animationWithKeyPath:@"transform.scale"];
    shrinkAnimation.timingFunction = [CAMediaTimingFunction
➥functionWithName:kCAMediaTimingFunctionEaseIn];
    shrinkAnimation.toValue = [NSNumber numberWithFloat:0.0];
    [[contentView layer] addAnimation:shrinkAnimation forKey:@"shrinkAnimation"];

    // fade it out
    CABasicAnimation *fadeAnimation = [CABasicAnimation
➥animationWithKeyPath:@"opacity"];
    fadeAnimation.toValue = [NSNumber numberWithFloat:0.0];
    fadeAnimation.timingFunction = [CAMediaTimingFunction functionWithName:
➥kCAMediaTimingFunctionEaseIn];
    [[contentView layer] addAnimation:fadeAnimation forKey:@"fadeAnimation"];

    [CATransaction commit];
}
```

Recipe: Swiping Views

Swipes are a convenient but often-overlooked iPhone interaction style. When a user quickly drags his or her finger across the screen, the UITouch objects returned for that gesture include an info property. This property defines the direction in which the user swiped the screen, (for example, up, down, left, or right). This behavior is best seen in the iPhone's Photos application, when users swipe left or right to move between album pictures.

Early versions of the iPhone SDK offered swipe detection as a standard part of the UITouch object, but later releases dropped that capability. Instead, Apple offered workaround code in its *iPhone Developers Guide*. Recipe 2-8 is based on that code. It ensures that a user continues finger movement in one direction by defining a safety zone around the movement. If the user strays diagonally more than 6 pixels off course, the swipe cancels. Stay on-course for at least 12 pixels and the swipe is set.

Recipe 2-8 applies a Core Animation Transition on completion of a successful swipe. It uses the swipe direction to set the animation's subtype. Subtypes are used in Core Animation to specify the overall movement of the animation, whether up, down, or sideways.

This sample mimics the interaction style used for browsing through album pictures in Photos but allows you to move up and down as well as left and right. If you comment out the `kCATransitionPush` animation type and replace it with the undocumented `oglFlip` in the line that immediately follows it, you'll receive an even nicer surprise. Far from being limited to the two core flip directions, the iPhone actually supports a full four-way flip style, albeit one that Apple has not included in its public SDK.

Note

In early releases of the iPhone SDK, swipes didn't work in the Simulator. In later versions, they did. Should you encounter platform limitations while developing (for example, when working with the Camera), you can easily add workarounds based on testing the platform. Add compiler directives such as `#if defined(TARGET_IPHONE_SIMULATOR)` to your source.

Recipe 2-8   Detecting and Responding to User Swipes in Your Views

```
- (CATransition *) getAnimation:(NSString *) direction
{
    CATransition *animation = [CATransition animation];
    [animation setDelegate:self];
    [animation setType:kCATransitionPush];
    // [animation setType:@"oglFlip"];
    [animation setSubtype:direction];
    [animation setDuration:1.0f];
    [animation setTimingFunction:[CAMediaTimingFunction
    ➥functionWithName:kCAMediaTimingFunctionEaseInEaseOut]];
    return animation;
}


#define HORIZ_SWIPE_DRAG_MIN 12
#define VERT_SWIPE_DRAG_MAX 4

- (void)touchesBegan:(NSSet *)touches withEvent:(UIEvent *)event
{
    UITouch *touch = [touches anyObject];
    startTouchPosition = [touch locationInView:self];
    dirString = NULL;
}


- (void)touchesMoved:(NSSet *)touches withEvent:(UIEvent *)event
{
```

Recipe 2-8   **Continued**

```
    UITouch *touch = touches.anyObject;
    CGPoint currentTouchPosition = [touch locationInView:self];


    if (fabsf(startTouchPosition.x - currentTouchPosition.x) >=
        HORIZ_SWIPE_DRAG_MIN &&
        fabsf(startTouchPosition.y - currentTouchPosition.y) <=
        VERT_SWIPE_DRAG_MAX)
    {
        // Horizontal Swipe
        if (startTouchPosition.x < currentTouchPosition.x) {
            dirString = kCATransitionFromLeft;
        }
        else
            dirString = kCATransitionFromRight;
    }
    else if (fabsf(startTouchPosition.y - currentTouchPosition.y) >=
        HORIZ_SWIPE_DRAG_MIN &&
        fabsf(startTouchPosition.x - currentTouchPosition.x) <=
        VERT_SWIPE_DRAG_MAX)
    {
        // Vertical Swipe
        if (startTouchPosition.y < currentTouchPosition.y)
            dirString = kCATransitionFromBottom;
        else
            dirString = kCATransitionFromTop;
    } else
    {
        // Process a non-swipe event.
        // dirString = NULL;
    }
}


- (void)touchesEnded:(NSSet *)touches withEvent:(UIEvent *)event
{
    if (dirString)
    {
        CATransition *animation = [self getAnimation:dirString];
        [[self superview] exchangeSubviewAtIndex:0 withSubviewAtIndex:1];
        [[[self superview] layer] addAnimation:animation forKey:kAnimationKey];


    }
}
```

Recipe: Transforming Views

Affine transforms enable you to change an object's geometry by mapping that object from one view coordinate system into another. The iPhone SDK fully supports standard affine 2D transforms. With them, you can scale, translate, rotate, and skew your views however your heart desires and your application demands.

Transforms are defined in Core Graphics, and consist of calls such as `CGAffineTransformMakeRotation` and `CGAffineTransformScale`. These build and modify the 3-by-3 transform matrices. Once built, use `UIView`'s `setTransform:` call to apply 2D affine transformations to `UIView` objects.

Recipe 2-9 demonstrates how to build and apply an affine transform of a `UIView`. To create the sample, I kept things simple. I build an `NSTimer` that ticks every 1/30th of a second. On ticking, it rotates a view by 1% of pi and scales over a cosine curve. I use the cosine's absolute value for two reasons. It keeps the view visible at all times, and it provides a nice bounce effect when the scaling changes direction. This produces a rotating and undamped bounce animation.

This is one of those samples that it's best to build and view as you read through the code. You'll be better able to see how the `handleTimer:` method correlates to the visual effects you're looking at.

Recipe 2-9   **Example of an Affine Transform of a** `UIView`

```
#import "math.h"
#define PI 3.14159265

@interface HelloController : UIViewController
{
    UIView *contentView;
    UIImageView *rotateView;
    int theta;
}
@end


@implementation HelloController
- (id)init
{
    if (self = [super init]) self.title = @"Affine Demo";
    return self;
}


- (void) handleTimer: (NSTimer *) timer
{
    // Rotate each iteration by 1% of PI
    float angle = theta * (PI / 100);
    CGAffineTransform transform = CGAffineTransformMakeRotation(angle);
    theta = (theta + 1) % 200;
```

Recipe 2-9   **Continued**

```objc
    // For fun, scale by the absolute value of the cosine
    float degree = cos(angle);
    if (degree < 0.0) degree *= -1.0f;
    degree += 0.5f;
    CGAffineTransform scaled = CGAffineTransformScale(transform, degree, degree);

    // Apply the affine transform
    [rotateView setTransform:scaled];
}

- (void)loadView
{
    theta = 0;

    contentView = [[UIView alloc] initWithFrame:[[UIScreen mainScreen]
➥applicationFrame]];
    rotateView = [[UIImageView alloc] initWithFrame:CGRectMake(0.0f, 0.0f, 240.0f,
➥240.0f)];
    [rotateView setImage:[UIImage imageNamed:@"rotateart.png"]];
    [rotateView setCenter:CGPointMake(160.0f, 208.0f)];
    [contentView addSubview:rotateView];
    [rotateView release];

    self.view = contentView;
    [contentView release];

    [NSTimer scheduledTimerWithTimeInterval: 0.03f target: self selector:
➥@selector(handleTimer:)
                                    userInfo: nil repeats: YES];
}

// Allow the view to respond to iPhone Orientation changes
-
(BOOL)shouldAutorotateToInterfaceOrientation:(UIInterfaceOrientation)
interfaceOrientation
{
    return NO;
}
-(void) dealloc
{
    [contentView release];
    [rotateView release];
    [super dealloc];
}
@end
```

Centering Landscape Views

Use the same affine transform approach to center landscape-oriented views. Listing 2-12 creates a 480-by-320 pixel view, centers it at [160, 240] (using portrait view coordinates), and then rotates it into place. Half of pi corresponds to 90 degrees, creating a landscape-right rotation. Centering keeps the entire view onscreen. All subviews, including text fields, labels, switches, and so on rotate into place along with the parent view.

If you want to work with a landscape keyboard for this view, make sure to call [[UIApplication sharedApplication] setStatusBarOrientation: UIInterfaceOrientationLandscapeRight]. This sets the status bar orientation, which controls the keyboard regardless of whether the status bar is hidden or shown.

Listing 2-12   **Rotating Landscape Views into Place**

```
@implementation HelloController
- (void)loadView
{
    contentView = [[UIView alloc] initWithFrame:CGRectMake(0.0f, 0.0f, 480.0f,
    ➥320.0f)];
    [contentView setCenter:CGPointMake(160.0f, 240.0f)];
    [contentView setBackgroundColor:[UIColor blackColor]];
    [contentView setTransform:CGAffineTransformMakeRotation(3.141592f / 2.0f)];
    self.view = contentView;
    [contentView release];
}

-(void) dealloc
{
    [contentView release];
    [super dealloc];
}
@end
```

Summary

UIViews provide the onscreen components your users see and interact with. As this chapter has shown, even in their most basic form, they offer incredible flexibility and power. You've discovered how to use views to build up elements on a screen, create multiple interaction objects, and introduce eye-catching animation. Here's a collection of thoughts about the recipes you've seen in this chapter that you might want to ponder before moving on:

- When dealing with multiple onscreen views, hierarchy should always remain front-most in your mind—no pun! Use your view hierarchy vocabulary (bringSubviewToFront:, sendSubviewToBack:, `exchangeSubviewAtIndex:withSubviewAtIndex:`) to take charge of your views and always present the proper visual context to your users.

- You're not limited to rectangles. Use `UIView` / Core Graphics clipping to create compelling interaction objects that don't necessarily have right corners.

- Be concrete. The iPhone has a perfectly good touch screen. Why not let your users drag items around the screen with their fingers? It adds to the reality and the platform's interactive nature.

- Animate everything. Animations don't have to be loud, splashy, or bad design. The iPhone's strong animation support enables you to add smooth transitions between user tasks. Short, smooth, focused changes are the iPhone's bread and butter.

- Users typically have five fingers per hand. Don't limit yourself to a one-finger interface when it makes sense to expand your interaction into multitouch territory.

- A solid grounding in Quartz graphics and Core Animation will be your friend. Using `drawRect:`, you can build any kind of custom `UIView` presentation you'd like, including text, Bézier curves, scribbles, and so forth.

- Explore! This chapter has only touched lightly on the ways you can use `UIViews` in your applications. Use this material as a jumping-off point to explore the full vocabulary of the `UIView` class.

3

View Controllers

The iPhone screen isn't big by any measure. It's just a few inches across by a few inches high. This diminutive size constrains programs by limiting a user's physical viewport. Although your virtual worlds may be very large indeed, the small physical screen means that iPhone classes must cleverly expand their practical interaction space. In this chapter, you're about to discover numerous ways to create virtual presentations that enlarge your application's physical reality through the use of view controllers. You'll discover how to use view controllers to build navigable worlds and how to connect to these classes using Interface Builder.

View Management

On the iPhone, view controllers centralize basic view management. They provide practical utility by linking the view functionality covered in Chapter 2, "Views," with the pragmatic reality of your device. View controllers handle reorientation events such as when users tip the iPhone on its side to landscape mode and navigation issues such as when users need to move their attention from view to view. The following sections introduce the kinds of view controllers used in the iPhone SDK. You see what classes are used in the view controller paradigm, including both core classes and specialized ones.

Core Classes

The iPhone SDK offers any number of view controllers and their subclasses. These range from the general to the specific. Just three of these represent core controller classes. They are as follows:

- **UIViewController.** This is the parent class for view controllers and the one you use to specifically link to a single view. It's the workhorse of view controllers and the kind you'll spend most of your time customizing. Most important, UIViewController handles all view reorientation tasks, enabling you to easily program for both landscape and portrait orientation.

- **UINavigationController.** Use navigation controllers for navigating up and down through tree-based view hierarchies (for example, drilling). As their name suggests, they create the blue- or gray-colored navigation bars that appear at the top of a standard iPhone application. They enable you to add buttons through the use of Navigation Items and automatically generate "back" buttons showing the title of the calling view controller. All navigation controllers use a "root" view controller to establish the top of their navigation tree.

- **UITabBarController.** Parallel views are like stations on a radio. A tab bar enables users to select which UIViewController to "tune in to," without there being a specific navigation hierarchy. You see this best in applications like YouTube and iPod, where users select whether to see a "Top 25" list or view albums or playlists. When TabBar instances offer more than five view controller choices at a time, users can customize them through the More > Edit screen. The More > Edit screen lets users drag their favorite controllers down to the button bar at the bottom of the screen.

Specialized Classes

In addition to the three general classes you just read about, Apple offers many highly adapted controllers. These specialized items leverage access to the iPhone's core databases and functions. While you can throw instances of these classes into your applications and use them like any other UIViewController, they're preloaded with advanced functionality. Here are a few examples of the kinds of specialized view controllers available in the SDK:

- **UIImagePickerController.** This utility controller enables users to select images from onboard albums or to snap a photo from the iPhone camera. Apple has added an advanced image-selection interface. The controller even lets the users orient and zoom an image before finishing.

- **ABNewPersonViewController.** This controller enables users to create a new contact for their Address Book. Other Address Book controller styles include ABPersonViewController, ABUnknownPersonViewcontroller, and ABPeoplePickerNavigationController.

- **UITableViewController.** Table view controllers simplify using tables in your iPhone projects. This controller class provides a standard already-connected UITableView instance and automatically sets delegation and data sources to point to itself. All you have to do is supply those delegate and data source methods to fill up the table with data and react to user taps. UITableViewController is discussed at length in Chapter 5, "Basic Tables."

- **MPMoviePlayerController.** When your user needs to watch a movie or listen to audio, this controller does the trick. Just supply it with a path to the media resource and drill down to its display. The controller provides a Done button for the user or automatically returns a delegate call when playback finishes.

In a way, these specialized controllers are both a blessing and a curse. On the positive side, they introduce enormous functionality, essentially with no additional programming burden. On the downside, they're so specialized that they often hide core features that developers might prefer to work with.

For example, there's no simple audio playing classes. You either work at the lowest level through `AudioQueue`, dealing with sample rates and encoding styles, or at the highest through `MPMoviePlayerController`. You have no access to a general scrubber bar or pause/play button. These are actually features that are hidden within the Media Player framework, but they have no publicly defined methods or classes. There used to be a public framework called Celestial that provided a QuickTime-like interface to audiovisual controllers and handy playback features, but Apple moved this framework to its Private Frameworks hierarchy for firmware versions after 1.1.4.

Creating a `UIViewController`

`UIViewController` instances provide tons of great core view management. What they don't supply is an actual view. It's up to you to create one and install it into the view controller via the `loadView` method. Every `UIViewController` and subclass implements this method, which is where you connect the controller to a view instance. You need to do two things: Initialize the view and then connect it to the controller:

- Initialize and size your content view by calling `initWithFrame:` using `[[UIScreen mainScreen] applicationFrame]` as its argument. This returns the standard bounds for the application. The math automatically takes any onscreen navigation bars and tab bars into account. The Hello World example in Chapter 1, "Introducing the iPhone SDK," provided a simple example of this layout in action.

- Connect the view to the controller by assigning `self.view` to a `UIView` instance of some kind. Do this in your `loadView` method (for example, `self.view = contentView`).

When working with specialized controllers, always make sure to call the superclass's version of the method from the child (that is, `[super loadView]`). This ensures that children inherit the parent's layout behavior as well as the class methods and variables. Other key `UIViewController` methods include the following.

init

Use the class `init` method to set the view controller's title and other features that need to be set up before the class is actually used. To match the title to the application name, assign `self.title` to `[[[NSBundle mainBundle] infoDictionary] objectForKey:@"CFBundleName"]`. This returns the name defined in the bundle's Info.plist file.

Unlike `UIView`, the `UIViewController` instance is an abstract object and has no physical onscreen presence. Do not set a frame the way you would with a normal `UIView`. `UIViews` use `initWithFrame:` and `UIViewControllers` use `init`. Set up any view frames in the well-named `loadView` method.

shouldAutorotateToInterfaceOrientation:

This method returns either `YES` or `NO`, depending on whether you want to support autorotation in your program. When returning `YES`, the view controller uses several flags to determine how the autorotation takes place. Listing 3-1 shows a typical code snippet from a `loadView` method that specifies that subviews should automatically resize both horizontally and vertically.

Listing 3-1   **Setting Up Autorotation Flags**

```
contentView.autoresizesSubviews = YES;
contentView.autoresizingMask = (UIViewAutoresizingFlexibleWidth |
    UIViewAutoresizingFlexibleHeight);
```

viewDidAppear: and viewDidDisappear:

These methods are called each time a `UIViewController`'s view is brought onscreen or pushed offscreen—typically due to navigation between views. Use these methods to refresh the view to reflect the current data state and update stored data. These methods enable you to claim or resign first-responder status for text elements, remove text selections if needed, or perform any other bookkeeping that needs to be done before returning control to the user.

didRotateFromInterfaceOrientation:

Programmatically catch orientation changes by implementing this method in your `UIViewController` subclass. This method enables you to respond to the new orientation and passes the previous orientation in case you want to perform a specific animation type based on the change involved. It is entirely possible to move from one orientation to another without passing through the intermediate phases you'd expect, so avoid assumptions. Use the actual data passed to this method.

> **Note**
>
> Apple has promised support for separate landscape and portrait views in the SDK at some point. At the time of writing, this functionality has not yet been implemented. It's up to you to rearrange your screen when the orientation changes. To force your application into landscape mode, return `NO` for `shouldAutorotateToInterfaceOrientation:`, call `[[UIApplication sharedApplication] setStatusBarOrientation: UIInterfaceOrientationLandscapeRight]` from your `applicationDidFinishLaunching:` method, and set `UIInterfaceOrientation` to `UIInterfaceOrientationLandscapeRight` in your Info.plist file.

Working with Interface Builder to Build Views for `UIViewControllers`

Interface Builder, with its interactive GUI layout tools, helps create `UIView` content. It makes it possible for you to add interactive controls, moving them around the screen by hand to design one-of-a-kind interfaces. Interface Builder excels at `UIView` layout. It offers little or no direct support for `UIViewController` behavior. That's because the `UIViewController` is an abstract class, and `UIView` is a concrete one.

While taking that limitation into account, you can use Interface Builder to embed your `UIView` material into `UIViewController` instances and into other view controller classes. The workflow you're about to read through lets you combine the power of Interface Builder's design tools with the convenience of view controller classes.

Temperature Conversion Example

This example creates a classic Fahrenheit to Celsius conversion using a combination of Xcode and Interface Builder. A `UIView` subclass defines the conversion behavior. This view connects the buttons and text fields and gives them meaning by adding a `convert:` function to perform the math.

The view is embedded into a trivial `UIViewController` subclass. This controller typically takes over any autorotation and view navigation tasks. In this example, it doesn't actually do much other than demonstrate how views are created and added to controllers using the Interface Builder tool.

In the following steps, you create a new Xcode project, populate it with the convert source code, and then lay out the GUI using Interface Builder's tools:

1. **Create a new Xcode project.**

   In Xcode, choose File, New Project. Create a new Cocoa Touch Application View-Based project and name it however desired. Keep the name short. Both Xcode and Interface Builder use that project name to define your application delegate, so a simple name works best.

2. **Clean up the project and replace the code.**

   Select the Classes subfolder and delete it. This leaves main.m as your sole remaining source file. Open it and replace its contents with Listing 3-2. Change the name of the application delegate (here `WalkThroughAppDelegate`) to match your project name. Notice the two `IBOutlet` text fields and the `IBAction` return type. The `IBOutlet` keyword indicates objects to be defined in Interface Builder. `IBAction` tells Interface Builder to treat methods as the action for target/action pairs. `IBAction` is functionally equivalent to (void).

Listing 3-2   **Converter Source**

```
#import <UIKit/UIKit.h>

// Custom view that converts temperatures
```

Listing 3-2 **Continued**

```objc
@interface MyView : UIView {
    IBOutlet UITextField *infield;
    IBOutlet UITextField *outfield;
}
@end

@implementation MyView
- (IBAction) convert: (id) sender
{
    float invalue = [[infield text] floatValue];
    float outvalue = (invalue - 32.0f) * 5.0f / 9.0f;
    [outfield setText:[NSString stringWithFormat:@"%3.2f", outvalue]];
}
@end

// View controller that autorotates
@interface MyViewController : UIViewController
@end

@implementation MyViewController
-(void) loadView
{
    [super loadView];
    self.view.autoresizesSubviews = YES;
    self.view.autoresizingMask = (UIViewAutoresizingFlexibleWidth |
    ➥UIViewAutoresizingFlexibleHeight);
}
- (BOOL)shouldAutorotateToInterfaceOrientation:(UIInterfaceOrientation)
interfaceOrientation
{
    return YES;
}
@end

// Application delegate that uses NIB objects
@interface WalkThroughAppDelegate : NSObject {
    IBOutlet UIWindow *window;
    IBOutlet MyView *contentView;
}
@end
@implementation WalkThroughAppDelegate
- (void)applicationDidFinishLaunching:(UIApplication *)application {

    [window addSubview:contentView];
    [window makeKeyAndVisible];
}
```

Listing 3-2   **Continued**

```
- (void)dealloc {
    [contentView release];
    [window release];
    [super dealloc];
}
@end


int main(int argc, char *argv[])
{
    NSAutoreleasePool * pool = [[NSAutoreleasePool alloc] init];
    int retVal = UIApplicationMain(argc, argv, nil, nil);
    [pool release];
    return retVal;
}
```

3. **Launch Interface Builder.**

    Double-click the MainWindow.xib file in your project (see Figure 3-1). This opens it in Interface Builder.

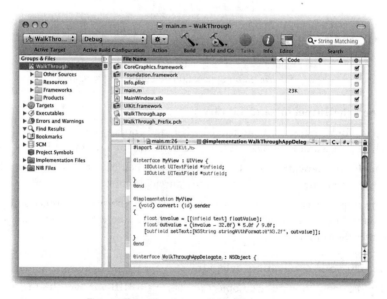

Figure 3-1   Xcode automatically creates a
MainWindow.xib file in your project. Double-click this
file to launch Interface Builder.

4. **Set up your windows.**

When Interface Builder launches, your MainWindow.nib project contains five objects: a file owner, an application delegate object (named with your project name), a First Responder object, a view controller, and a window (see Figure 3-2).

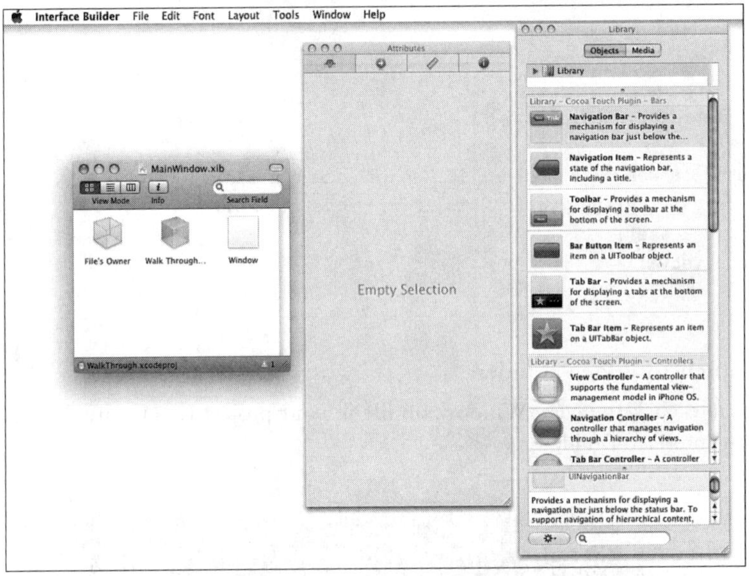

Figure 3-2   The default Xcode XIB file contains a
file owner, an application delegate, and a window.

5. **Open the Inspector and Library.**

Select Tools, Inspector (Command-Shift-I) and Tools, Library (Command-Shift-L). These two windows provide two of the key tools for working in Interface Builder:

- The Library provides a set of reusable Cocoa Touch objects. You can drag these objects from the Library window into your application.

- The Inspector enables you to view and customize the interface objects in your project. Use the Inspector to see how objects are connected together and what classes they link to.

6. **Set Up your application delegate.**

Tap the application delegate object in your main XIB window. (It's the one that's not the file's owner or window). Then either tap the rightmost tab in the Inspector or press Command-4. Both of these actions open the Identity Inspector. In the Identity Inspector, locate the class name at the top of the window (see Figure 3-3).

If you want to change the class name used by your application delegate, here is where you update it.

The owner, delegate, and window objects mirror the classes used in standard applications. The file's owner object defines the class that "owns" the XIB file (that is, the shared `UIApplication` instance). The application delegate object connects to the delegate, which is responsible for handling the applicationDidLaunch eventsapplicationDidFinishLaunching: callback and setting up the primary window and ordering it out for display.

7. **Add outlets to the delegate.**

   Add two outlets: `window` and `contentView`. Change the window class from id to `UIWindow`, and the view class to `MyView`. Typing these outlets adds a layer of control to your IB setup. When you make your connections, they'll only connect to objects of the proper class. Adding class types isn't required—and in a few steps you'll see how to do this without typing—but it's something you should be aware of as a developer.

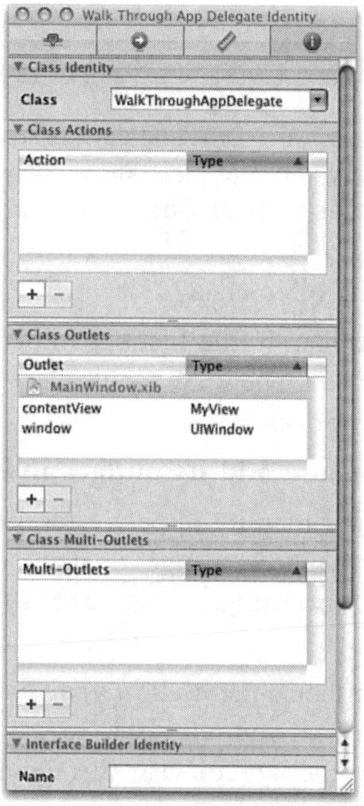

Figure 3-3   Use the Identity Inspector to add
outlets or actions and update class names
associated with Interface Builder objects.

8. **Add an object to your project window.**

In your Library locate the `UIViewController` (it's toward the top of the library) and `UIView` (it's near the bottom). Drag one of each into your project window. Figure 3-4 shows the project window after adding these objects. These two items use this object. This item will be used to represent instances of the classesan instance of the MyView class you defined in the code: `MyView` and `MyViewController`.

Figure 3-4   Dragging objects from the Library into your main XIB window adds instances of those classes to your project.

9. **Change the View Controller class.**

Tap the new View Controller. In the Identity Inspector (Command-4), change its class to `MyViewController`. The View Controller's name in the project window updates to My View Controller.

10. **Change the view class and add its outlets and action.**

Tap the new view. Use the Identity Inspector to change its class to `MyView`. The view in the project window changes its name to My View. Add one action (`convert:`) and two outlets (`infield` and `outfield`) to the view, as shown in Figure 3-5.

Actions correspond to instance methods in your source code, and outlets correspond to instance variables. If you refer back to the code from Step 2 of these instructions, you see that the `MyView` class was defined with two `IBOutlet` instances and with a method to do the conversion. In the next steps, you see how to connect onscreen objects with these instance variables and methods.

11. **Edit the view.**

Double-click My View in the project window to open its editor. From the Library, drag over two labels, one button and two fields, as shown in Figure 3-6.

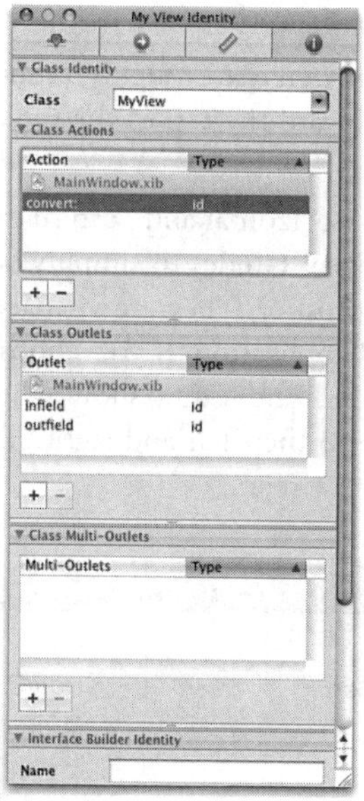

Figure 3-5   The Identity Inspector enables you to add outlets and actions to your objects. These correspond to instance variables and instance methods in your source code.

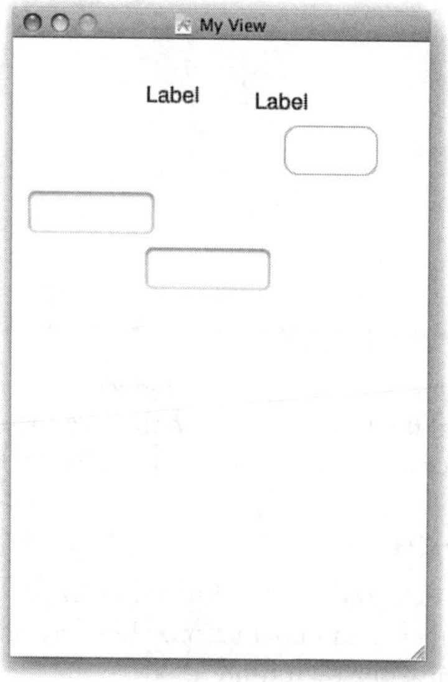

Figure 3-6   Drag interface elements from the Interface Builder Library (Tools, Library) onto a view to begin laying out its GUI.

12. **Edit the view.**

Arrange the elements in your view to roughly mimic the layout shown in Figure 3-7. Putting items toward the top of the screen leaves room for the keyboard at the bottom.

If you like, use the built-in horizontal and vertical guides (Layout, Add Horizontal Guide and Layout, Add Vertical Guide) to simplify layout. These guides are similar to the ones you find in Photoshop. They are virtual placement helpers only. They do not appear in your final application. If you choose to use them, pay attention to the left and right numeric indicators they show while being moved. They let you know how many pixels are to their left and right. A vertical guide at 160 | 160 is directly in the middle of the screen.

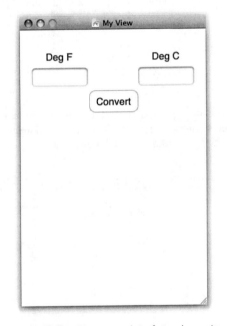

Figure 3-7   Place your interface elements toward the top of the screen to leave room for the keyboard, which will appear at the bottom.

13. **Edit the left field traits.**

Select the left (input) field and use the Attributes Inspector (Command-1) to set its keyboard type to numbers and punctuation. There are additional traits here you will want to explore on your own time.

14. **Connect the application delegate to its window and view.**

While holding down the Control key, drag from the application delegate object in the project window to the `Window` object. Select Window from the pop-up. This assigns the `Window` object to the `window` instance variable of your application delegate.

Next, Control-drag from the application delegate to the `My View` object. Select contentView from the pop-up.

These actions set up the application delegate's instance variables, creating associations between the `IBOutlet` instances declared in the code with the actual window and view laid out in Interface Builder.

15. **Connect the view to its outlets.**

Open the My View window so that it can be seen. Control-drag between the `My View` object and the left text field. Select Infield from the pop-up. Then Control-drag from the view to the right text field and select Outfield. Again, you're assigning objects to instance variables.

16. **Connect the button to the view.**

Right-tap Control-drag from the Convert button you added to the custom view to the `My View` object. A customization pop-up appears. Scroll down the pop-up to find TouchUpInside. Drag from the circle to its right to the `MyView` instance in the XIB project window. Select, select convert: from the pop-up.

This action connects a touch inside the button to the conversion action you defined in your object. Check on the connection by right-tapping the Convert button again. The pop-up confirms this connection, as shown in Figure 3-8.

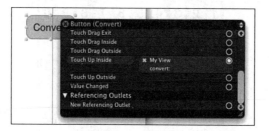

Figure 3-8   Once connected, you can view both the target and the action associated with a touch event.

17. **Add the view to its controller.**

Double-tap My View Controller to open its editor. Drag the `My View` instance from the project window onto this editor. It automatically jumps into place. Notice the right-pointing arrow at the top right of the View Controller editor.

This allows you to preview your view in landscape as well as in portrait mode. Go ahead and do this, and make any adjustments needed to provide a satisfactory landscape presentation.

By assigning the view to a controller, you enable that view controller to assume responsibilities for that view in your application. You do not need to make any further formal connections in Interface Builder.

18. **Save.**

Save your changes in Interface Builder and return to Xcode.

19. **Run.**

In Xcode, set your active SDK to either the device or the Simulator and run the completed application. Figure 3-9 shows the final result with a view whose elements have been fully defined in Interface Builder connected to a simple `UIViewController` of your design.

Figure 3-9   The completed application binds the custom-built view to the `UIViewController` you specified.

Loading XIB Files Directly

Cocoa Touch lets you recover objects from any XIB file by calling `loadNibNamed:owner:options:`. This returns an array of objects initialized from the NIB/XIB bundle, which you can then grab and use in your program.

```
NSArray *niblets = [[NSBundle mainBundle] loadNibNamed:@"sample" owner:self
options:NULL];
for (id theObject in niblets) {
    if ([theObject isKindOfClass:[UIViewController class]])
        [self.navigationController pushViewController:theObject
        ➥animated:YES];
}
```

Navigation Controllers

The `UINavigationController` class provides all the high-calorie goodness of a
`UINavigationBar`-based interface with little programming. Navigation controllers
enable you to smoothly move between views using built-in animation. You also get
history control. The controller handles all the Back button functionality. This means that
parent view titles automatically appear as Back buttons and you can "pop the stack," so
to speak, without any programming.

And if that weren't enough, the navigation controller also offers a simple menu bar.
You can add buttons—or even more complicated controls—into the bar to build actions
into your application. Between these three features of navigation, history, and menus,
navigation controllers build a lot of wow into a simple-to-program package.

The following recipes introduce these core navigation controller features from building menus to building a history stack. In these examples, you see how to use the
`UINavigationBar` class to create a variety of novel and useful interfaces.

Setting Up a Navigation Controller

Whether you plan to use a navigation controller to simplify moving between views—its
intended use—you should understand how the navigation controller works. At their simplest level, navigation controllers manage view controller stacks.

Every navigation controller owns a root view controller. This controller forms the
base of the stack. You can push other controllers onto the stack. This extends the navigation breadcrumb trail and automatically builds a Back button. You can pop controllers off
the stack by tapping one of these Back buttons. And you can pop back until you reach
the root. Then you can go no further. The root is the root, and you cannot pop below
that root.

This stack-based design lingers even when you plan to use just one view controller.
You might want to leverage the `UINavigationController`'s built-in navigation bar to
build a two-button menu, for example. This would disregard any navigational advantage
of the stack. You still need to set that one controller as the root via
`initWithRootViewController:`.

Listing 3-3 shows the creation and initialization of a navigation controller from a
typical `applicationDidFinishLaunching:` method. The controller is allocated,
initialized with a root view, and then added to the main window via its `view` property.

Listing 3-3   **Initializing a Navigation Controller**

```
- (void)applicationDidFinishLaunching:(UIApplication *)application
{
    UIWindow *window = [[UIWindow alloc] initWithFrame:[[UIScreen mainScreen]
    ➥bounds]];
    UINavigationController *nav = [[UINavigationController alloc]
initWithRootViewController: [[HelloController alloc] init]];
    [window addSubview:nav.view];
    [window makeKeyAndVisible];
}
```

Pushing and Popping View Controllers

Add new items onto the navigation stack by pushing a new controller with
pushViewController: animated:. Send this call to the parent navigation controller
of any UIViewController (for example, [self navigationController]). When
pushed, the new controller slides onscreen (assuming you set animated to YES). A left-
pointing Back button appears, leading you one step back on the stack. The Back button
uses the title of the previous view controller.

There are many reasons you'd push a new view. Typically, these involve navigating to
subviews like detail views or drilling down a file structure. You normally push controllers
onto the navigation controller stack after your user taps a button, a table item, or a
disclosure accessory.

Perform push requests and other navigation bar customization inside your
UIViewController subclasses. There's no reason or need to subclass
UINavigationController. You have direct access to the navigation bar and its features.
Here is a line from a loadView method that customizes the navigation bar style using a
chain of properties:

```
self.navigationController.navigationBar.barStyle = UIBarStyleBlackTranslucent;
```

Modal Presentation

Modal presentation offers another way to present a view controller. After sending the
presentModalViewController: animated: message, a new view controller
slides up into the screen and takes control until it's dismissed with
dismissModalViewControllerAnimated:. This enables you to add special-purpose
dialogs into your applications. Typically, modal controllers are used to pick data such as
contacts from the Address Book or photos from the Library. Chapters 7, "Media," and 9,
"People, Places, and Things," show modal view controllers in action.

The Navigation Item Class

The objects that populate the navigation bar are put into place using the
UINavigationItem class. This class enables you to attach buttons, text, and other UI

objects into three key locations: the left, the center, and the right of the navigation bar. Typically, this works out to be a regular button on the right, some text (usually the `UIViewController`'s title) in the middle, and a Back-styled button on the left. But you're not limited to that layout. You can add custom controls to any of these three locations. So you can build navigation bars with search fields, with segment controls, with toolbars, with pictures, and more.

Assign these items via `SetCustomLeftItem: animated:`, `SetCustomRightItem: animated:` and by updating the `customTitleView` property to point to a view of your choice. Listing 3-4 shows how to add a custom button to the right navigation item view. This is a standard navigation-style `UIButton` (`UIButtonTypeNavigation`). In this example, it invokes the `randomize` method when pushed.

Listing 3-4   **Adding a Custom Button to a `UINavigationItem`**

```
// Add a randomize button
UIBarButtonItem *randomButton = [[[UIBarButtonItem alloc]
              initWithTitle:@"Randomize"
              style:UIBarButtonItemStylePlain
              target:self
              action:@selector(randomize)] autorelease];
self.navigationItem.rightBarButtonItem = randomButton;
```

Adding a custom view to the title space is just as simple. Instead of adding a control, assign a view. This example (from the first recipe in Chapter 5) adds a custom `UILabel`:

```
self.navigationItem.titleView = [[UILabel alloc] initWithFrame:CGRectMake(0.0f,
➥4.0f, 320.0f, 36.0f)];
```

Recipe: Building a Simple Two-Item Menu

Although many applications demand serious user interfaces, often you don't need complexity. A simple one- or two-button menu can accomplish a lot. Use these steps to create basic interfaces for simple utilities:

1. Create a UIViewController subclass that you'll use as your primary interaction space.
2. Allocate a navigation controller and assign an instance of your custom view controller to its root view.
3. In the custom view controller, create one or two buttons and add them to the view's navigation item.
4. Build the callback routines that get triggered when a user taps a button.

Recipe 3-1 demonstrates these steps. It creates a simple view controller called `HelloController` and assigns it as the root view for a `UINavigationController`. In the `loadView` method, two buttons populate the left and right custom slots for the

view's navigation item. When tapped, these update the background color for the main
view. This recipe is not feature rich, but it provides an easy-to-build two-item menu.
Figure 3-10 shows the interface in action.

If you're looking for more complexity than two items can offer, consider having the
buttons trigger UIActionSheet menus. Action sheets, which are discussed in Chapter 4,
"Alerting Users," enable you to select actions from a short list of options (usually
between two and five options) and can be seen in use in the Photos and Mail applications for sharing and filing data.

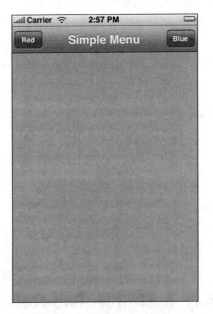

Figure 3-10   Create a basic two-button menu for
simple iPhone applications by adding custom
buttons to a UINavigationController.

> **Note**
>
> You can add images in addition to or instead of text to the UIButtons used in your
> navigation bar.

Recipe 3-1   Creating a Two-Item Menu Using a Navigation Controller

```
- (void) goRed
{
    contentView.backgroundColor = [UIColor colorWithRed: 1.0f green:0.45f
    ➥blue:0.45f alpha:1.0f];
```

```
}

- (void) goBlue
{
    contentView.backgroundColor = [UIColor colorWithRed: 0.45f green:0.45f
    ➥blue:1.0f alpha:1.0f];
}

- (void)loadView
{
    contentView = [[UIView alloc] initWithFrame:[[UIScreen mainScreen]
    ➥applicationFrame]];
    self.view = contentView;
    contentView.backgroundColor = [UIColor whiteColor];
    [contentView release];

    // Add a left button
    self.navigationItem.leftBarButtonItem = [[[UIBarButtonItem alloc]
                                            initWithTitle:@"Red"
                                            style:UIBarButtonItemStylePlain
                                            target:self
                                            action:@selector(goRed)]
                                            autorelease];

    // Add a right button
    self.navigationItem.rightBarButtonItem = [[[UIBarButtonItem alloc]
                                            initWithTitle:@"Blue"
                                            style:UIBarButtonItemStylePlain
                                            target:self
                                            action:@selector(goBlue)]
                                            autorelease];

}
```

Recipe: Adding a Segmented Control

The preceding recipe showed how to use the two available button slots in your navigation bar to build mini-menus. Recipe 3-2 expands on that idea by introducing a four-item UISegmentedControl and adding it to a navigation bar's custom title view, as shown in Figure 3-11. When tapped, each item updates the main view with its number.

The key thing to pay attention to in this recipe is the momentary attribute assigned to the segmented control. This transforms the interface from a radio button style into an actual menu, where items can be selected independently and more than once. So after tapping item three, for example, you can tap it again. That's an important behavior for menu interaction.

Unlike Recipe 3-1, all items in the segmented control trigger the same action (in this case, segmentAction:). Determine which action to take by querying the control for its selectedSegmentIndex and matching that value to the appropriate behavior.

Figure 3-11   Adding a segmented control to the custom title view enables you to build a multi-item menu. Notice that no items remain highlighted even after an action takes place. (In this case, the three button was pressed.)

Recipe 3-2   **Adding a Segmented Control to the Navigation Bar**

```
- (void)loadView
{
    // Set up the content view
    contentView = [[UITextView alloc] initWithFrame:[[UIScreen mainScreen]
    ➥applicationFrame]];
    contentView.autoresizesSubviews = YES;
    contentView.textAlignment = UITextAlignmentCenter;
    contentView.font = [UIFont fontWithName:@"Georgia" size:64.0f];
    contentView.autoresizingMask = (UIViewAutoresizingFlexibleWidth |
    ➥UIViewAutoresizingFlexibleHeight);
    [contentView setEditable:NO];
    self.view = contentView;
    [contentView release];
```

Recipe 3-2   **Continued**

```
// Build the Segmented Control
NSArray *buttonNames = [NSArray arrayWithObjects:@"One", @"Two", @"Three",
➥@"Four", nil];
UISegmentedControl* segmentedControl = [[UISegmentedControl alloc]
➥initWithItems:buttonNames];
segmentedControl.momentary = YES;
[contentView setText:@""];

// Customize the Segmented Control
segmentedControl.autoresizingMask = UIViewAutoresizingFlexibleWidth;
segmentedControl.segmentedControlStyle = UISegmentedControlStyleBar;
segmentedControl.frame = CGRectMake(0, 0, 400, 30);
[segmentedControl addTarget:self action:@selector(segmentAction:)
➥forControlEvents:UIControlEventValueChanged];

// Add the control to the navigation bar
self.navigationItem.titleView = segmentedControl;
[segmentedControl release];
}

-(void) segmentAction: (id) sender
{
    switch([sender selectedSegmentIndex] + 1)
    {
        case 1: [contentView setText:@"\n\nOne"]; break;
        case 2: [contentView setText:@"\n\nTwo"]; break;
        case 3: [contentView setText:@"\n\nThree"]; break;
        case 4: [contentView setText:@"\n\nFour"]; break;
        default: break;
    }
}
```

Recipe: Adding a `UIToolbar` to a Navigation Bar

This next recipe builds on the essence of Recipe 3-2, which used a segment control in the navigation bar and takes it a step further. Recipe 3-3 adds a UIToolbar into the navigation item's custom title view and adds it to the basic interface seen in Recipe 3-1. This accomplishes two things:

- It adds the power of a toolbar without taking up space at the bottom of the screen.
- It works without interfering with the two core button slots of the navigation bar.

Clutter should be a concern when using this approach. Figure 3-12 shows the updated interface, including both the menu buttons and the toolbar while retaining a clean look. The toolbar uses flexible spaces to the left and right of the arrows to center the controls and maintain a simple presentation. Also beware of landscape presentation. The toolbar height, which works perfectly with the portrait navigation bar, might not match the landscape bar in newer SDK releases.

Note

The two arrows use custom art, up.png and down.png, which are loaded from the application bundle at runtime and added to the toolbar buttons. Created in Photoshop, they're basic PNG images, white on a clear background, saved with transparency.

Figure 3-12   A well-designed custom toolbar takes advantage of the space between navigation bar buttons while freeing up room at the bottom of the screen.

Recipe 3-3   **Adding a Toolbar into the Custom Title View**

```
- (void)loadView
{
    // Set up the text view to show the current value
    contentView = [[UITextView alloc] initWithFrame:[[UIScreen mainScreen]
            applicationFrame]];
    contentView.autoresizesSubviews = YES;
```

Recipe 3-3   **Continued**

```
contentView.autoresizingMask = (UIViewAutoresizingFlexibleWidth |
                               UIViewAutoresizingFlexibleHeight);
contentView.editable = NO;
contentView.textAlignment = UITextAlignmentCenter;
contentView.font = [UIFont fontWithName:@"American Typewriter" size:120];
self.view = contentView;
[contentView release];

// Initialize at 50
[contentView setText:@"\n50"];
value = 50;

// The app style is black
self.navigationController.navigationBar.barStyle = UIBarStyleBlackTranslucent;

NSMutableArray *buttons = [[NSMutableArray alloc] init];

UIBarButtonItem *flexibleSpaceItem;
flexibleSpaceItem = [[UIBarButtonItem alloc]
                        initWithBarButtonSystemItem:
                        UIBarButtonSystemItemFlexibleSpace
                        target:nil action:NULL];
[buttons addObject:flexibleSpaceItem];
[flexibleSpaceItem release];

// Add the up and down items
UIBarButtonItem *item;
item = [[UIBarButtonItem alloc]
        initWithImage:[UIImage imageNamed:@"down.png"]
        style:UIBarButtonItemStylePlain
        target:self
        action:@selector(decrement:)];
[buttons addObject:item];
[item release];

item = [[UIBarButtonItem alloc]
        initWithImage:[UIImage imageNamed:@"up.png"]
        style:UIBarButtonItemStylePlain target:self
        action:@selector(increment:)];
[buttons addObject:item];
[item release];

flexibleSpaceItem = [[UIBarButtonItem alloc]
                        initWithBarButtonSystemItem:
                        UIBarButtonSystemItemFlexibleSpace
```

Recipe 3-3   **Continued**

```
                          target:nil action:NULL];
    [buttons addObject:flexibleSpaceItem];
    [flexibleSpaceItem release];

    UIToolbar *toolbar = [[UIToolbar alloc] init];
    toolbar.barStyle = UIBarStyleBlackOpaque;
    [toolbar setItems:buttons animated:YES];
    [toolbar sizeToFit];
    self.navigationItem.titleView = toolbar;
    [toolbar release];

    // Add a left button
    self.navigationItem.leftBarButtonItem = [[[UIBarButtonItem alloc]
                                    initWithTitle:@"Red"
                                    style:UIBarButtonItemStylePlain
                                    target:self
                                    action:@selector(goRed)]
                                    autorelease];

    // Add a right button
    self.navigationItem.rightBarButtonItem = [[[UIBarButtonItem alloc]
                                    initWithTitle:@"Blue"
                                    style:UIBarButtonItemStylePlain
                                    target:self
                                    action:@selector(goBlue)]
                                    autorelease];
}

-(void) increment: (id) sender
{
    [contentView setText:[NSString stringWithFormat:@"\n%d", ++value]];
}

-(void) decrement: (id) sender
{
    [contentView setText:[NSString stringWithFormat:@"\n%d", —value]];
}
```

Recipe: Navigating Between View Controllers

In addition to providing spiffy menus, navigation controllers do the job they are
designed to do: managing hierarchy as you navigate between views. Recipe 3-4
introduces the navigation controller as an actual navigation controller, pushing views on
the stack. These views consist of three UIViewController subclasses, each with an

identifying color: lime, pink, and orange. In real use, you'd use more meaningful view controllers. This sample demonstrates things at their simplest level. Here are a couple of points to keep in mind about this recipe:

- The navigation controller automatically creates the Back button shown in Figure 3-13 (Lime) as an effect of pushing the new (Orange) controller from the (root) Lime controller. The rightmost button (Pink) triggers navigation to the next controller by calling `pushViewController: animated:`. When pushed, the next Back button would read Orange.

- The interface works in both landscape and portrait orientations. When testing, you may want to try out both styles. In the Simulator, choose Hardware, Rotate Left (Command-Left arrow) or Hardware, Rotate Right (Command-Right arrow) to see this in action.

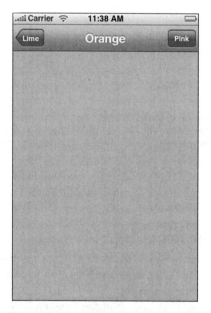

Figure 3-13   The navigation controller automatically creates Back and Forward buttons.

Recipe 3-4   Drilling Through Views with `UINavigationController`

```
@implementation OrangeController
- (id) init
{
    // The view controller title sets the name for back buttons
    // once it's been pushed
    if (self = [super init]) self.title = @"Orange";
```

Recipe 3-4   **Continued**
```
       return self;
}

- (void) loadButton
{
    // Create the button that activates the switch
    self.navigationItem.rightBarButtonItem = [[[UIBarButtonItem alloc]
      initWithTitle:@"Pink"
      style:UIBarButtonItemStylePlain
      target:self
      action:@selector(switch:)] autorelease];
}

- (void) loadView
{
    [super loadView];
    contentView.backgroundColor = ORANGE;
}

- (void) switch: (id) sender
{
    // On a button press, push the next controller into place
    [[self navigationController] pushViewController:[[PinkController alloc] init]
    ➥animated:YES];
}
@end
```

Popping Back to the Root

Although you'll usually want to pop to the previous view controller upon hitting the
Back button, be aware that there are times you'll want to pop the entire stack instead. For
example, you might have just given an interactive quiz, or a museum visitor might have
finished his walking tour. For both cases, it makes little sense to move back up a long
complex tree a screen at a time. Instead, use popToRootViewControllerAnimated: to
return all the way back to the root or popToViewController: animated: to stop
somewhere short of the root. These pop view controllers until either the root or the specified controller becomes the top controller, updating the display accordingly.

Loading a View Controller Array

You can also create and assign an NSArray of UIViewController objects to a
UINavigationController's viewControllers property. The top (that is, active)

`viewController` occupies the last position (*n-1*) in that array while the root object lives at index 0. Arrays are handy when jumping within a conceptual tree. For example, you might be navigating directories and then need to jump through a symbolic link to somewhere else. By setting the entire array, you avoid the detail work of popping and then pushing the stack.

View controller arrays also help restore previous states after quitting and then returning to an application. Store a state list to your local defaults and then re-create the same array on launch. Assign the re-created array to `viewControllers` and you return your user to the same place he or she left from.

Tab Bars

The `UITabBarController` class enables users to move between multiple view controllers and to customize the bar at the bottom of the screen. This is best seen in the YouTube and iPod applications. Both offer one-tap access to different views, and both offer a More button leading to user selection and editing of the bottom bar.

With tab bars, you don't push views the way you do with navigation bars. Instead, you assemble a collection of controllers (they can individually be `UIViewControllers`, `UINavigationControllers`, or any other kind of view controllers) and add them into a tab bar. Just set the bar's `viewControllers` property. It really is that simple. Cocoa Touch does all the rest of the work for you. Set `allowsCustomizing` to `YES` to enable user reordering of the bar.

Recipe 3-5 creates 11 simple view controllers of the `BrightnessController` class. This class builds a `UIView` and sets it background to a specified gray level, in this case from 0% to 100% in steps of 10%. These 11 view controllers, in the form of an array, become the options a user can navigate through and select from, as shown in Figure 3-14.

Notice that this recipe adds those 11 controllers twice. The first time assigns them to the list of view controllers available to the user:

```
tbarController.viewControllers = controllers;
```

The second time specifies that the user can select from the entire list when interactively customizing the bottom tab bar:

```
tbarController.customizableViewControllers = controllers;
```

The second line is optional, the first mandatory. After setting up the view controllers, you can add all or some to the customizable list. If you don't, you'll still be able to see the extra view controllers using the More button, but users won't be able to include them in the main tab bar on demand.

Note that art appears inverted in color on the More screen. According to Apple, this is the expected and proper behavior. They have no plans to change this. It does provide an interesting view contrast when your 100% white swatch appears as pure black on that screen.

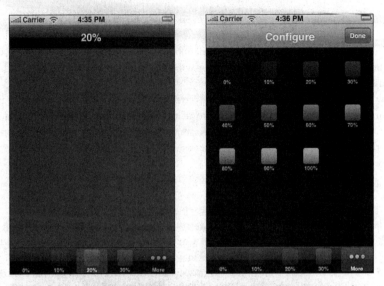

Figure 3-14   Tab bar controllers enable users to pick view controllers from a bar at the bottom of the screen (left side of the figure) and to customize the bar from a list of available view controllers (right side of the figure).

Recipe 3-5   **Creating a Tab View Controller**

```
@interface BrightnessController : UIViewController
{
    UIView *contentView;
    int brightness;
}
@end

@implementation BrightnessController

-(BrightnessController *) initWithBrightness: (int) aBrightness
{
    self = [super init];
    brightness = aBrightness;
    self.title = [NSString stringWithFormat:@"%d%%", brightness * 10];
    [self.tabBarItem initWithTitle:self.title image:createImage(((float)
brightness / 10.0f)) tag:NULL];
    return self;
}

- (void)loadView
{
    // Create each view with the given brightness
    contentView = [[UIView alloc] init];
    float percent = brightness * 0.1;
```

Recipe 3-5 **Continued**

```
    contentView.backgroundColor = [UIColor colorWithRed:percent green:percent
➡blue:percent alpha:1.0];
    contentView.autoresizesSubviews = YES;
    contentView.autoresizingMask = (UIViewAutoresizingFlexibleWidth |
➡UIViewAutoresizingFlexibleHeight);
    self.view = contentView;
    [contentView release];
}


-(void) dealloc
{
    [contentView release];
    [super dealloc];
}


@end


@interface SampleAppDelegate : NSObject <UIApplicationDelegate,
➡UITabBarControllerDelegate> {
}
@end


@implementation SampleAppDelegate


- (void)applicationDidFinishLaunching:(UIApplication *)application {

    UIWindow *window = [[UIWindow alloc] initWithFrame:[[UIScreen mainScreen]
➡bounds]];

    // Create the array of UIViewControllers
    NSMutableArray *controllers = [[NSMutableArray alloc] init];

    for (int i = 0; i < 11; i++) {
        BrightnessController *bControl = [[BrightnessController alloc]
                                initWithBrightness:i];
        UINavigationController *nav = [[UINavigationController alloc]
                                initWithRootViewController:bControl];
        nav.navigationBar.barStyle = UIBarStyleBlackTranslucent;
        [controllers addObject:nav];
        [bControl release];
        [nav release];
    }

    UITabBarController *tbarController = [[UITabBarController alloc] init];
    tbarController.viewControllers = controllers;
    tbarController.customizableViewControllers = controllers;
```

```
        tbarController.delegate = self;
        tbarController.allowsCustomizing = YES;
        [window addSubview:tbarController.view];
        [window makeKeyAndVisible];
        [controllers release];
    }

    - (void)dealloc {
        [super dealloc];
    }
@end
```

Summary

This chapter introduced the `UIViewController`, `UINavigationController`, and
`UITabBarController` classes and showed how to use them. These classes handle
view management and user navigation. Between them, developers can expand virtual
interaction space and create multipage interfaces as demanded by their applications.

Between the walk-through and recipes, you've learned how you can connect view
controllers to interfaces designed in Interface Builder and how to create interfaces
entirely within Xcode. Before moving on to the next chapter, here are a few points to
consider about view controllers:

- Interface Builder excels at laying out the content of `UIView` instances. Use its
  tools to connect those instances to the view controllers in your program and
  use Interface Builder to refine WYSIWYG-style interfaces like the temperature
  converter example covered in this chapter.

- Know when Interface Builder isn't the right solution. When you're building tab
  bars and navigation controllers with minimal window design (such as for table-
  based or text-based applications), you don't especially need IB's view layout tools.
  When skipping IB, make sure to delete the XIB file from your project and remove
  the main NIB window key from Info.plist.

- Use navigation trees to build hierarchical interfaces. They work great for looking at
  file structures or building a settings tree. When you think "disclosure view" or
  "preferences," consider pushing a new controller onto a navigation stack.

- Don't be afraid to use conventional UI elements in unconventional ways. A large
  part of this chapter covered innovative uses for the `UINavigationController`
  that didn't involve any navigation. The tools are there for the using.

Alerting Users

At times, you need to grab your user's attention. New messages might arrive or the system status might change. You might want to tell your user that there's going to be a wait before anything more happens—or that the wait is over and it's time to come back and pay attention. The iPhone offers many ways to provide that heads-up to the user: from alerts and progress bars to audio pings and status bar updates. In this chapter, you discover how to build these indications into your applications and expand your user-alert vocabulary. You're about to see real-life examples that showcase these classes and discover how to make sure your user pays attention at the right time.

Talking Directly to Your User Through Alerts

`UIActionSheet` and `UIAlertView` objects speak to your user. They pop up or scroll in above other views to deliver their message. These lightweight classes add two-way dialog to your apps. Alerts visually "speak" to users and can prompt them to reply. You present your alert onscreen, get user acknowledgment, and then dismiss the alert to move on with other tasks.

If you think that alerts are nothing more than messages with an attached OK button (as in Figure 4-1), think again. `UIAlertSheet` objects provide incredible versatility—assuming that Apple continues to let you access that incredible versatility. With alert sheets, you can actually build menus, text input, queries, and more. Unfortunately, much of this behavior falls into the undocumented or barely supported category. In this chapter's recipes, you see how to create a wide range of useful alerts that you can use in your own programs.

Much of the functionality covered in this chapter was removed from the official SDK yet remains within the public frameworks. Because this chapter relies so heavily on "unofficial" calls, think long and hard about the trade-offs between reliability and power programming. Apple discourages developers from using private routines because they change them at will. But the bottom line is the same story as with Mac OS X. If you figure out how to use private routines in public frameworks, you can use them. You cross the line when you start accessing private frameworks in your applications.

> **Note**
>
> In early releases of the iPhone firmware, `UIActionSheet` and `UIAlertView` were
> implemented by the same class, `UIAlertSheet`. This one class provided both pop-up
> alert and menu functionality. Then Apple replaced alert sheets with `UIModalView` and
> subclassed these new objects from that base class. Later, Apple removed `UIModalView`,
> and in new versions of the SDK, `UIActionSheet` and `UIAlertView` are no longer
> derived from that class. (They both descend from `UIView`.) Like their predecessors, they
> remain siblings in their behavior and use similar underlying technology to present them-
> selves onscreen.

Logging Your Results

Due to their sample nature, most of these recipes use `printf` to output their results into a
viewable format. During the initial SDK beta period, `printf` provided the most reliable
way to examine internal program data. `NSLog()` is now fully implemented and stable in
recent iPhone SDK releases. In addition, here are a few tricks you may want to use.

Redirecting `stderr`

The standard `freopen()` function redirects `stderr` output to a log file of your choice.
Supply it a local path. Here, `logPath` is a standard `NSString` such as `@"/tmp/mylog"`,
which is converted to a local file system representation. After this call, all `stderr` results
(this includes `NSLog`) go directly to your log file. Use `"w"` (write) rather than `"a"`
(append) to restart the log when your program runs:

```
freopen([logPath fileSystemRepresentation], "a", stderr);
```

Building a Custom Log Function

Building your own log function allows you to add functionality that goes beyond standard `NSLog`. Here is a basic log function that mimics `NSLog`'s functionality. It's not hard
to adapt this to produce, for example, an alert notification or a text view update rather
than a print to `stderr`:

```
#include <stdarg.h>
void dolog(id formatstring,...)
{
    va_list arglist;
    if (formatstring)
    {
        va_start(arglist, formatstring);
        id outstring = [[NSString alloc] initWithFormat:formatstring argu-
ments:arglist];
        fprintf(stderr, "%s\n", [outstring UTF8String]);
        [outstring release];
        va_end(arglist);
    }
    }
```

Building Alerts

To create alert sheets, allocate a `UIAlertView` object. Initialize it with a title and a button array, along with a few other options. The title is an `NSString`, and the button array includes `NSStrings`, where each string represents a single button. Listing 4-1 creates a very simple alert, as shown in Figure 4-1.

When working with alerts, space is often at a premium. Placing buttons on a single line minimizes the alert height and is the default presentation. When you define more buttons, they're added side by side. So, limit the number of buttons you add at any time to no more than three or four. Fewer buttons work better, one or two being ideal.

`UIAlertView` objects provide no visual "default" button highlights. In the iPhone context, button highlights are more confusing than helpful. (For example, should users press on the light button or the dark?) There's no way to match the interface to user expectations because the presentation is ambiguous. So unlike OS X, Apple has omitted highlights in newer iPhone firmware.

Note

The Cancel button appears at the bottom of menus and at the left of pop-up alerts.

Listing 4-1   **Creating a Basic Alert**

```
UIAlertView *baseAlert = [[UIAlertView alloc]
                           initWithTitle:@"Alert" message:@""
                           delegate:self cancelButtonTitle:nil
                           otherButtonTitles:@"OK", nil];
```

Figure 4-1   Use the `UIAlertView`
class to build simple pop-up alerts.

Unless you have some compelling reason to do otherwise, set the delegate to your primary `UIViewController` object. The delegate implements the `UIAlertViewDelegate` protocol. `UIAlertView` instances require this delegate support to handle button taps, at a minimum.

Delegate methods enable you to customize your responses when different buttons are pressed. You can actually omit that delegate support if all you need to do is throw up some message with an OK button.

After the user has seen and interacted with your alert, they raise the following delegate method call: `alertView: clickedButtonAtIndex:`. From this call, you can determine which button was pressed and recover any options that have been set on the sheet. Button numbering begins with zero.

Displaying the Alert

Use the `show` method to tell your alert to appear onscreen (that is, `[myAlert show]`). When shown, the alert works in a modal fashion. That is, it dims the screen behind it and blocks user interaction with your application. This modal interaction continues until your user acknowledges the alert through a button tap, typically by selecting OK or Cancel.

> **Note**
>
> After creating the alert sheet, you may customize the alert by updating its `message`. That's optional text that appears below the alert title and above its buttons. Other customizable properties include `title`, `delegate`, and `visible`.

Recipe: Creating Multiline Button Displays

By default, iPhone alerts present their buttons in a single line. Figure 4-2 shows this standard look on the left. You can override the single row presentation using an undocumented call. This call creates a multiline alert, as shown on the right. Use `setNumberOfRows:` to build alerts that use one row per button, as demonstrated in Listing 4-2. Supply a single argument, an integer, specifying the requested number of rows.

> **Note**
>
> See Chapter 1, "Introducing the iPhone SDK," for further discussion about using undocumented calls and features in your programs.

Earlier versions of the iPhone software worked in reverse. The standard was originally multiple rows, and you had to use `setNumberOfRows:` to get the phone to move the buttons onto a single line.

The sample created by Recipe 4-1 pop ups its alert midscreen, dimming the screen around it. Because it runs modal by default, everything waits until the user taps the OK button. Once tapped, the alert closes, passing control to the `modalView:` `clickedButtonAtIndex:` delegate method. This method, as defined here, does little more than print out the tapped button's number.

Note

You can disable background dimming using `setDimsBackground:NO`. This is another undocumented call. I can't recommend it for general use. It breaks the Apple human interface standards and may confuse your user as to whether the background can be tapped during the lifetime of the alert.

Figure 4-2   An undocumented `UIKit` call allows you to select whether to lay out your buttons in a row or a column.

Recipe 4-1   Creating `UIAlertViews` with One Button per Line

```
- (void) presentSheet
{
    UIAlertView *baseAlert = [[UIAlertView alloc]
                             initWithTitle:@"Alert"
                             message:@"Please select a button"
                             delegate:self cancelButtonTitle:nil
                             otherButtonTitles:@"One", @"Two", @"Three", nil];
    [baseAlert setNumberOfRows:3];
    [baseAlert show];
}
```

Recipe 4-1   **Continued**

```
- (void)alertView:(UIAlertView *)alertView
➥clickedButtonAtIndex:(NSInteger)buttonIndex
{
    printf("User Pressed Button %d\n", buttonIndex + 1);
    [alertView release];
}
```

Recipe: Autotimed No-Button Alerts

No-button alerts present a special challenge because they do not properly call back to a delegate method. They do not autodismiss, even when tapped. Figure 4-3 shows a simple no-button alert. As you can see from this screenshot, removing buttons produce awkward-looking alerts. You can enhance presentation by adjusting the message text. Add carriage returns (@"\n") to balance the bottom (where buttons normally go) with the spacing at the top.

Because alerts run modally, you need to add a safeguard to ensure that the alert goes away at some point and users can continue using their iPhone. A simple NSTimer that dismisses the alert after a set period of time must return control back to the standard GUI. Recipe 4-2 creates an alert and dismisses it using a timer and either the undocumented dismiss method or the UIAlertView class's dismissWithClickedButtonIndex: animated: method.

Figure 4-3   Use the undocumented dismiss method to return control to your program after displaying a button-free UIAlertView. It helps to balance the extra bottom space where the missing buttons would go by adding carriage returns to the message property.

Recipe 4-2   **Creating No-Button UIAlertViews with Timer Fail-Safe**

```
- (void) performDismiss: (NSTimer *)timer
{
    [baseAlert dismissWithClickedButtonIndex:0 animated:NO];
}


- (void) presentSheet
{
    baseAlert = [[UIAlertView alloc]
                            initWithTitle:@"Alert"
                            message:@"Message to user with asynchronous
                            information"
                            delegate:self cancelButtonTitle:nil
                            otherButtonTitles: nil];
    [NSTimer scheduledTimerWithTimeInterval:3.0f target:self selector:
    ➥@selector(performDismiss:)
                            userInfo:nil repeats:NO];
    [baseAlert show];
}
```

Recipe: Soliciting Text Input from the User

Leaving official SDK calls aside, alert views provide an especially simple way to prompt
your user for text. The `UIAlertView` class takes total command of presenting and dismissing an associated keyboard. All you have to do is add the text input fields, tell the
alert how to handle them, and let it take care of the rest.

To add a text field, use the undocumented `addTextFieldWithValue: label:` call.
Send the default text as the first argument and the text that displays in an otherwise-
empty field as the second. Figure 4-4 shows both a filled and empty field.

You can recover each field via `[alert textFieldAtIndex:0]` and then pull the text
from the text field with `text`. Because each field is addressable, you can set its attributes
before presenting the alert. Customize the autocaps, the autocorrection, and the preferred
keyboard, as demonstrated in Recipe 4-3.

Space is an important consideration. If you manage your space carefully, you can place
the alert onscreen leaving enough room for the keyboard to present itself. By skipping a
title and body text, you can fit three (but not four) text entry fields onscreen at once.
Two fields is a more practical maximum, as Figure 4-4 reveals.

Recipe 4-3   **Using UIAlertView to Solicit Text from Users**

```
- (void)alertView:(UIAlertView *)alertView
clickedButtonAtIndex:(NSInteger)buttonIndex
{
    printf("User Pressed Button %d\n", buttonIndex + 1);
    printf("Text Field 1: %s\n", [[[modalView textFieldAtIndex:0] text]
    ➥cStringUsingEncoding:1]);
```

Figure 4-4   Using careful space management and omitting the
title and body text, you can add up to three text entry fields to a
UIAlertSheet at once. You probably want to limit your
UIAlertSheets to one or two text fields.

Recipe 4-3 **Continued**

```
   printf("Text Field 2: %s\n", [[[modalView textFieldAtIndex:1] text]
➥cStringUsingEncoding:1]);
   [alertView release];
}

- (void) presentSheet
{
   UIAlertView *alert = [[UIAlertView alloc]
                         initWithTitle: @"Enter Information"
                         message:@"Specify the Name and URL"
                         delegate:self
                         cancelButtonTitle:@"Cancel"
                         otherButtonTitles:@"OK", nil];
   [alert addTextFieldWithValue:@"" label:@"Enter Name"];
   [alert addTextFieldWithValue:@"http://" label:@"Enter URL"];

   // Name field
   UITextField *tf = [alert textFieldAtIndex:0];
   tf.clearButtonMode = UITextFieldViewModeWhileEditing;
   tf.keyboardType = UIKeyboardTypeAlphabet;
   tf.keyboardAppearance = UIKeyboardAppearanceAlert;
```

```
    tf.autocapitalizationType = UITextAutocapitalizationTypeWords;
    tf.autocorrectionType = UITextAutocorrectionTypeNo;

    // URL field
    tf = [alert textFieldAtIndex:1];
    tf.clearButtonMode = UITextFieldViewModeWhileEditing;
    tf.keyboardType = UIKeyboardTypeURL;
    tf.keyboardAppearance = UIKeyboardAppearanceAlert;
    tf.autocapitalizationType = UITextAutocapitalizationTypeNone;
    tf.autocorrectionType = UITextAutocorrectionTypeNo;

    [alert show];
}
```

Recipe: Presenting Simple Menus

When it comes to menus, `UIActionSheet` instances supply the iPhone answer. They slide choices, basically a list of buttons representing possible actions, onto the screen and wait for the user to respond. Action sheets are different from pop-ups. Pop-ups stand apart from the interface and are better used for demanding attention. Menus slide into a view and better integrate with ongoing application work. Cocoa Touch supplies two ways to present menus:

- **showInView.** Presenting your sheet in a view is pretty much the ideal way to use menus and is the method used here. This method slides the menu up from the exact bottom of the view (see Figure 4-5).

- **showFromToolBar: and showFromTabBar.** When working with toolbars, tab bars, or any other kinds of bars that provide those horizontally grouped buttons that you see at the bottom of many applications, these methods align the menu with the top of the bar and slide it out exactly where it should be.

Recipe 4-4 shows how to initialize and present a simple `UIActionSheet` instance. Its initialization method introduces a concept missing from `UIAlertView`: the destructive button. Colored in red, a destructive button indicates an action from which there is no return, such as permanently deleting a file (see Figure 4-5). Its bright red color warns the user about the choice. Obviously, this option should be used sparingly.

Note

Missing in action sheets, at least as far as the official SDK is concerned, is the `UIAlertView`'s message. Action sheet instances do not officially support adding a message in addition to presenting a title. In reality, messages are implemented, even if they're not especially pretty. Use the undocumented `setMessage:` call to add a message to your menu. When used, messages appear below the sheet title, in slightly larger text.

Figure 4-5   Use showInView: to create simple menu presentations. The menu slides in from the bottom of the view. Although the "Delete File" menu button appears gray here, it is red on your iPhone and indicates permanent actions with possible negative consequences to your users.

Recipe 4-4   **Presenting a Menu**

```
- (void)actionSheet:(UIActionSheet *)actionSheet
clickedButtonAtIndex:(NSInteger)buttonIndex
{
    printf("User Pressed Button %d\n", buttonIndex + 1);
    [actionSheet release];
}

- (void) presentSheet
{
    UIActionSheet *menu = [[UIActionSheet alloc]
                        initWithTitle: @"File Management"
                        delegate:self
                        cancelButtonTitle:@"Cancel"
                        destructiveButtonTitle:@"Delete File"
                        otherButtonTitles:@"Rename File", @"Email File", nil];
    [menu showInView:contentView];
}
```

"Please Wait": Showing Progress to Your User

Waiting is an intrinsic part of the computing experience and will remain so for the foreseeable future. It's your job as a developer to communicate that fact to your users. Cocoa Touch provides several classes that tell your user to wait for a process to complete. These progress indicators come in two forms: as a spinning wheel that persists for the duration of its presentation; and as a bar, which fills from left to right as your process moves forward from start to end. The classes that provide these indications are as follows:

- **UIActivityIndicatorView.** A progress indicator offers a spinning circle that tells your user to wait without providing specific information about its degree of completion. The iPhone activity indicator is small, but its live animation catches the user's eye and is best-suited for quick disruptions in a normal application.

- **UIProgressView.** This view presents a progress bar. The bar provides concrete feedback as to how much work has been done and how much remains while occupying a relatively small onscreen space. It presents as a thin, horizontal rectangle that fills itself from left to right as progress takes place. This classic user interface element works best for long delays, where users want to know to what degree the job has finished.

And from the undocumented features point of view, you have the following:

- **UIProgressHUD.** The undocumented "heads up display" version of the progress indicator floats over all other views within a window and adds a status message to the basic progress indicator. The HUD provides a middle ground between the bar and the simple indicator. You do not need to quantify your progress, the way you do with progress bars, but the associated text enables you to narrate your progress. Progress HUDs work especially well when you want to indicate what's happened along a process (for example, "Contacting Server," "Authenticating," "Requesting Data," and so forth).

Recipe: Invoking the Basic Undocumented `UIProgressHUD`

The `UIProgressHUD` class overlays your window with a status dialog. This dialog contains a rotating progress indicator and a short message that you specify. As far as programming goes, all you have to do is instantiate the object, initialize it using your main window, and tell it to go by sending `show:YES`. Figure 4-6 shows a `UIProgressHUD` display in action, and Recipe 4-5 shows the code that created that display.

`UIProgressHUD` enables you to update its text as needed. Send a new `setText:` message at any time. When you've finished, dismiss it using `show:NO`. You can adjust the font size via `setFontSize:` if needed, but I urge you to keep your messages short and to the point.

> **Note**
>
> It's disappointing that Apple did not include this as a standard SDK class. I've presented the workaround here. By the time this book publishes, hopefully Apple will have added it back to Cocoa Touch.

Figure 4-6   The `UIProgressHUD`'s name means that it is an HUD. It adds a progress overlay above your window. You tell it when to show, when to hide, and what to say.

When using HUD displays with data intense code, you'll want to let it run in its own thread so the UI updates do not block. To do this, use `NSThread`'s `detatchThreadSelector: toTarget: withObject:` method. Use separate threads to start it going, to update the HUD's text, and to dismiss the HUD when finished.

Recipe 4-5   Creating a `UIProgressHUD` for Your Window

```
@interface UIProgressHUD : NSObject
- (void) show: (BOOL) yesOrNo;
- (UIProgressHUD *) initWithWindow: (UIView *) window;
- (void) setText: (NSString *) theText;
@end

- (void) killHUD: (id) aHUD
{
    [aHUD show:NO];
    [aHUD release];
```

Recipe 4-5   **Continued**

```
}
- (void) presentSheet
{
    id HUD = [[UIProgressHUD alloc] initWithWindow:[contentView superview]];
    [HUD setText:@"Downloading File. Please wait."];
    [HUD show:YES];

    [self performSelector:@selector(killHUD:)
            withObject:HUD afterDelay:5.0];
}
```

Recipe: Using UIActivityIndicatorView

UIActivityIndicatorView instances offer lightweight views that display a standard rotating progress wheel. The keyword to keep in mind when working with these views is *small*. The sharpest display for most indicator styles occurs at a view size of just 20 by 20 pixels. Any larger, and the indicator starts to blur. Figure 4-7 shows a 40-pixel version.

You need not center the indicator on the screen. Place it wherever it works best for you. As a clear-backed view, the indicator will blend over whatever backdrop view lies behind it. The predominant color of that backdrop helps select which style of indicator to use.

For general use, just add the activity indicator as a subview to the window, view, toolbar or navigation bar you want to overlay. Allocate the indicator and initialize it with a frame, preferably centered within whatever parent view you're using.

Start the indicator in action by updating its animating property to YES. To stop, set the property to NO. Cocoa Touch takes care of the rest, hiding the view when not in use.

The iPhone offers several different styles of the UIActivityIndicatorView class. UIActivityIndicatorViewStyleWhite and UIActivityIndicatorViewStyleGray are the cleanest. The white version looks best against a black background, and the gray (shown in Figure 4-7) looks best against white. It's a thin, sharp style. Take care when choosing whether to use white or gray. An all-white presentation will not show at all against a white backdrop. Unfortunately, UIActivityIndicatorViewStyleWhiteLarge is available only for use on dark backgrounds. It provides the largest, clearest indicator. Recipe 4-6 shows the code used to create these simple UIActivityIndicatorView instances.

Recipe 4-6   **Adding a UIActivityIndicatorView to Your Program**

```
- (void) performAction
{
        if (progressShowing) [activityIndicator stopAnimating];
            else [activityIndicator startAnimating];
        progressShowing = !progressShowing;
}
- (void)loadView
{
```

Recipe 4-6   **Continued**

```
contentView = [[UIView alloc] initWithFrame:[[UIScreen mainScreen]
➥applicationFrame]];
self.view = contentView;
contentView.backgroundColor = [UIColor whiteColor];
[contentView release];
// Add an action button
self.navigationItem.rightBarButtonItem = [[[UIBarButtonItem alloc]
                                 initWithTitle:@"Do It"
                                 style:UIBarButtonItemStylePlain
                                 target:self
                                 action:@selector(performAction)]
                                 autorelease];

// Add the progress indicator but do not start it
progressShowing = NO;
activityIndicator = [[UIActivityIndicatorView alloc]
➥initWithFrame:CGRectMake(0.0f, 0.0f, 32.0f, 32.0f)];
[activityIndicator setCenter:CGPointMake(160.0f, 208.0f)];
[activityIndicator
➥setActivityIndicatorViewStyle:UIActivityIndicatorViewStyleGray];
[contentView addSubview:activityIndicator];
[activityIndicator release];
}
```

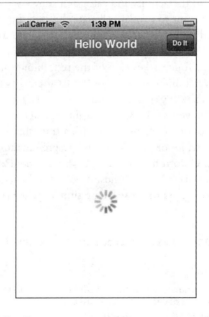

Figure 4-7   The `UIActivityIndicatorView`
class provides a simple rotating wheel that's meant to
display at relatively small sizes.

Recipe: Building a `UIProgressView`

Progress views enable your users to follow task progress as it happens rather than just saying "Please wait." They present bars that fill from left to right. These bars indicate the degree to which a task has finished. Progress bars work best for long waits where providing state feedback enables your users to retain the feel of control.

To create a progress view, allocate it and set its frame. To use the bar, issue `setProgress:`. This takes one argument, a floating-point number that ranges between 0.0 (no progress) and 1.0 (finished). Progress view bars come in two styles: basic white or light gray. The `setStyle:` method chooses the kind you prefer.

Unlike the other kinds of progress indicators, it's completely up to you to show and hide the progress bar's view. There's no `setVisible:` method. I like adding progress bars to action sheets. This simplifies both bringing them onto the screen and dismissing them. Another advantage is that when alert sheets display, the rest of the screen dims. This forces a modal presentation as your task progresses. Users cannot interact with the GUI until you dismiss the alert. Recipe 4-7 shows a `UIActionSheet`/`UIProgressView` sample that produces the display shown in Figure 4-8.

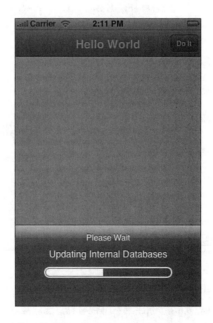

Figure 4-8   Use `UIProgressView` instances to track progress over an extended delay. Adding them to a `UIActionSheet` simplifies their presentation and dismissal.

This recipe uses the undocumented `setNumberOfRows:` call. To stay within SDK standards, add a bunch of new lines (\n) to the title.

> **Note**
>
> When embedding a progress bar into an action sheet, you need to implement the `UIActionSheet` delegate protocol. Adding a button click method satisfies the required methods for that protocol, even if the method itself does nothing.

Recipe 4-7   **Adding a Progress Bar to an Alert Sheet**

```
@interface UIActionSheet (extended)
- (void) setNumberOfRows: (NSInteger) rows;
@end

@implementation HelloController

// This callback fakes progress via setProgress:
- (void) incrementBar: (id) timer
{
    amountDone += 1.0f;
    [progbar setProgress: (amountDone / 20.0)];
    if (amountDone > 20.0) {[baseSheet dismissWithClickedButtonIndex:0
    ➥animated:YES]; [timer invalidate];}
}

// Dismiss the action sheet backdrop used here
- (void)actionSheet:(UIActionSheet *)actionSheet
clickedButtonAtIndex:(NSInteger)buttonIndex
{
    [actionSheet release];
}
// Load the progress bar onto an actionsheet backing
- (void) presentSheet
{
if (!baseSheet) {
        baseSheet = [[UIActionSheet alloc]
                    initWithTitle:@"Please Wait"
                    delegate:self
                    cancelButtonTitle:nil
                    destructiveButtonTitle: nil
                    otherButtonTitles: nil];
        [baseSheet setNumberOfRows:5];
        [baseSheet setMessage:@"Updating Internal Databases"];

        progbar = [[UIProgressView alloc] initWithFrame:CGRectMake(50.0f, 70.0f,
        ➥220.0f, 90.0f)];
        [progbar setProgressViewStyle: UIProgressViewStyleDefault];
```

```
        [baseSheet addSubview:progbar];
        [progbar release];
    }


    // Create the demonstration updates
    [progbar setProgress:(amountDone = 0.0f)];
    [NSTimer scheduledTimerWithTimeInterval: 0.5 target: self selector:
➥@selector(incrementBar:) userInfo: nil repeats: YES];
    [baseSheet showInView:contentView];
}

- (void)loadView
{

    contentView = [[UIView alloc] initWithFrame:[[UIScreen mainScreen]
➥applicationFrame]];
    self.view = contentView;
    contentView.backgroundColor = [UIColor whiteColor];
    [contentView release];

    // Add an action button
    self.navigationItem.rightBarButtonItem = [[[UIBarButtonItem alloc]
                                        initWithTitle:@"Do It"
                                        style:UIBarButtonItemStylePlain
                                        target:self
                                        action:@selector(presentSheet)]
                                        autorelease];

}
```

Recipe: Adding Custom, Tappable Overlays

When communicating to users, you need not limit yourself to standard (even when undocumented) UIKit objects. Fading an overlay onto a view offers unlimited possibilities. You can throw up text, images, animation, and what have you. You can make the overlay interactive (as shown in this recipe) or allow any taps to fall through to the interface below. You can add simple status information (think white, gray, or black text on a transparent background) or you can build an elaborate presentation. The choice is up to you.

Figure 4-9 shows the custom "Please Wait" overlay built in Recipe 4-8. Adding UIView animations, as discussed in Chapter 2, "Views," smoothes this overlay's entrance and exit presentations. A tap on the overlay dismisses it, returning you to the interface beneath. This overlay is, as you can see, busy and intended to go over a clean, bright background. To use this kind of overlay with a complicated interface, you might fill in the transparent areas with a translucent white, which would partially hide the interface and add a backdrop that allows any message to remain visible.

If you want to add an overlay like this and provide your own `UIProgressHUD`-like backdrop, use care that you match Apple's overall graphic design. Users are particularly sensitive to errors in custom interface elements.

Figure 4-9   Combine transparency with animation to create view overlays that pop.

Recipe 4-8   Creating a Custom Animated `UIView` Overlay

```
@interface PleaseWaitView : UIImageView
@end

@implementation PleaseWaitView
- (PleaseWaitView *) initWithFrame: (CGRect) rect
{
    self = [super initWithFrame:rect];
    [self setImage:[UIImage imageNamed:@"PlsWait.png"]];

    UIImageView *imgView = [[UIImageView alloc] initWithFrame:CGRectMake(40.0f,
    ➥300.0f, 60.0f, 60.0f)];
    [self addSubview:imgView];
    [imgView release];

    // load in the animation cells for the butterfly
```

Recipe 4-8 **Continued**

```objc
    NSMutableArray *bflies = [[NSMutableArray alloc] init];
    for (int i = 1; i <= 17; i++) {
        NSString *cname = [NSString stringWithFormat:@"bf_%d.png", i];
        UIImage *img = [UIImage imageNamed:cname];
        if (img) [bflies addObject:img];
    }

    // begin the animation
    [imgView setAnimationImages:bflies];
    imgView.animationDuration = 0.75f;
    [imgView startAnimating];
    [bflies release];

    return self;
}

- (void)touchesBegan: (NSSet *) touches withEvent:(UIEvent *)event
{
    // fade away the overlay
    CGContextRef context = UIGraphicsGetCurrentContext();
    [UIView beginAnimations:nil context:context];
    [UIView setAnimationCurve:UIViewAnimationCurveEaseInOut];
    [UIView setAnimationDuration:1.0];

    [self setAlpha:0.0f];

    // Complete the animation
    [UIView commitAnimations];
    [pleaseWait setUserInteractionEnabled:YES];
}

@end

@interface HelloController : UIViewController
{
    UIView *contentView;
    PleaseWaitView *pleaseWait;
}
@end

@implementation HelloController

CGPoint randomPoint() { return CGPointMake(random() % 256, random() % 256); }

- (void) moveButterfly: (NSTimer *) timer
```

Recipe 4-8 **Continued**

```
{
    if ([pleaseWait alpha] == 0.0f) {[timer invalidate]; return;}

    // Create an animation block around moving the butterfly to a new origin
    CGContextRef context = UIGraphicsGetCurrentContext();
    [UIView beginAnimations:nil context:context];
    [UIView setAnimationCurve:UIViewAnimationCurveEaseInOut];
    [UIView setAnimationDuration:1.0];

    // Move the butterfly
    UIImageView *iv = [[pleaseWait subviews] objectAtIndex:0];
    CGRect frame = [iv frame];
    frame.origin = randomPoint();
    [iv setFrame:frame];

    // Complete the animation
    [UIView commitAnimations];
}

- (void) presentSheet
{
    if ([pleaseWait alpha] != 0.0f) return;

    // Create an animation block around fading in the overlay
    CGContextRef context = UIGraphicsGetCurrentContext();
    [UIView beginAnimations:nil context:context];
    [UIView setAnimationCurve:UIViewAnimationCurveEaseInOut];
    [UIView setAnimationDuration:1.0];

    [pleaseWait setAlpha:1.0f];

    // Complete the animation
    [UIView commitAnimations];

    // Give life to the butterfly
    [NSTimer scheduledTimerWithTimeInterval: 4.0f target: self selector:
    ➥@selector(moveButterfly:)
                                    userInfo: nil repeats: YES];

}

- (id) init
{
    if (self = [super init]) self.title = @"Hello World";
    return self;
```

Recipe 4-8 **Continued**

```
}

- (void) loadView
{
    contentView = [[UIView alloc] initWithFrame:[[UIScreen mainScreen]
    ➥applicationFrame]];
    self.view = contentView;
    contentView.backgroundColor = [UIColor whiteColor];
    [contentView release]; // reduce retain count by one

    // Add an action button
    self.navigationItem.rightBarButtonItem = [[[UIBarButtonItem alloc]
                                        initWithTitle:@"Do It"
                                        style:UIBarButtonItemStylePlain
                                        target:self
                                        action:@selector(presentSheet)]
                                        autorelease];

    // Create and hide the "Please Wait" view
    pleaseWait = [[PleaseWaitView alloc] initWithFrame:[[UIScreen mainScreen]
    ➥applicationFrame]];
    [contentView addSubview:pleaseWait];
    [pleaseWait setAlpha:0.0f];
}

-(void) dealloc
{
    [pleaseWait release];
    [contentView release];
    [super dealloc];
}
@end
```

Recipe: Building a Scroll-Down Alert

Building off the preceding recipe's animation block, you can apply the same kind of approach to create a more traditional scroll-down alert. Recipe 4-9 animates a view's frame location to create the illusion that a view has scrolled onscreen. The frame starts offscreen and animates itself onscreen to present itself as shown in Figure 4-10. When the user clicks OK, the process reverses. You can use this method to build any kind of alert.

The view in this recipe contains a title, a block of text, and a simple button. Add any UIView elements or controls as needed to your own implementation. An example in Chapter 5, "Basic Tables," builds on this recipe by adding a user-selectable scrolling table to the slide-down view.

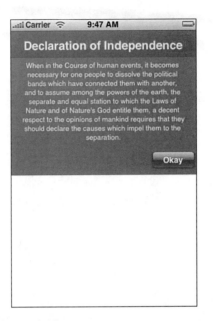

Figure 4-10   Use `UIViewAnimation` to
create custom scroll-down alert sheets.

Recipe 4-9   **Building a Custom Slide-Down Alert**

```
// Create a color of blue that mimics the official gray highlighting
UIColor *sysBlueColor(float percent) {
    float red = percent * 255.0f;
    float green = (red + 20.0f) / 255.0f;
    float blue = (red + 45.0f) / 255.0f;
    if (green > 1.0) green = 1.0f;
    if (blue > 1.0f) blue = 1.0f;

    return [UIColor colorWithRed:percent green:green blue:blue alpha:1.0f];
}
@interface TopAlert : UIView
{
    UILabel *title, *message;
}
- (void) setTitle: (NSString *)titleText;
- (void) setMessage: (NSString *)messageText;
@end

@implementation TopAlert

- (void) setTitle: (NSString *)titleText
{
```

Recipe 4-9   **Continued**

```
    [title setText:titleText];
}
- (void) setMessage: (NSString *)messageText
{
    [message setText:messageText];
}

- (TopAlert *) initWithFrame: (CGRect) rect
{
    rect.origin.y = 20.0f - rect.size.height; // Place above status bar
    self = [super initWithFrame:rect];

    [self setAlpha:0.9];
    [self setBackgroundColor: sysBlueColor(0.4f)];

    // Add button
    UIButton *button = [[UIButton buttonWithType:UIButtonTypeCustom]
➥initWithFrame:CGRectMake(220.0f, 200.0f, 80.0f, 32.0f)];
    [button setBackgroundImage:[UIImage imageNamed:@"whiteButton.png"]
➥forState:UIControlStateNormal];
    [button setTitle:@"Okay" forState: UIControlStateHighlighted];
    [button setTitle:@"Okay" forState: UIControlStateNormal];
    [button setFont:[UIFont boldSystemFontOfSize:14.0f]];
    [button addTarget:self action:@selector(removeView)
➥forControlEvents:UIControlEventTouchUpInside];
    [self addSubview:button];

    // Add title
    title = [[UILabel alloc] initWithFrame:CGRectMake(0.0f, 8.0f, 320.0f, 32.0f)];
    title.text = @"Declaration of Independence";
    title.textAlignment = UITextAlignmentCenter;
    title.textColor = [UIColor whiteColor];
    title.backgroundColor = [UIColor clearColor];
    // Alternative framed title:
    // title.backgroundColor = [UIColor colorWithRed:1.0f green:1.0f blue:1.0f
➥alpha:0.25f];
    title.font = [UIFont boldSystemFontOfSize:20.0f];
    [self addSubview:title];
    [title release];

    // Add message
    message = [[UILabel alloc] initWithFrame:CGRectMake(20.0f, 40.0f, 280.0f,
➥200.0f - 48.0f)];
    message.text = @"When in the Course of human events, it becomes necessary for
➥one people to dissolve the political bands which have connected them with
➥another, and to assume among the powers of the earth, the separate and equal
```

Recipe 4-9   **Continued**

```
➥which the Laws of Nature and of Nature's God entitle them, a decent respect
➥to the opinions of mankind requires that they should declare the causes
➥which impel them to the separation.";
    message.textAlignment = UITextAlignmentCenter;
    message.numberOfLines = 999;
    message.textColor = [UIColor whiteColor];
    message.backgroundColor = [UIColor clearColor];
    message.lineBreakMode = UILineBreakModeWordWrap;
    message.font = [UIFont systemFontOfSize:[UIFont smallSystemFontSize]];
    [self addSubview:message];
    [message release];

    return self;
}


- (void) removeView
{
    // Scroll away the overlay
    CGContextRef context = UIGraphicsGetCurrentContext();
    [UIView beginAnimations:nil context:context];
    [UIView setAnimationCurve:UIViewAnimationCurveEaseInOut];
    [UIView setAnimationDuration:0.5];

    CGRect rect = [self frame];
    rect.origin.y = -10.0f - rect.size.height;
    [self setFrame:rect];

    // Complete the animation
    [UIView commitAnimations];
}


- (void) presentView
{
    // Scroll in the overlay
    CGContextRef context = UIGraphicsGetCurrentContext();
    [UIView beginAnimations:nil context:context];
    [UIView setAnimationCurve:UIViewAnimationCurveEaseInOut];
    [UIView setAnimationDuration:0.5];

    CGRect rect = [self frame];
    rect.origin.y = 0.0f;
    [self setFrame:rect];

    // Complete the animation
    [UIView commitAnimations];
}
```

```
-(void) dealloc
{
    [title release];
    [message release];
    [super dealloc];
}
@end
```

Recipe: Adding Status Bar Images

The bar at the top of your iPhone offers a wealth of status information. These application-triggered status symbols appear to the right of the time display. Familiar icons include pause/play indicators, battery use, and so forth. `UIApplication` instances can add existing images to the status bar using undocumented methods, but I've been unable to convince the status bar call to use data from the Application package itself. All status bar images are stored in SpringBoard.app, in /System/Library/CoreServices/ SpringBoard.app. So as you can guess, this is clearly marching into App Store–agreement boundary conditions.

This limitation has two profound consequences. First, you can only use this very limited range of images (they are just standard PNGs, using transparency) but also, second, it's a pretty bad move security-wise and just overall OS-wise to rely on adding custom images to your user's System folder. It's bad manners, and it's not secure, and there are your agreements (and sandboxes!) between you and Apple that stand in the way.

Recipe 4-10 shows how to load and remove these images. To set an icon, call `addStatusBarImageNamed:`, using one argument, the trimmed icon name without an extension. As a rule, there are two versions of each image, one for a black status bar (each name starts with FSO_) and one for a white/gray status bar (names start with Default_). All changes last beyond quitting the program. That, too, indicates why you should use status bar updates sparingly.

When passed, for example, @"Airplane" (the airplane mode icon), SpringBoard displays `Default_Airplane.png` for a black status bar. You do not pass either the extension or the prefix. Remove the icon with `removeStatusBarImageNamed:`. Figure 4-11 shows the airplane icon, as displayed.

Status bar images persist beyond the life of the application. When you add an airplane to the status bar and then quit, the airplane remains. If you decide to use status bar images, consider cleaning up the bar before suspending or terminating your program. By definition, these images are meant to indicate behavior that exceeds the span of any application session. Because Apple insists on the "one application at a time" metaphor, use this technology sparely and meaningfully within that limitation.

Figure 4-11   Status bar icons allow you to communicate mode information to your users.

Recipe 4-10   **Adding and Removing Status Bar Icons**

```
@interface UIApplication (extended)
- (void) addStatusBarImageNamed:(NSString *)aName;
- (void) removeStatusBarImageNamed:(NSString *)aName;
@end

- (void) performAction
{
    isShowing = !isShowing;

    if (isShowing)
        [[UIApplication sharedApplication] addStatusBarImageNamed:@"Airplane"];
    else
        [[UIApplication sharedApplication] removeStatusBarImageNamed:@"Airplane"];
}
```

Adding Application Badges

If you've used the iPhone or iPod touch for any time, you've likely seen the small, red badges that appear over applications on the home screen. These might indicate the number of missed phone calls or unread emails that have accumulated since the user last opened Phone or Mail.

There are actually three ways to go about badging applications: one, an extremely simple `UIApplication` call; the other a slightly more involved tunneling into `UIKit`; and the last using the announced SDK push features from a Web server. To set an application badge from within the program itself, use either the undocumented `setApplicationBadge:` call or set the official `applicationIconBadgeNumber` property. Pass an `NSString` as a general badge argument, limiting the string size to four or five characters at most or an `NSInteger` for the badge number property. For example, you could badge an application with the three-letter abbreviation for the current month, as shown by Listing 4-2.

> **Note**
>
> To hide badges, either set `applicationIconBadgeNumber` to 0 (the number zero) or `setApplicationBadge:` to @"" (the empty string).

Listing 4-2   Badging an Application Icon with the Current Month

```
NSDate *now = [NSDate dateWithTimeIntervalSinceNow:0];
NSString *caldate = [[now
        dateWithCalendarFormat:@"%b"
        timeZone:nil] description];
[[UIApplication sharedApplication] setApplicationBadge:caldate];
```

To remove an application badge, pass the empty string (for example, @""). This removes any existing badge from the icon. If you want an "empty" badge, pass it a space character instead, @" ".

The problem with the UIApplication approach is that to use it you must place your requests directly from the application and then only as a number. You may want to badge icons from outside the application itself. This is something developers will want to know about—especially if you do not intend to distribute certain applications through App Store. Listing 4-3 demonstrates how to badge applications using dynamic links to the public UIKit framework. This code does not require that the badging be done by the application itself. Instead, it calls SpringBoard to perform the dirty work.

This function relies on dynamic linking. Reverse engineering the UIKit framework revealed how UIApplication's setApplicationBadge worked. It calls SBSetApplicationBadge with a string and an application identifier. Dynamic linking isn't an approach I generally endorse for day-to-day programming. Figure 4-12 shows the result of using this function to badge a few icons.

Figure 4-12   Application badges appear as small, red containers on the top-right corner of an application's icon.

Be aware that recent iPhone firmware versions have behaved inconsistently with badging. Second-party badging continues to work reliably for items in the /Applications folder but not for those applications residing in sandboxes.

> **Note**
>
> It remains unclear whether SpringBoard calls fall into the undocumented-but-acceptable category or the undocumented-and-bad-evil-evil-evil category as far as App Store submission is concerned. Use dynamic linking with care.

Listing 4-3   **General Badging Through Reverse Engineering and Dynamic Linking**

```
#include <dlfcn.h>
void badge(char *appid, char *badge)
{
    // link to UIKit
    void *uikit = dlopen("/System/Library/Frameworks/UIKit.framework/UIKit",
                RTLD_LAZY);

    // Recover the SpringBoard Port
    int (*SBSSpringBoardServerPort)() =
                    dlsym(uikit, "SBSSpringBoardServerPort");
    mach_port_t *p;
    p = SBSSpringBoardServerPort();

    // Perform the badging
    int (*doBadge)(mach_port_t* port, char* x, char *y) =
                    dlsym(uikit, "SBSetApplicationBadge");
    doBadge(p, appid, badge);
    dlclose(uikit);
}
```

Recipe: Simple Audio Alerts

Audio alerts "speak" directly to your users. They produce instant feedback—assuming users are not hearing impaired. Fortunately, Apple built basic sound playback into the Cocoa Touch SDK through System Audio services. This works very much like system audio on a Macintosh. The alternative, using Audio Queue calls to create audio alerts, comes with a pretty high price. Audio Queue playback is "expensive" to program and involves much more complexity than simple alert sounds need. In contrast, you can load and play system audio with just a few lines of code.

Alert sounds work best when kept short, preferably two seconds or less according to Apple. That being said, I've tested using sounds up to a minute in length, and they played back fine with the System Audio services. System Audio plays PCM and IMA audio only. That means limiting your sounds to AIFF, WAV, and CAF formats.

To build a system sound, call `AudioServicesCreateSystemSoundID` with a file URL pointing to the sound file. This call returns an initialized system sound object, which you can then play at will. Just call `AudioServicesPlaySystemSound` with the sound object. That single call does all the work.

You can add an optional system sound completion callback to notify your program when a sound finishes playing (call `AudioServicesAddSystemSoundCompletion`), but you really don't need to do that in practice, especially when using short Apple-approved sounds.

To clean up your sounds, dispose them when you're through using them. Call `AudioServicesDisposeSystemSoundID` with the sound object in question.

> **Note**
>
> To use these system sound services, make sure to include `AudioToolbox/AudioServices.h` in your code and link to the Audio Toolbox framework.

Recipe 4-11   **Playing Simple Audio Alerts**

```
@interface HelloController : UIViewController
{
    UIView *contentView;
    SystemSoundID pmph;
}
@end


@implementation HelloController

- (void) playSound
{
    AudioServicesPlaySystemSound (pmph);
}

- (void)loadView
{
    contentView = [[UIView alloc] initWithFrame:[[UIScreen mainScreen]
    ➥applicationFrame]];
    self.view = contentView;
    contentView.backgroundColor = [UIColor whiteColor];
    [contentView release];

    // Add an action button
    self.navigationItem.rightBarButtonItem = [[[UIBarButtonItem alloc]
                                       initWithTitle:@"Do It"
                                       style:UIBarButtonItemStylePlain
                                       target:self
```

```
                                        action:@selector(playSound)]
                                        autorelease];

    // Load the sound
    id sndpath = [[NSBundle mainBundle] pathForResource:@"pmph1" ofType:@"wav"
    ➥inDirectory:@"/"];
    CFURLRef baseURL = (CFURLRef)[[NSURL alloc] initFileURLWithPath:sndpath];
    AudioServicesCreateSystemSoundID (baseURL, &pmph);
}

-(void) dealloc
{
    if (pmph) AudioServicesDisposeSystemSoundID(pmph);
    [contentView release];
    [super dealloc];
}
@end
```

Vibration

As with audio alerts, vibration immediately grabs a user's attention. What's more, vibration works for nearly all users, including those who are hearing or visually impaired. Using the same System Audio services you just used in Recipe 4-11, you can vibrate as well as play a sound. All you need is the following one-line call to accomplish it:

```
AudioServicesPlaySystemSound (kSystemSoundID_Vibrate);
```

You cannot vary the vibration parameters. Each call produces a short one- to two-second buzz. On platforms without vibration support (like the iPod touch), this call does nothing—but will not produce an error.

Summary

This chapter has introduced ways to interact directly with your user. You've seen how to build alerts—visual, auditory, and tactile—that grab your user's attention and can request immediate feedback. Use these examples to enhance the interactive appeal of your programs and leverage some unique iPhone-only features. Here are a few thoughts to carry away from this chapter:

- Many recipes in this chapter rely on undocumented UIKit calls or, worse, dynamic linking. I've included these recipes into a book that is otherwise focused on official SDK development because their functionality is both useful and passes the test of being needed by a large segment of iPhone developers. All calls in this chapter are limited to public SDK frameworks and do not, at least theoretically, cross the line according to Apple's stated policies.

- Whenever any task will take a noticeable amount of time, be courteous to your user and display some kind of progress feedback. The iPhone offers many ways to do this, from heads-up displays to status bar indicators and beyond.

- Alerts take users into the moment. They're designed to elicit responses while communicating information. And, as you've seen in this chapter, they're almost insanely customizable. It's possible to build entire applications around the simple `UIAlertSheet`.

- Badges and status bar icons both allow you to extend application state beyond the running of the application itself. Use these features sparingly to deliver the greatest information punch.

- Audio feedback-like clicks and beeps can enhance your programs and make your interaction richer. Using system sound calls means that your sounds play nicely with iPod functionality and won't ruin the ongoing listening experience.

Basic Tables

Tables provide an interaction class that works particularly well on a small, cramped device. Many if not most apps that ship with the iPhone and iPod touch center on tables, including Settings, iPod, YouTube, Stocks, and Weather. The iPhone's limited screen size makes tables, with their scrolling and individual item selection, an ideal way to deliver information and content in simple easy-to-manipulate form. In this chapter, you discover how iPhone tables work, what kinds of tables are available to you as a developer, and how you can use table features in your own programs.

Introducing `UITableView` and `UITableViewController`

The standard iPhone table consists of a simple scrolling list of individual cells, providing an interactive data index. Users may scroll or flick their way up and down until they find an item they want to interact with. Then, they can work with that item independently of other rows. On the iPhone, tables are ubiquitous. Nearly every standard software package uses them, and they form the core of many third-party applications, too. In this section, you'll discover how tables function and what elements you need to bring together to create your own.

The iPhone SDK supports several kinds of tables, all of which are implemented as flavors of the `UITableView` class. In addition to the standard scrolling list of cells, which provides the most generic table implementation, you can create several specialized tables. These include the kind of tables you see in the preferences application, with their gray background and rounded cell edges, tables with sections and an index like the ones used in the Contacts application, and a `UITableView` subclass with wheeled tables, like those used to set appointment dates and alarms. Chapter 6, "Advanced Tables," introduces the how-tos for these specialized table styles. No matter what type of table you use, they all work in the same general way. They contain a column of cells provided from a data source and respond to user interactions by calling well-defined methods.

`UITableViewControllers` are a subclass of `UIViewController`. Like their parent class, they enable you to build onscreen views with minimal programming and maximum convenience. As you'll read in this section, the UITableViewController class greatly simplifies the process of creating a UITableView, reducing or eliminating the repetitive steps required for working directly with table instances. UITableViewController handles the fussy details for view layout and provides table-specific convenience by adding a local tableView instance variable and automatic table protocol support for delegates and data sources.

Creating the Table

To implement tables, you must define three key elements: how the table is laid out, the kind of things that are used to fill the table, and how the table reacts to user interaction. To specify these elements, you add descriptions and methods to your application. You create the visual layout when building your views, you define a data source that feeds table cells on demand, and you implement delegate methods that respond to user interactions such as row-selection changes.

Laying Out the View

UITableViews are, as the name suggests, views. They present interactive tables on the iPhone screen. The UITableView class inherits from the UIScrollView class. This inheritance provides the up and down scrolling capabilities used by the table. Like other views, UITableView instances define their boundaries through frames, and they can be children or parents of other views. To create a table view, you allocate it (alloc), initialize it with a frame just like any other view (initWithFrame:), and then add all the bookkeeping details by assigning data source and delegate objects.

UITableViewControllers take care of the layout work for you. The UITableViewController class creates a standard UIViewController and populates it with a UITableView, setting its frame to allow for any navigation bars or toolbars. You may access that table view via the tableView instance variable.

One important note: When creating a custom UITableViewController subclass, make sure to call [super layoutView] from the child's layoutView method. This properly sets up the view within the controller and enables you to add customize features in the subclass such as navigation item buttons.

Assigning a Data Source

Tables do not directly own or copy the cells they use. Table cells exist independently of each table. UITableView instances rely on an external source to feed either new or existing table cells on demand. This external source is called a "data source" and refers to the object whose responsibility it is to return a cell to a table's query.

Data sources provide table cells based on an index path. Index paths, members of the NSIndexPath class, describe the path through a data tree to a particular node. It's the data source's job to connect that path to a concrete UITableViewCell instance and return that cell on demand.

The iPhone SDK provides a built-in mechanism for reusing table cells. You can tag cells for reuse and then pop them off a stack as needed. This saves memory and provides a fast, efficient way to feed cells when users scroll quickly through long lists onscreen.

Use `setDataSource:` to assign an object to a table as its data source. That object must implement the `UITableViewDataSource` protocol. Most typically, the `UITableViewController` that owns the table view acts as the data source for that view. When working with `UITableViewController` subclasses, you need not assign the `<UITableViewDataSource>` protocol. The `UITableViewController` class implicitly supports that protocol.

After you've assigned a data source, you can go ahead and load your table up with its cells. Call the table's `reloadData` method and the table starts querying its data source to load the actual onscreen cells into your table.

Assigning a Delegate

Like many other interaction objects, `UITableView` instances use delegates to respond to user interactions and implement a meaningful response. Your table's delegate can respond to events like the table scrolling or row selection changes. Delegation tells the table to hand off responsibility for reacting to these interactions to the object you specify, typically the `UITableViewController` object that owns the table view. If you're working directly with a `UITableView`, use the standard `setDelegate:` method to set your table's delegate. The delegate must implement the `UITableViewDelegate` protocol. When working with `UITableViewController`, omit the `setDelegate:` method and protocol assignment. That class automatically handles this. A full set of delegate methods is listed in the Apple SDK documentation.

Note

UITableView instances provide notifications in addition to delegate method calls. Notifications enable different threads of your application to communicate with each other by broadcasting updates. You can subscribe your application to these notifications (using standard NSNotificationCenter calls) to find out when the table states change.

What the `UITableViewController` Does

The `UITableViewController` class embeds a `UITableView` into a `UIViewController` object that manages its table view. Its view is called `tableView`, which you can access directly through calls to `self.tableView`. It automatically sets the data source and delegate methods for the table view to itself. And it automatically implements editing mode when you add an Edit|Done button to its parent's navigation bar via `setEditing: animated:` calls.

Recipe: Creating a Simple List Table

Pretty much any array of strings can be used to set up and populate a table. This recipe leverages the UIFont class's capability to list available system fonts. A call to [UIFont familyNames] returns an NSArray populated with those font names—handy for setting up a table data source. Recipe 5-1 creates a basic table based on those font names. Figure 5-1 shows the interface produced by this code, as run on the iPhone simulator. (Running on the Simulator produces a different set of fonts because they're based on the available fonts from the Macintosh running the SDK rather than the fonts on the iPhone itself.)

Figure 5-1   It's easy to fill a UITableView with cells based on any array of strings. Here, the font family list from the UIFont class is listed. When tapped, the font chosen will update the title bar font.

Data Source Functions

To display a table, every table data source (UITableViewDelegate) must provide three core methods. These methods are presented in the following list along with comments about their use in a simple list view, as shown in Figure 5-1:

- **numberOfSectionsInTableView.** Tables must determine whether they display their data in sections or as a single list. For simple tables, always return 1, as in one single section for the table.

- **tableView: numberOfRowsInSection.** Because simple lists contain only one section, return the number of rows for the entire table here. For more complex lists, you'll want to provide a way to report back per section.

- **`tableView: cellForRowAtIndexPath.`** This is the method that actually returns a cell. Use the index path's `row` to determine which cell to provide.

Reusing Cells

One of the ways the iPhone conserves memory is by reusing cells. You can assign an ID string to each cell. This specifies what kind of cell it is. Use different IDs for different kinds of cells. For simple tables, a single identifier does the job. In the case of Recipe 5-1, it is `@"any-cell"`. The strings are arbitrary. Define them the way you like, but when using multiple cell types keep the names meaningful.

Before allocating a new cell, always check whether a reusable cell is available. If your table returns NULL from a request to `dequeueReusableCellWithIdentifier:`, go ahead and allocate that new cell. If it returns a cell, customize that cell with the information that's meaningful for the current row index. You do not need to add cells to the reuse queue. Cocoa Touch handles all those details for you.

Font Table Sample

Recipe 5-1 demonstrates how to build a simple list-based table. It creates a table and fills that table with all available font families. When tapped, the view controller assigns that font to the label in the blue navigation bar at the top of the screen and prints a list of available fonts for that family out to the debugger console. This behavior is defined in the `tableView:  didSelectRowAtIndexPath:` delegate method.

Using the `UITableViewController` as a delegate is a good choice here because the table's user interactions affect its views. If you'd rather use the application delegate, you can call `setDelegate:` with that object by querying the application: `[[UIApplication sharedApplication] delegate]` instead. This overrides the standard `UITableViewController` settings.

> **Note**
>
> Tables enable you to set the color for the selected cell by choosing between a blue or gray overlay. Set the `selectionStyle` property to either `UITableViewCellSelectionStyleBlue` or `UITableViewCellSelectionStyleGray`. If you'd rather not show a selection, use `UITableViewCellSelectionStyleNone`. The cell can still be selected, but the overlay will not display.

Recipe 5-1   **Creating a Simple List-Based Table**

```
@interface HelloController : UITableViewController
@end

@implementation HelloController

- (HelloController *) init
```

Recipe 5-1   **Continued**

```
{
    if (self = [super init]) self.title = @"Fonts";
    return self;
}

#pragma mark UITableViewDataSource Methods

// Only one section in this table
- (NSInteger)numberOfSectionsInTableView:(UITableView *)tableView
{
    return 1;
}

// Return the number of rows in the table
- (NSInteger)tableView:(UITableView *)tableView
numberOfRowsInSection:(NSInteger)section
{
    return [[UIFont    familyNames] count];
}

// Return a cell for the specified index path
- (UITableViewCell *)tableView:(UITableView *)tableView
➥cellForRowAtIndexPath:(NSIndexPath *)indexPath
{
    UITableViewCell *cell = [tableView
➥dequeueReusableCellWithIdentifier:@"any-cell"];
    if (cell == nil) {
        cell = [[[UITableViewCell alloc] initWithFrame:CGRectZero
        ➥reuseIdentifier:@"any-cell"] autorelease];
    }
    // Set up the cell
    cell.text = [[UIFont familyNames] objectAtIndex:[indexPath row]];
    return cell;
}

#pragma mark UITableViewDelegateMethods

// Respond to user selection
- (void)tableView:(UITableView *)tableView
➥didSelectRowAtIndexPath:(NSIndexPath *)newIndexPath
{
    printf("User selected row %d\n", [newIndexPath row] + 1);
    NSString *fontName = [[UIFont familyNames] objectAtIndex:[newIndexPath row]];
    CFShow([UIFont fontNamesForFamilyName:fontName]);
    [(UILabel *)self.navigationItem.titleView setFont:[UIFont fontWithName:
    ➥fontName size:[UIFont systemFontSize]]];
}

#pragma mark Controller's loadView method
```

Recipe 5-1   **Continued**

```
- (void)loadView
{
    [super loadView];

    // Add the custom title bar label
    self.navigationItem.titleView = [[UILabel alloc]
    ➥initWithFrame:CGRectMake(0.0f, 4.0f, 320.0f, 36.0f)];
    [(UILabel *)self.navigationItem.titleView setText:@"Font Families"];
    [(UILabel *)self.navigationItem.titleView setBackgroundColor:[UIColor
    ➥clearColor]];
    [(UILabel *)self.navigationItem.titleView setTextColor:[UIColor whiteColor]];
    [(UILabel *)self.navigationItem.titleView
    ➥setTextAlignment:UITextAlignmentCenter];
    [(UILabel *)self.navigationItem.titleView setFont:[UIFont
    ➥boldSystemFontOfSize:[UIFont systemFontSize]]];
}

-(void) dealloc
{
    [super dealloc];
}
@end
```

Recipe: Creating a Table-Based Selection Sheet

The preceding recipe showed you how to create an extremely simple table of font families. This recipe takes that idea to the next level by embedding that table into a view and presenting it for user selection (see Figure 5-2). Tables provide an excellent way to offer your users a selection of similar options. Mobile Safari has standardized on a UIPickerTableView presentation, but I think a simple flat scrolling list has a lot to offer. The metallic look used by Picker views can be jarring, and although my design skills are limited, this UITableView alternative should be able to find a home in many applications.

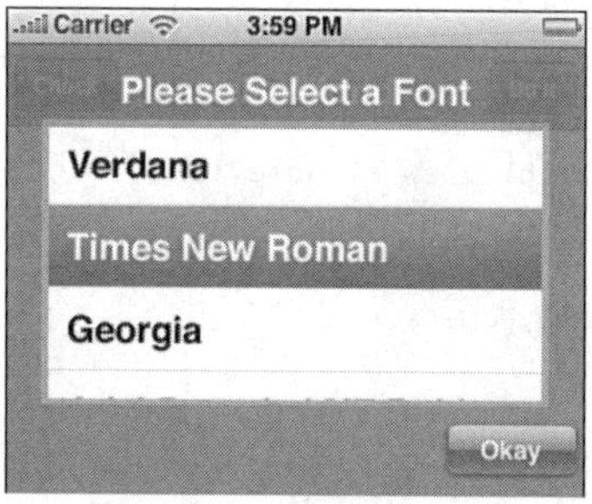

Figure 5-2   Embed tables into other views to create
another way for your users to pick from lists.

Note that this recipe does not use UITableViewController. The solution wraps around a custom view with a table and a button to indicate selection. This falls outside the province of UIViewControllers and is presented by animating a UIView subclass into position.

This recipe, shown in Recipe 5-2, creates a custom view, the FontPickerSheet, and slides it onto the screen on demand using a UIView animation block (see Chapter 2, "Views"). User selections are stored in a local property, the selection, which can be queried from the UIViewController. A value of NULL means that the user failed to make a selection. Otherwise, it returns an NSString, the name of the selected font.

What I have not included here, which you might want to consider, is a semitranslucent UIView sitting between the sheet and the view below it. Such a view would serve two purposes. First, it would dim your main application view, and second, it would block interactions with that view. This forces a modal presentation, the interaction style that limits your user to a single view before returning control to the main application.

Recipe 5-2   Embedding a Table into a Sheet and Recovering the Selection

```
@interface FontPickerSheet : UIView <UITableViewDataSource, UITableViewDelegate>
{
    UILabel *title;
    UITableView *tableView;
    NSString *selection;
}
@property (nonatomic, retain) NSString *selection;
@end

@implementation FontPickerSheet
@synthesize selection;

#pragma mark UITableViewDataSource Methods

// Only one section in this table
- (NSInteger)numberOfSectionsInTableView:(UITableView *)tableView
{
    return 1;
}

// One row for each family font name
- (NSInteger)tableView:(UITableView *)tableView
➥numberOfRowsInSection:(NSInteger)section
{
    return [[UIFont    familyNames] count];
}

// Return a cell for the ith row
- (UITableViewCell *)tableView:(UITableView *)tView
➥cellForRowAtIndexPath:(NSIndexPath *)indexPath
{
    UITableViewCell *cell = [tView dequeueReusableCellWithIdentifier:@"any-cell"];
```

Recipe 5-2 **Continued**

```objc
    if (cell == nil) {
        cell = [[[UITableViewCell alloc] initWithFrame:CGRectZero
        ➥reuseIdentifier:@"any-cell"] autorelease];
    }
    // Set up the cell
    cell.text = [[UIFont familyNames] objectAtIndex:[indexPath row]];
    return cell;
}

#pragma mark UITableViewDelegateMethods

// Respond to user selection
- (void)tableView:(UITableView *)tableView didSelectRowAtIndexPath:(NSIndexPath *)
➥newIndexPath
{
    selection = [[[UIFont familyNames] objectAtIndex:[newIndexPath row]] retain];
}

#pragma mark FontPickerSheet customization

- (FontPickerSheet *) initWithFrame: (CGRect) rect
{
    rect.origin.y = 0.0f - rect.size.height; // Place above status bar
    self = [super initWithFrame:rect];
    [self setAlpha:0.9];
    [self setBackgroundColor:sysBlueColor(0.4f)];

    // Add button
    UIButton *button = [[UIButton buttonWithType:UIButtonTypeCustom]
    ➥initWithFrame:CGRectMake(220.0f, 200.0f, 80.0f, 32.0f)];
    [button setBackgroundImage:[UIImage imageNamed:@"whiteButton.png"]
    ➥forState:UIControlStateNormal];
    [button setTitle:@"Okay" forState: UIControlStateHighlighted];
    [button setTitle:@"Okay" forState: UIControlStateNormal];
    [button setFont:[UIFont boldSystemFontOfSize:14.0f]];
    [button addTarget:self action:@selector(removeView)
    ➥forControlEvents:UIControlEventTouchUpInside];
    [self addSubview:button];

    // Add title
    title = [[UILabel alloc] initWithFrame:CGRectMake(0.0f, 8.0f, 320.0f, 32.0f)];
    title.text = @"Please Select a Font";
    title.textAlignment = UITextAlignmentCenter;
    title.textColor = [UIColor whiteColor];
    title.backgroundColor = [UIColor clearColor];
    title.font = [UIFont boldSystemFontOfSize:20.0f];
    [self addSubview:title];
    [title release];
```

Recipe 5-2 **Continued**

```
    // Add border for the table
    CGRect bounds = CGRectMake(20.0f, 40.0f, 280.0f, 200.0f - 48.0f);
    UIView *borderView = [[UIView alloc] initWithFrame:bounds];
    [borderView setBackgroundColor:sysBlueColor(0.55f)];
    [self addSubview:borderView];
    [borderView release];

    // Add table
    tableView = [[UITableView alloc] initWithFrame:CGRectInset(bounds, 4.0f, 4.0f)
    ➥style:UITableViewStylePlain];
    tableView.backgroundColor = [UIColor whiteColor];
    tableView.delegate = self;
    tableView.dataSource = self;
    [tableView reloadData];
    [self addSubview:tableView];
    [tableView release];

    return self;
}

- (void) removeView
{
    [tableView deselectRowAtIndexPath:[tableView indexPathForSelectedRow]
    ➥animated:NO];

    // Scroll away the overlay
    CGContextRef context = UIGraphicsGetCurrentContext();
    [UIView beginAnimations:nil context:context];
    [UIView setAnimationCurve:UIViewAnimationCurveEaseInOut];
    [UIView setAnimationDuration:0.5];

    CGRect rect = [self frame];
    rect.origin.y = 0.0f - rect.size.height;
    [self setFrame:rect];

    // Complete the animation
    [UIView commitAnimations];
}

- (void) presentView
{
    selection = NULL;

    // Scroll in the overlay
    CGContextRef context = UIGraphicsGetCurrentContext();
    [UIView beginAnimations:nil context:context];
    [UIView setAnimationCurve:UIViewAnimationCurveEaseInOut];
    [UIView setAnimationDuration:0.5];

    CGRect rect = [self frame];
    rect.origin.y = 0.0f;
```

Recipe 5-2   **Continued**

```
    [self setFrame:rect];

    // Complete the animation
    [UIView commitAnimations];
}

-(void) dealloc
{
    [title release];
    [tableView release];
    [super dealloc];
}
@end
```

Recipe: Loading Images into Table Cells

Add images to tables by assigning them to individual cells. The UITableViewCell class enables you to place a small thumbnail to the left side of any cell without any special programming by setting the cell's image property to a UIImage. The image does not interfere with the normal text property of that cell. Any text appears to the right of the image, with spacing automatically taken into account.

You must know the approximate size of the images you'll use and adjust the table view's rowHeight property accordingly. This example sets the row height to 64, with plenty of space to accommodate 57-pixel square application icons.

This example scans for application icons on your iPhone. It uses NSFileManager to access your /Applications folder and scans each application for icon.png. When found, it uses this icon to label each cell. When not found, it adds the icon for its own application instead. You can expect to see icons for most apps, including Calculator and Maps but not for the two MobileSlideshow applications (Photos and Camera) because they do not provide individual icon.png files.

> **Note**
>
> If you'd like to launch the selected application, call the undocumented UIApplication method launchApplicationWithIdentifier: suspended:. Pass it the application ID (for example, com.apple.Calculator). Launching applications is, however, strictly prohibited by App Store agreements.

Recipe 5-3   **Adding Image Thumbnails to a Table**

```
// Return a cell for the ith row
- (UITableViewCell *)tableView:(UITableView *)tView
➥cellForRowAtIndexPath:(NSIndexPath *)indexPath
{
    UITableViewCell *cell = [tView dequeueReusableCellWithIdentifier:@"any-cell"];
```

Recipe 5-3   **Continued**

```
    if (cell == nil) {
        cell = [[[UITableViewCell alloc] initWithFrame:CGRectZero
        ➥reuseIdentifier:@"any-cell"] autorelease];
    }
    // Set up the cell
    NSString *appname = [[[NSFileManager defaultManager]
    ➥directoryContentsAtPath:@"/Applications"] objectAtIndex:[indexPath row]];
    cell.text = appname;

    NSString *imagePath = [NSString stringWithFormat:@"/Applications/%@/icon.png",
    ➥appname];
    printf("app: %s\n", [imagePath UTF8String]);
    if ([[NSFileManager defaultManager] fileExistsAtPath:imagePath])
        cell.image = [UIImage imageWithContentsOfFile:imagePath];
    else
        cell.image = [UIImage imageWithContentsOfFile:[[NSBundle mainBundle]
        ➥pathForResource:@"Icon" ofType:@"png" inDirectory:@"/"]];
    return cell;
}

- (void)loadView
{
    [super loadView];
    [self.tableView setRowHeight:64];
}
```

Figure 5-3   `UITableViewCells` makes it easy to add
thumbnail pictures to your tables as well as text labels.

Recipe: Setting a Cell's Text Traits

Each `UITableViewCell` provides full text trait support. You can set the cell label's color, font, size, alignment, and so forth. Recipe 5-4 shows data source methods that create a simple three-item table, assigning unique colors and fonts to each cell. Although this produces a visual mishmash, as shown in Figure 5-4, you can see how you might assign visual cues to differentiate table rows from their mates.

You might use different text styles to indicate which table elements are "busy" and cannot be accessed or which items have not yet been examined. In one of my early iPhone utilities (SendFile, see ericasadun.com), I used color to tell users which file was being shared over Bonjour's configuration-free networking. To assign text traits, use the standard text properties such as `textColor` and `font`.

Recipe 5-4 assigns these kinds of traits arbitrarily, to produce a proof of concept. It demonstrates that each cell can own its own text styling.

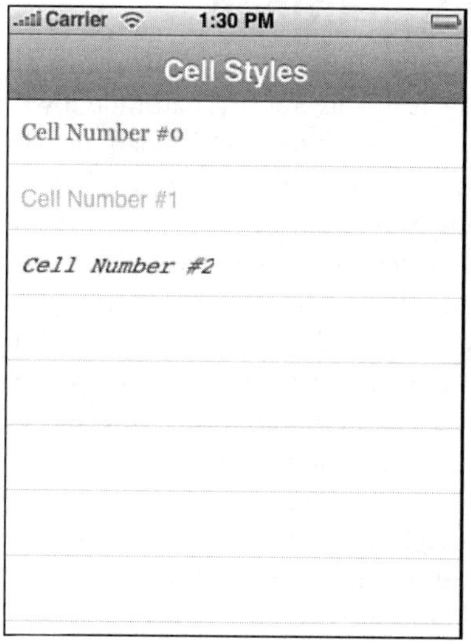

Figure 5-4   `UITableViewCell`s gives you direct access to their label's text traits.

Recipe 5-4   **Assigning Text Traits to Table Cells**

```
// Return a cell for the ith row
- (UITableViewCell *)tableView:(UITableView *)tView
➥cellForRowAtIndexPath:(NSIndexPath *)indexPath
{
    UITableViewCell *cell = [tView dequeueReusableCellWithIdentifier:@"any-cell"];
    if (cell == nil) {
        cell = [[[UITableViewCell alloc] initWithFrame:CGRectZero
        ➥reuseIdentifier:@"any-cell"] autorelease];
    }
```

```
    // Set up the cell
    cell.text = [NSString stringWithFormat:@"Cell Number #%d", [indexPath row]];
    cell.font = [UIFont fontWithName:[[NSArray arrayWithObjects:@"Georgia",
    ➥@"Helvetica", @"Courier", nil]
                                            objectAtIndex:[indexPath row]] size:16];
    cell.textColor = [[NSArray arrayWithObjects:
                        [UIColor redColor],
                        [UIColor lightGrayColor],
                        [UIColor blueColor], nil] objectAtIndex: [indexPath row]];

    return cell;
}
```

Removing Cell Selections

If there's one thing I hated about the UITableView class (and by association UITableViewController), it was its historical attitude toward cell reselection. Depending on the iteration of the iPhone SDK beta program, UITableView instances wouldn't let you reselect the currently selected cell and trigger a delegate method call—as you can now do in recent SDK releases. There was always at least one way you could use to get a table cell to allow itself to be selected twice—and that was by removing the current selection so that the table was ready for the next tap.

When working with delegate methods, you can't just tell the selected cell to deselect itself. There is no [aCell setSelected:NO]; method. Instead, you must talk to the table and have it deselect the cell in question, as shown in Listing 5-1. Here, each user selection triggers a delayed deselection (the deselect method) after a half a second.

Now that cells support multiple tapping, instead of deselecting for functionality use deselection semantically. A table with a selected item may present different options than a table with no selection. For example, in an audio application, you might show only a Play or Pause button when users select a sound from a list.

Listing 5-1   **Removing a Table Cell Selection**

```
- (void) deselect: (id) sender
{
    [tableView deselectRowAtIndexPath:[tableView indexPathForSelectedRow]
    ➥animated:YES];
}

// Respond to user selection
- (void)tableView:(UITableView *)tableView didSelectRowAtIndexPath:(NSIndexPath *)
➥newIndexPath
{
    printf("User selected row %d\n", [newIndexPath row] + 1);
    [self performSelector:@selector(deselect:) withObject:nil afterDelay:0.5f];
}
```

When moving between views (which often happens as a result of table selection), delay this method until the view that contains this table is fully redrawn. Perform deselection in the `viewDidAppear` method of the table's parent `UIViewController`.

Recipe: Creating Complex Cells

Table cells can be more than a text label with an optional image. Table cells are much more flexible and complex than that. They are, in the end, views. And as such, you can customize them the way you'd customize any other view with arbitrary frame sizes and child subviews.

Recipe 5-5 demonstrates how to create a custom table cell with children. In this example, I modify a standard `UITableViewCell`. A cell constructor (`newCell:url: note:`) creates a 320-by-100-pixel cell and populates it with several `UITextLabels` with distinct text traits (see Figure 5-5). My design strengths, as you can see from this image, are limited. Developers with better-developed graphic skills will be able to do much more than this after mastering the notion that each cell can be a canvas. Chapter 6 demonstrates more table cell customization examples.

Please note that this example does not subclass `UITableCell`. It customizes the standard cell. Also note that unlike standard table cells, this presentation does not invert the black fonts to white on selection. You might have to play with your cell-selection behavior if you don't like the standard blue-over-black display. This involves catching the selection, restoring the colors for any previously selected cell, and either inverting or changing the text color for the labels in the newly selected cell.

Figure 5-5 Create complex cell types by adding subviews to your `UITableCells`.

Recipe 5-5 Creating a Customized `UITableViewCell`

```
- (void) modCell:(UITableViewCell *)aCell withTitle:(NSString *)title
                    url: (NSString *) url note: (NSString *) comment
{
    // Title
    CGRect tRect1 = CGRectMake(0.0f, 5.0f, 320.0f, 40.0f);
    id title1 = [[UILabel alloc] initWithFrame:tRect1];
    [title1 setText:title];
    [title1 setTextAlignment:UITextAlignmentCenter];
    [title1 setFont: [UIFont fontWithName:@"American Typewriter" size:36.0f]];
    [title1 setBackgroundColor:[UIColor clearColor]];

    // URL
    CGRect tRect2 = CGRectMake(0.0f, 45.0f, 320.0f, 20.0f);
    id title2 = [[UILabel alloc] initWithFrame:tRect2];
    [title2 setText:url];
    [title2 setTextAlignment:UITextAlignmentCenter];
    [title2 setFont: [UIFont fontWithName:@"Helvetica" size:18.0f]];
    [title2 setBackgroundColor:[UIColor clearColor]];

    // Comment
    CGRect tRect3 = CGRectMake(0.0f, 70.0f, 320.0f, 20.0f);
    id title3 = [[UILabel alloc] initWithFrame:tRect3];
    [title3 setText:comment];
    [title3 setTextAlignment:UITextAlignmentCenter];
    [title3 setFont: [UIFont fontWithName:@"Helvetica" size:18.0f]];
    [title3 setBackgroundColor:[UIColor clearColor]];

    // Add to cell
    [aCell addSubview:title1];
    [aCell addSubview:title2];
    [aCell addSubview:title3];

    [title1 release];
    [title2 release];
    [title3 release];
}

// Return a cell for the ith row
- (UITableViewCell *)tableView:(UITableView *)tableView
➥cellForRowAtIndexPath:(NSIndexPath *)indexPath
{
    UITableViewCell *cell = [[[UITableViewCell alloc] initWithFrame:CGRectZero
    ➥reuseIdentifier:@"any-cell"] autorelease];
    }
```

Recipe 5-5   **Continued**

```
// Set up the cell
int row = [indexPath row];
switch (row)
{
    case 0:
        [self modCell:cell withTitle:@"Digital Media"
                url: @"http://digitalmedia.oreilly.com/"
                note: @"Developer Issues"];
        break;
    case 1:
        [self modCell:cell withTitle:@"TUAW"
                url: @"http://tuaw.com/"
                note: @"Consumer Apple Use"];
        break;

    case 2:
        [self modCell:cell withTitle:@"Erica Sadun"
                url: @"http://ericasadun.com"
                note: @"Software Updates"];
        break;
}
    return cell;
}
```

Recipe: Creating Checked Selections

Accessory views enable you to expand normal UITableViewCell functionality. The most common accessories are the Delete buttons and drag bars for reordering, but you can also add check marks to create interactive one-of-n or n-of-n selections. With these kinds of selections, you can ask your users to pick what they want to have for dinner or choose which items they want to update. This kind of radio button/check box behavior provides a richness of table interaction. Recipe 5-6 demonstrates how to create this kind of table.

Figure 5-6 shows checks in action: a standard UITableView with accessorized cells. Check marks appear next to selected items. When tapped, the checks toggle on or off. Query your table by iterating through the cells. Checked items use the UITableViewCellAccessoryCheckmark accessory type.

Note very carefully that it's the cell that's being checked here, not the logical item associated with the cell. As you scroll your table, your cells get reused. And as they do, the reused cells remain checked or unchecked. In the next chapter, Recipe 6-6 demonstrates how to store and update state information that's tied to data.

.ııl Carrier 🛜   2:25 PM   ▭
Fonts
AppleGothic
Hiragino Kaku Gothic ProN... ✓
Arial
STHeiti
Courier
Courier New   ✓
Zapfino   ✓
Hiragino Kaku Gothic ProN W6
Arial Unicode MS

Figure 5-6   Check mark accessories offer a convenient
way of making one-of-n or n-of-n selections from a list.

You control the way items are selected. To simply toggle items on and off, keep track
of the current `accessoryType` setting. To create a one-of-n selection instead, remove
the accessory from the old index path, and add it to the cell at the new index path.

Recipe 5-6   **Implementing Table Cell Checks**

```
// Respond to user selection
- (void)tableView:(UITableView *)tableView didSelectRowAtIndexPath:(NSIndexPath
➥*)newIndexPath
{
    printf("User selected row %d\n", [newIndexPath row] + 1);
    if ([[tableView cellForRowAtIndexPath:newIndexPath] accessoryType] ==
➥UITableViewCellAccessoryCheckmark)
        [[tableView cellForRowAtIndexPath:newIndexPath]
        ➥setAccessoryType:UITableViewCellAccessoryNone];
    else
        [[tableView cellForRowAtIndexPath:newIndexPath]
        ➥setAccessoryType:UITableViewCellAccessoryCheckmark];

    [self performSelector:@selector(deselect) withObject:nil afterDelay:0.5f];
}
```

Recipe: Deleting Cells

The iPhone deletion accessory makes table management simple and elegant. Every iPhone user quickly becomes familiar with the small, red circles that enable them to delete cells from tables, and many users pick up on basic swipe-to-delete functionality. Recipe 5-7 shows how to build a table that responds meaningfully to cell deletion. In this sample, users may add new cells by tapping an Add button and may remove cells either by swiping or entering edit mode and using the red remove controls (see Figure 5-7).

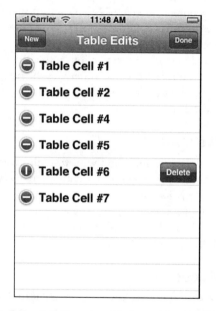

Figure 5-7   Red remove controls enable your users to interactively delete items from an interactive table.

Remove controls belong to the UIRemoveControl class, which is not a public class. Like the check marks discussed in Recipe 5-6, remove controls are a kind of accessory view. Accessories enable you to add user-tappable elements to your UITableViewCells. Accessory types include the remove controls seen here, add controls, check marks, and disclosures.

Creating and Displaying Remove Controls

There are actually two steps you need to take when adding remove controls to your cells. When creating the cell, you must specify what kind of accessory view it uses (in this case, the remove control). You do this by assigning the cell's editingStyle to UITableViewCellEditingStyleDelete. Implement this in the tableView: cellForRowAtIndexPath: data source routine.

In addition to creating the control, you must tell the table to enter edit mode. You do this through two calls. First, animate the table into an edit mode, revealing the edit controls next to each cell title and performing the indentation that makes room for the controls. To do this, call [tableView setEditing:YES animated:YES]. If for some reason you'd rather not animate the change, you can pass NO instead of YES, but I urge you not to. Whenever possible, add animations to your iPhone user interfaces to lead your users from one state to the next, so they're prepared for the mode changes that happen onscreen.

Next, call [tableView beginUpdates]. This tells your table to enter the mode that enables you to change its contents interactively. This means removing cells with remove controls or adding cells with insert controls. (This latter requires an editingStyle of UITableVFiewCellEditingStyleInsert.)

In Recipe 5-7, I've combined these latter actions into a single method enterEditMode. This method is called when a user taps the navigation bar's Edit button. This method also swaps out the title from Edit to Done and updates the target-action settings for that button to call leaveEditMode.

Dismissing Remove Controls

When you've completed your edit mode and want to return to normal table display, proceed in reverse. Conclude your table updates with [tableView endUpdates]. Then dismiss the controls ([tableView setEditing:NO animated:YES]). You can reenter editing mode at will without having to update cell attributes or performing any other work. Once the editing style has been set for your cell, it can show and hide its remove controls strictly through UITableView calls.

Handling Delete Requests

On row deletion, the table communicates with your application by issuing a tableView: commitEditingStyle: forRowAtIndexPath: callback. This method lets you update your data source and respond to the row deletion that the user just performed.

Here is where you actually delete the item from the data structure that supplies the data source methods (in this recipe, through an NSMutableArray of titles) and handle any real-world action such as deleting files that occur as a consequence. In this sample code, the cell goes away but there's no real-world consequence for the deletion. The sample is not based on a real-life model. Instead, the title list just loses that particular numbered cell title.

Swiping Cells

Swiping provides an elegant method for removing items from your UITableViews. You don't have to do anything to enable swipes other than set a cell's editingStyle. The table takes care of the rest. To swipe, users drag swiftly from the left to the right side of the cell. The rectangular delete confirmation appears to the right of the cell, but the cells do *not* display the round remove controls on the left.

After users swipe and confirm, the `tableView: commitEditingStyle:`
`forRowAtIndexPath:` method handles data updates just as if the deletion had occurred
in edit mode.

Adding Cells

Recipe 5-7 introduces an Add button. This button lets users add new table cells. To
accomplish this, an add method appends a new cell title at the end of the `tableTitles`
array and then tells the table to update the data source using `reloadData`. So rather
than actually creating new cells, this enables the normal table mechanism to check the
data and re-create the table view using that updated data source.

Recipe 5-7   **Deleting Cells On-the-Fly**

```
// Initialize and set up the table title array
- (HelloController *) init
{
    if (![self = [super init]]) return self;

    self.title = @"Table Edits";
    tableTitles = [[NSMutableArray alloc] init];
    ithTitle = NCELLS;
    for (int i = 1; i <= NCELLS; i++)
        [tableTitles addObject:[NSString stringWithFormat:@"Table Cell #%d", i]];

    return self;
}

// Add a row to the table
- (void) add
{
    [tableTitles addObject:[NSString stringWithFormat:@"Table Cell #%d",
    ➥++ithTitle]];
    [self.tableView reloadData];
}

// Finished with edit mode, so restore the buttons and commit changes
-(void) leaveEditMode
{
    // Add the edit button
    self.navigationItem.rightBarButtonItem = [[[UIBarButtonItem alloc]
                                    initWithTitle:@"Edit"
                                    style:UIBarButtonItemStylePlain
                                    target:self
                                    action:@selector(enterEditMode)]
                                    autorelease];
    [self.tableView endUpdates];
    [self.tableView setEditing:NO animated:YES];
```

Recipe 5-7   **Continued**

```
}

// Handle deletion requests
- (void)tableView:(UITableView *)tableView
➥commitEditingStyle:(UITableViewCellEditingStyle)editingStyle
➥forRowAtIndexPath:(NSIndexPath *)indexPath
{
    printf("About to delete item %d\n", [indexPath row]);
    [tableTitles removeObjectAtIndex:[indexPath row]];
    [tableView reloadData];
}

// Enter edit mode by changing "Edit" to "Done"
-(void)enterEditMode
{
    // Add the edit button
    self.navigationItem.rightBarButtonItem = [[[UIBarButtonItem alloc]
                                          initWithTitle:@"Done"
                                          style:UIBarButtonItemStylePlain
                                          target:self
                                          action:@selector(leaveEditMode)]
                                          autorelease];
    [self.tableView setEditing:YES animated:YES];
    [self.tableView beginUpdates];
}

// Initialize the view with its buttons
- (void)loadView
{
    [super loadView];

    // Add an add button
    self.navigationItem.leftBarButtonItem = [[[UIBarButtonItem alloc]
                                          initWithTitle:@"New"
                                          style:UIBarButtonItemStylePlain
                                          target:self
                                          action:@selector(add)] autorelease];
    // Add the edit button
    self.navigationItem.rightBarButtonItem = [[[UIBarButtonItem alloc]
                                          initWithTitle:@"Edit"
                                          style:UIBarButtonItemStylePlain
                                          target:self
                                          action:@selector(enterEditMode)]
                                          autorelease];

}
```

Recipe: Reordering Cells

You empower your users when you enable them to directly reorder the cells of a table. They can apply this interaction to sort to-do items by priority or choose which songs should go first in a playlist. The iPhone ships with built-in reordering support that's easy to add to your applications. Recipe 5-8 shows how. Just set `showsReorderControl:` to YES for your cells.

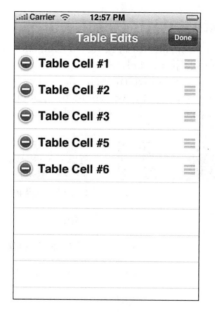

Figure 5-8   Reorder controls appear at the right of each cell during edit mode. They appear as three stacked gray lines.

To make your cells reorder properly, you must implement one method in addition to setting the `showsReorderControl` property: `tableView: moveRowAtIndexPath: toIndexPath:`. This method synchronizes your data source with the onscreen changes, much as committing edits worked with cell deletion. This data source method enables you to move the object from an original path to an updated one. In the case of this example, this means moving the cell title to an updated location in the `tableTitles` mutableArray.

Recipe 5-8   Reordering Table Cells

```
// Perform the reorder
-(void) tableView: (UITableView *) tableView moveRowAtIndexPath: (NSIndexPath *)
➥oldPath toIndexPath:(NSIndexPath *) newPath
```

```
{
    NSString *title = [tableTitles objectAtIndex:[oldPath row]];
    [tableTitles removeObjectAtIndex:[oldPath row]];
    [tableTitles insertObject:title atIndex:[newPath row]];
}
```

Recipe: Working with Disclosures

Disclosures refer to those small, blue or gray, right-facing chevrons found on the right of table cells. Disclosures enable you to link from a cell to a view that supports that cell. For example, in the Contacts list and Calendar applications, these chevrons link to screens that enable you to customize contact information and appointments. Figure 5-9 shows two UITable examples where each cell displays a disclosure control.

Figure 5-9   The right-pointing chevrons indicate disclosure controls, allowing you to link individual table items to another view.

The blue and gray chevrons have two roles. The blue UITableViewCellAccessoryDetailDisclosureButton versions are actual buttons. They respond to touches and are supposed to indicate that the button leads to a full interactive detail view. The gray UITableViewCellAccessoryDisclosureIndicator does not track touches and should lead your users to a further options view, specifically options about that choice.

You see these two accessories in play in the Settings application. In the Wi-Fi Networks screen, the detail disclosures lead to specific details about each WiFi network: its IP address, subnet mask, router, DNS and so forth. The disclosure indicator for "Other" enables you to add a new network by scrolling up a screen for entering network information. A new network then appears with its own detail disclosure.

You also see disclosure indicators whenever one screen leads to a related submenu. When working with submenus, stick to the simple gray chevron. The rule of thumb is this: Submenus use gray chevrons, and object customization uses blue ones.

Recipe 5-9 demonstrates how to use disclosures in your applications. This code sets the `accessoryType` for each cell to `UITableViewCellAccessoryDetailDisclosureButton`. Importantly, it also sets `hidesAccessoryWhenEditing` to YES. When your delete or reorder controls appear, your disclosure chevron will hide, enabling your user full control over their edits without accidentally popping over to a new view.

To handle user taps on the disclosure, the `tableView:` `accessoryButtonTappedForRowWithIndexPath:` method enables you to check the row that was tapped and implement some appropriate response. This sample merely pushes a new `UIViewController` that displays the application's Default.png image. In real life, you'd move to a view that explains more about the selected item or that enables you to choose from additional options.

Recipe 5-9   Adding Disclosure Views

```
// Return a cell for the ith row
- (UITableViewCell *)tableView:(UITableView *)tView
➥cellForRowAtIndexPath:(NSIndexPath *)indexPath
{
    UITableViewCell *cell = [tView dequeueReusableCellWithIdentifier:@"any-cell"];
    if (cell == nil) {
        cell = [[[UITableViewCell alloc] initWithFrame:CGRectZero
        ➥reuseIdentifier:@"any-cell"] autorelease];
    }
    // Set up the cell
    cell.text = [tableTitles objectAtIndex:[indexPath row]];
    cell.editingStyle = UITableViewCellEditingStyleDelete;
    cell.accessoryType = UITableViewCellAccessoryDetailDisclosureButton;
    cell.hidesAccessoryWhenEditing = YES;
    return cell;
}
- (void)tableView:(UITableView *)tableView
➥accessoryButtonTappedForRowWithIndexPath:(NSIndexPath *)indexPath
{
    [[self navigationController] pushViewController:[[ImageController alloc] init]
    ➥animated:YES];
}
```

Summary

This chapter has introduced all the basic iPhone table features: from simple tables to edits to reordering. The skills covered in this chapter should enable you to build a wealth of basic table-based applications for the iPhone and iPod touch. Here are some key points to take away from this chapter:

- When it comes to understanding tables, make sure you know the difference between data source and delegate methods. Data sources fill up your tables with meaningful cells. Delegate methods respond to user interactions.

- Don't overlook notifications as a useful part of programming not just tables but all UI elements. With tables, notifications can sometimes move you past some of the SDK's inherent limitations.

- `UITableViewControllers` simplify applications built around a central `UITableView`. Do not hesitate to use `UITableView` instances directly, however, if your application requires it. Just make sure to explicitly support the `UITableViewDelegate` and `UITableViewDataSource` protocols.

- There's more than one way to skin a cat or remove a cell. If you'd rather avoid introducing an "edit/done" mode switch, support swipe-to-delete by setting your cells' `editingStyle`.

Advanced Tables

iPhone tables do not begin and end with simple scrolling lists. You can build tables with titled sections, with multiple scrolling columns, and more. You can add controls such as switches, create translucent cell backgrounds, and include custom fonts. You can display a quick-access index like the one used in the Address Book or build preferences screens like the kind you see in Settings. This chapter starts from where Chapter 5, "Basic Tables," left off. It introduces advanced table recipes for you to use in your iPhone programs. Discover what it takes to design and implement more complex tables by exploring these recipes and discussions.

Recipe: Grouping Table Selections

On the iPhone, tables come in two formats: grouped tables and plain table lists. You've already seen the latter. Chapter 5 focused on creating them. They use a single section without intrinsic element grouping. But you've surely already seen the former, too. The Settings application on the iPhone offers grouped lists in action. These lists display on a blue-gray background, and each subsection appears within a slightly rounded rectangle. Figure 6-1 shows the grouped list built by Recipe 6-1.

Grouped lists depend on properly setting a table's style. This happens during object initialization. Unfortunately, you cannot go back later and change a table's style from one kind to the other, so you have to begin right. Decide which kind of list you're building and add that into your view controller's init or loadView routine as follows.

With lists, you may be working either with table view controllers (used here) or directly with UITableView instances. For table view controllers, use initWithStyle: to set the table's style to UITableViewStyleGrouped. With UITable instances, use initWithFrame: style:. At this time, the SDK supports just these two styles mentioned: the grouped style and the (default) plain style, UITableViewStylePlain.

> **Note**
>
> Apple seems to be moving from the "plain" terminology to "indexed," so these names may change without notice.

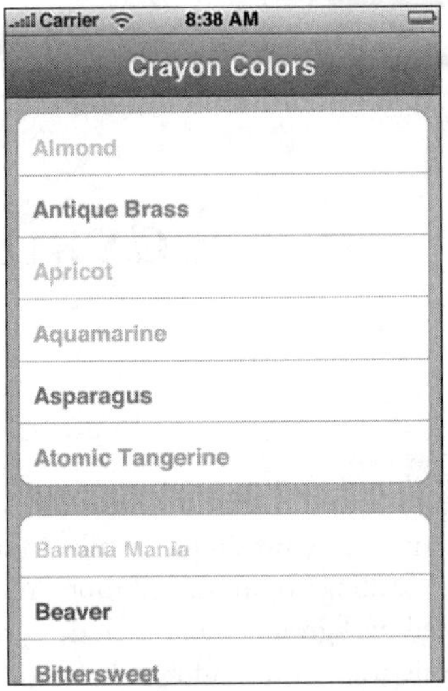

Figure 6-1   Grouped lists enable you to create blocks of
cells that scroll over a blue-gray background.

Style initialization is optional. If you'd rather go with the default, just use `init` or `initWithFrame:` to create your table. This produces the same result as initializing it with the plain style.

Building a Section-Based Data Source

When working with groups and sections, think two dimensionally. A section array lets you store and access the members of each section. Recipe 6-1 implements this by creating an array of arrays. The section array stores one array for each section, which in turn contains the titles and, in this case, colors for each cell.

The way this works in this recipe is through the `createSectionList` method. This method takes a sorted array of words and iterates through them. As it does, it adds each name to an array based on the index of the first letter of that word.

To work, this particular implementation relies on two things: first, that the words are already sorted—each subsection adds the words in the order they're found in the array; and second, that the sections match the words. Entries that start with punctuation or numbers will cause this loop to fail. You can trivially add an "other" section to take care of these cases, which this (simple) sample omits.

Although alphabetic sections are useful and probably the most common grouping, you can use any kind of grouping structure you like. For example, you might group people by departments, gems by grades, or appointments by date. No matter what kind of grouping you choose, an array of arrays provides the table view data source that best matches sectioned tables.

Grouped tables require two key data source methods in addition to the standard UITable data source routines, as follows:

- **numberOfSectionsInTableView.** This method specifies how many sections appear in your table. This establishes the number of groups to display. When using a section array, as recommended here, return the number of items in the section array (that is, [mySectionArray count]).

- **tableView: numberOfRowsInSection.** This method is called with a section number. Specify how many rows appear in that section. With the recommended data structure, just return the count of items at the nth subarray:
  [[mySectionArray objectAtIndex: sectionNumber] count].

In addition to these data source methods, be sure to use both the row and section information to find the cell data in question. Recipes in Chapter 5 used a flat array with a row number index. Recipes in this chapter must look up the section array and then find the row indexed in that section.

Recipe 6-1 **Creating a Grouped Table**

```
@interface HelloController : UITableViewController
{
    NSMutableArray *sectionArray;
    int fullCount;
}
@end

@implementation HelloController
#define ALPHA @"ABCDEFGHIJKLMNOPQRSTUVWXYZ"

// Initialize the table view controller with the grouped style
- (HelloController *) init
{
    if (self = [super initWithStyle:UITableViewStyleGrouped]) self.title =
➥@"Crayon Colors";
    return self;
}


// One section for each alphabet member
- (NSInteger)numberOfSectionsInTableView:(UITableView *)tableView
{
    return [sectionArray count];
}


// Each row array object contains the members for that section
- (NSInteger)tableView:(UITableView *)tableView
➥numberOfRowsInSection:(NSInteger)section
```

Recipe 6-1   **Continued**

```objc
{
    return [[sectionArray objectAtIndex:section] count];
}


// Convert a 6-character hex color to a UIColor object
- (UIColor *) getColor: (NSString *) hexColor
{
    unsigned int red, green, blue;
    NSRange range;
    range.length = 2;

    range.location = 0;
    [[NSScanner scannerWithString:[hexColor substringWithRange:range]]
    ➥scanHexInt:&red];
    range.location = 2;
    [[NSScanner scannerWithString:[hexColor substringWithRange:range]]
    ➥scanHexInt:&green];
    range.location = 4;
    [[NSScanner scannerWithString:[hexColor substringWithRange:range]]
    ➥scanHexInt:&blue];

    return [UIColor colorWithRed:(float)(red/255.0f) green:(float)(green/255.0f)
    ➥blue:(float)(blue/255.0f) alpha:1.0f];
}


// Return a cell for the row and section
- (UITableViewCell *)tableView:(UITableView *)tableView
➥cellForRowAtIndexPath:(NSIndexPath *)indexPath
{
    NSInteger row = [indexPath row];
    NSInteger section = [indexPath section];

    // Create a cell if one is not already available
    UITableViewCell *cell = [self.tableView
    ➥dequeueReusableCellWithIdentifier:@"any-cell"];
    if (cell == nil)
        cell = [[[UITableViewCell alloc] initWithFrame:CGRectZero
        ➥reuseIdentifier:@"any-cell"] autorelease];

    // Set up the cell by coloring its text
    NSArray *crayon = [[[sectionArray objectAtIndex:section] objectAtIndex:row]
    ➥componentsSeparatedByString:@"#"];
    cell.text = [crayon objectAtIndex:0];
    cell.textColor = [self getColor:[crayon objectAtIndex:1]];
    return cell;
}
```

Recipe 6-1   **Continued**

```
// Remove the current table row selection
- (void) deselect
{
    [self.tableView deselectRowAtIndexPath:[self.tableView
    ➥indexPathForSelectedRow] animated:YES];
}


// Respond to user selection by coloring the navigation bar
- (void)tableView:(UITableView *)tableView didSelectRowAtIndexPath:
➥(NSIndexPath *)newIndexPath
{
    // Retrieve named color
    int row = [newIndexPath row];
    int section = [newIndexPath section];
    NSArray *crayon = [[[sectionArray objectAtIndex:section] objectAtIndex:row]
    ➥componentsSeparatedByString:@"#"];

    // Update the nav bar color
    self.navigationController.navigationBar.tintColor = [self getColor:[crayon
    ➥objectAtIndex:1]];

    // Deselect
    [self performSelector:@selector(deselect) withObject:NULL afterDelay:0.5];
}


// Build a section/row list from the alphabetically ordered word list
- (void) createSectionList: (id) wordArray
{
    // Build an array with 26 sub-array sections
    sectionArray = [[NSMutableArray alloc] init];
    for (int i = 0; i < 26; i++) [sectionArray addObject:[[NSMutableArray alloc]
    ➥init]];

    // Add each word to its alphabetical section
    for (NSString *word in wordArray)
    {
        if ([word length] == 0) continue;

        // determine which letter starts the name
        NSRange range = [ALPHA rangeOfString:[[word substringToIndex:1]
        ➥uppercaseString]];

        // Add the name to the proper array
        [[sectionArray objectAtIndex:range.location] addObject:word];
    }
}
```

```
// Prepare the Table View
- (void)loadView
{
    [super loadView];

    // Retrieve the text and colors from file
    NSString *pathname = [[NSBundle mainBundle]  pathForResource:@"crayons"
    ➥ofType:@"txt" inDirectory:@"/"];
    NSString *wordstring = [NSString stringWithContentsOfFile:pathname];
    NSArray *wordArray = [wordstring componentsSeparatedByString:@"\n"];

    // Build the sorted section array
    [self createSectionList:wordArray];
}

// Clean up
-(void) dealloc
{
    [sectionArray release];
    [super dealloc];
}
@end
```

Adding Section Headers

It takes little work to add section headers to your grouped table. Listing 6-1 shows the optional `tableView: titleForHeaderInSection:` method that titles each section. It's passed an integer. In return, you supply a title.

Listing 6-1   Adding Titles to Sections

```
#define ALPHA_ARRAY [NSArray arrayWithObjects: @"A", @"B", @"C", @"D", @"E", @"F",
@"G", @"H", @"I", @"J", @"K", @"L", @"M", @"N", @"O", @"P", @"Q", @"R", @"S",
@"T", @"U", @"V", @"W", @"X", @"Y", @"Z", nil]

// Add a title for each section
- (NSString *)tableView:(UITableView *)tableView
➥titleForHeaderInSection:(NSInteger)section
{
    return [NSString stringWithFormat:@"Crayon names starting with '%@'",
    ➥ [ALPHA_ARRAY objectAtIndex:section]];
}
```

As Figure 6-2 (left) shows, when you supply this (optional) method, titles automatically appear. Title names appear above each group, on the blue-gray background. And as Figure 6-2 (right) shows, these titles display whether you supply section members. You may want to weed through your titles and section data to remove empty sections to avoid the double headings shown here.

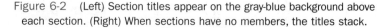

Figure 6-2   (Left) Section titles appear on the gray-blue background above each section. (Right) When sections have no members, the titles stack.

Recipe: Building a Section Table with an Index

Section lists need not be grouped. In fact, if you want to use an index, as shown in Figure 6-3 (left), avoid grouped lists. That is to say, it's completely possible to use an index with groups. It just looks ugly.

Create your section lists exactly as you would for a grouped table, but use the plain table style when initializing and add a method to supply the index title array. This data source method is called `sectionIndexTitlesForTableView`. When used, as in Recipe 6-2, it tells the table to build a new `UIControl` for the index and add it to your table.

The method returns an array of strings. For Recipe 6-2, it's a list of single characters, one per letter of the alphabet, but don't let this limit your design. As Figure 6-3 (right) shows, you can return words as well as characters. It's ugly, but it might be what you need for your design.

Recipe 6-2   **Building an Indexed Section List**

```
- (HelloController *) init
{
    if (self = [super initWithStyle:UITableViewStylePlain]) self.title = @"Crayon
    ➥Colors";
```

```
    return self;
}

#define ALPHA_ARRAY [NSArray arrayWithObjects: @"A", @"B", @"C", @"D", @"E", @"F",
@"G", @"H", @"I", @"J", @"K", @"L", @"M", @"N", @"O", @"P", @"Q", @"R", @"S",
@"T", @"U", @"V", @"W", @"X", @"Y", @"Z", nil]

// Adding a section index here
- (NSArray *)sectionIndexTitlesForTableView:(UITableView *)tableView
{
    return ALPHA_ARRAY;
}
```

Figure 6-3   (Left) Indexed lists enable you to jump directly to sections by tapping on their titles. (Right) Indices aren't limited to single characters. If desired, use entire words to create your index object.

Recipe: Custom Cell Backgrounds

The standard `UITableView` class contains a list of cells with white backgrounds. You can change your table's overall background color by setting its `backgroundColor` property. Set it to a color, and your cells take on that background color. Set it to clear, and any contents behind your table leak through.

This is the way Apple has built the classes, and this is the way it intends your tables to look. Getting around this behavior is not hard, but at the same time it's nontrivial. Although not especially intuitive or straightforward, you can customize your tables, their cells and any index control by diving into the UIView hierarchy used in the table. The steps needed to build this effect in your own application are presented in this section. Figure 6-4 shows the results: a custom UITableView with individual colors for each cell.

As you can see from this image, the method does not affect section headers. You may want to omit them from your table when making these modifications. (It looks a lot better without the section headers and runs more smoothly on the iPhone, but because Recipe 6-3 builds directly off Recipe 6-2, I kept them for continuity.)

There are three basic steps to follow to change the background:

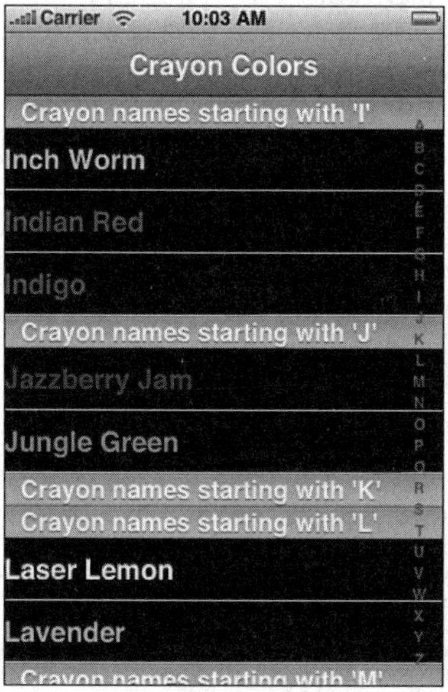

Figure 6-4   Customize your cells and index for custom backdrops.

1. **Access the index and clear its background.**

   The index control at the right side of the table is a subview of your table view. Its class is UITableViewIndex. To customize, you can set its background color individually from the table. Otherwise, it inherits whatever color the table uses.

   To let backgrounds leak through, use [UIColor clearColor]. Fortunately, you need only do this once. Unfortunately, the index is not placed into the table until after the loadView method returns. So, you have to delay modifying it.

   In Recipe 6-3, I wait until tableView: cellForRowAtIndexPath: is called during table creation. Then, I use a Boolean variable, clearedIndex, to make sure this modification is run just once.

   To perform the modification, you need to find the actual index control object. After searching through the tableView's subviews for the index object, I set the index's background color to clear. If you want, you can perform other index modifications here. For example, you might update its font to another style as desired.

2. **Create a custom label view for cells.**

   Standard `UITableView` cells are composed with a cell background view onto which is added a custom `UILabel`. Unfortunately, even though you can access this standard `UILabel` by browsing through subviews, it does not properly update its traits when requested.

   You can try clearing its background color, but the custom behavior prevents this action from completing, leaving you with a fixed color behind the text that matches the table's background color. Instead, you need to add a standard `UILabel` and use that for your cell labels. This approach is a workaround, but it's reliable and consistent.

   The workaround involves adding new `UILabel` labels when a cell is actually created. This gives them a fresh `UILabel` without any of the behavior issues associated with the `UITableViewCell`'s version. If you initialize your cells properly, they'll retain these labels when dequeued from the reuse stack.

   Recipe 6-3 works like this. During cell creation, it allocates those new labels and adds them to the cell as a subview. It then tags the label so it can be retrieved for setting text.

   This differs slightly from the standard `UITableViewCell` structure, where labels are usually children of the background, not a direct child of the cell itself.

3. **Tagging the cell background.**

   The `UITableViewCell`'s first child is its background view. Recipe 6-3 tags this view so that it can be recovered and colored on demand. To tint the background, adjust its `backgroundColor` property. To add custom image, create a `UIImageView` subview.

These three steps ensure that table elements, namely the index, cell titles, and cell backgrounds, can be customized.

Recipe 6-3   Creating Custom Cell Backgrounds

```
// Return a cell on demand
- (UITableViewCell *)tableView:(UITableView *)tableView
➥cellForRowAtIndexPath:(NSIndexPath *)indexPath
{
    // if the Index background has not yet been cleared, clear it
    if (!clearedIndex) {
        for (UIView *view in [tableView subviews])
            if ([[[view class] description]
            ➥isEqualToString:@"UITableViewIndex"]) {
                [view setBackgroundColor:[UIColor clearColor]];
            }
        clearedIndex = YES;
```

Recipe 6-3   **Continued**

```
}

    // Recover section and row info
    NSInteger row = [indexPath row];
    NSInteger section = [indexPath section];

    // Pull the cell
    UITableViewCell *cell = [tableView dequeueReusableCellWithIdentifier:@"any-
    ➥cell"];
    UILabel *labelView = NULL;

    // If there's a new cell needed, add a custom label
    if (cell == nil) {
        cell = [[[UITableViewCell alloc] initWithFrame:CGRectZero
        ➥reuseIdentifier:@"any-cell"] autorelease];
        cell.selectionStyle = UITableViewCellSelectionStyleGray;

        // Tag the background view
        [[[cell subviews] objectAtIndex:0] setTag:111];
        // Add and tag the label view
        labelView = [[UILabel alloc] initWithFrame: CGRectMake(0, 0, 300, 44)];
        [labelView setBackgroundColor:[UIColor clearColor]];
        [labelView setShadowColor:[UIColor whiteColor]];
        [labelView setFont:[UIFont boldSystemFontOfSize:20]];
        [labelView setTag:222];
        [cell addSubview:labelView];
        [labelView release];
    }

    // Set up the cell
    NSArray *crayon = [[[sectionArray objectAtIndex:section] objectAtIndex:row]
    ➥componentsSeparatedByString:@"#"];

    // Recover the label
    UILabel *labelView = (UILabel *)[cell viewWithTag:222];
    [labelView setText:[crayon objectAtIndex:0]];

    // recover the background
    UIView *bgView = [cell viewWithTag:111];
    [bgView setBackgroundColor:[self getColor:[crayon objectAtIndex:1]]];

    return cell;
}
```

Customizing the Table View

Further customize your tables by using a normal `UIViewController` and decoupling the table view. Figure 6-5 shows a partially translucent table set in the middle of a `UIImageView`. Listing 6-2 shows the table creation. It is built with a small frame, set with an alpha level of just 0.35, and added to the background as a subview. This kind of modification lets you break out of the "my application is the table, my table is the application" mindset and use scrolling tables more flexibly but again at a computational cost. Make sure you test on the iPhone to catch any performance issues introduced by your customization.

Figure 6-5   Tables can use translucency
as shown in this highly customized table view.

Listing 6-2   **Creating a Floating Semitranslucent Table**

```
- (void)loadView
{
        // Add a background
        CGRect frame = [[UIScreen mainScreen] applicationFrame];
        self.view = [[[UIImageView alloc] initWithImage:[UIImage
        ➥imageNamed:@"bg.png"]] autorelease];
        self.view.userInteractionEnabled = YES;
        [self.view setFrame:frame];

        // Set up the table -- allowing for customizations
        frame = CGRectMake(30.0f, 40.0f, 260.0f, 300.0f);
```

Listing 6-2 **Continued**

```
tableView = [[UITableView alloc] initWithFrame:frame style:
➥UITableViewStylePlain];
[tableView setDelegate:self];
[tableView setDataSource:self];
[tableView setBackgroundColor:[UIColor colorWithRed:1.0f green:1.0f
➥blue:1.0f alpha:0.35f]];
[self.view addSubview:tableView];
[tableView release];

// Retrieve the text and colors from file
NSString *pathname = [[NSBundle mainBundle]  pathForResource:@"crayons"
➥ofType:@"txt" inDirectory:@"/"];
NSString *wordstring = [NSString stringWithContentsOfFile:pathname];
NSArray *wordArray = [wordstring componentsSeparatedByString:@"\n"];

// Build the sorted section array
[self createSectionList:wordArray];

clearedIndex = NO;
}
```

Recipe: Creating Alternate Blue and White Cells

Although blue and white cell alternation is a common and highly requested table feature, Apple did not include that style in its iPhone SDK. The custom cell techniques
shown in the last few recipes enable you to build the alternating white/blue cell structure, as shown in Figure 6-6. Recipe 6-4 provides the cell creation method.

As with earlier recipes, this code uses a custom UILabel to blend text over whatever
background is used. A simple even/odd check (row % 2) specifies whether to fill the
background in with blue or white. Because this table uses just one section, it simplifies
the math considerably. Blue/white alternating cells work best for nongrouped, nonsec-
tion tables both visually and programmatically.

Recipe 6-4   **Creating Alternating Blue and White Cells**

```
- (UITableViewCell *)tableView:(UITableView *)tView
➥cellForRowAtIndexPath:(NSIndexPath *)indexPath
{

    NSInteger row = [indexPath row];

    // Pull the cell
    UITableViewCell *cell = [tView dequeueReusableCellWithIdentifier:@"any-cell"];
    UILabel *labelView = NULL;

    // If there's a new cell needed, add a custom label
    if (cell == nil) {
```

```
        cell = [[[UITableViewCell alloc] initWithFrame:CGRectZero
    ➥reuseIdentifier:@"any-cell"] autorelease];
        cell.selectionStyle = UITableViewCellSelectionStyleGray;
        [[[cell subviews] objectAtIndex:0] setTag:111];

        labelView = [[UILabel alloc] initWithFrame: CGRectMake(8, 0, 300, 44)];
        [labelView setBackgroundColor:[UIColor clearColor]];
        [labelView setTag:222];
        [labelView setFont:[UIFont boldSystemFontOfSize:20]];
        [cell addSubview:labelView];
        [labelView release];
    }

    UIView *cellView = [cell viewWithTag:111];
    if (row % 2)
        [cellView setBackgroundColor:[UIColor whiteColor]];
    else
        [cellView setBackgroundColor:[UIColor colorWithRed:0.90f green:0.95f
    ➥blue:1.0f alpha:1.0f]];

    // recover labelView from the cell
    [(UILabel *)[cell viewWithTag:222] setText:[[[sectionArray objectAtIndex:row]
    ➥componentsSeparatedByString:@"#"] objectAtIndex:0]];

    return cell;
}
```

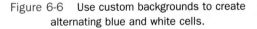

Figure 6-6　Use custom backgrounds to create
alternating blue and white cells.

Recipe: Framing Tables

Framed tables represent another frequently requested table feature not supplied within the SDK. Unlike the rounded sections used for group tables, a framed table enables users to scroll cells within a rounded frame. Figure 6-7 shows a framed table. Here, the rounded border stays still. All cell movement happens within and behind that border.

To make framing work, your table must be an independent view. This limits you to adding a `UITableView` to a `UIViewController` instead of using the `UITableViewController` class directly. The framing in turn is nothing but `UIImage` art added to a `UIImageView` (see Figure 6-7, right). This view is added directly on top of the `UITableView` and set to be noninteractive with `userInteractionEnabled = NO`. That means that all user touches redirect to the table below. The overlay provides art without interfering with interaction.

Recipe 6-5 shows how to set up the table and add its frame using the art shown in Figure 6-7. The table is sized to match the frame opening, and the art is layered on top of the table.

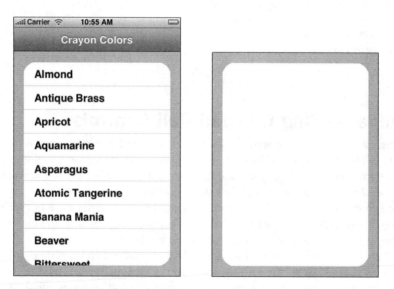

Figure 6-7   (Left) Framing tables add an iPhone style component to selections that aren't meant to occupy the entire screen. (Right) This is the art used to overlay the table to produce the desired framing.

Recipe 6-5   **Framing a List View**

```
- (void)loadView
{
    // Add a background for the main content view
    UIImageView *bg = [[[UIImageView alloc] initWithImage:[UIImage
    ➥imageNamed:@"BG.png"]] autorelease];
```

```
    bg.userInteractionEnabled = YES;
    self.view = bg;
    [bg release];

    // Build the table frame and add the table as a subview
    CGRect frame = CGRectMake(10.0f, 20.0f, 300.0f, 440.0f);
    tableView = [[UITableView alloc] initWithFrame:frame style:
    ➥UITableViewStylePlain];
    [tableView setDelegate:self];
    [tableView setDataSource:self];
    [bg addSubview:tableView];
    [tableView release];

    // Load the frame art, add it as a subview and set it
    // to be non-interactive
    UIImageView *fg = [[[UIImageView alloc] initWithImage:[UIImage
    ➥imageNamed:@"cutbg.png"]] autorelease];
    fg.userInteractionEnabled = NO;
    [bg addSubview:fg];
    [fg release];
}
```

Recipe: Adding Coupled Cell Controls

You can increase a cell's interactivity by adding UIControl items. Figure 6-8 shows a table with on/off switches. Adding this kind of cell extra depends on two things. First, you need to carefully manage your cell reuse. Second, you must expand your data source implementation to include addressable state information for the controls.

As with custom labels used in previous recipes, Recipe 6-6 uses a cell queue. It adds controls as new cells are created and recovers them from dequeued ones. This limits the number of actual control items used to about ten per program at most.

As for the state information, it's held in a simple mutable dictionary (boolDict) and indexed by the cell name. The cells are added to the dictionary when used so that the dictionary remains sparse and controls are assumed to be "off" until specified otherwise. Between the reusable cell queue and the sparse dictionary, this recipe produces a lot of visual bang for little memory buck.

Recipe 6-6   **Building Table Cells with Custom Controls**

```
// respond to user switches by updating the Boolean dictionary
- (void) switchEm: (UIControl *) sender
{
    UITableViewCell *cell = (UITableViewCell *)[sender superview];
    NSString *whichCell = [cell text];
```

```
    NSNumber *value = [boolDict objectForKey:whichCell];
    if (!value) // no value assigned, false
    {
        [boolDict setObject:[NSNumber numberWithBool:YES] forKey:whichCell];
// initialize
    } else {
        value = [NSNumber numberWithBool:(![value boolValue])]; // toggle
        [boolDict setObject:value forKey:whichCell];
    }
}


// Return a cell on demand
- (UITableViewCell *)tableView:(UITableView *)tableView
cellForRowAtIndexPath:(NSIndexPath *)indexPath
{
    // Recover section and row info
    NSInteger row = [indexPath row];
    NSInteger section = [indexPath section];
    // Pull the cell
    UITableViewCell *cell = [tableView dequeueReusableCellWithIdentifier:@"any-
    ➥cell"];
    UISwitch *switchView = NULL;

    // If there's a new cell needed, add a custom switch
    if (cell == nil) {
        cell = [[[UITableViewCell alloc] initWithFrame:CGRectZero
        ➥reuseIdentifier:@"any-cell"] autorelease];
        cell.selectionStyle = UITableViewCellSelectionStyleGray;
        cell.indentationLevel = 5;

        switchView = [[UISwitch alloc] initWithFrame: CGRectMake(4.0f, 16.0f,
        ➥100.0f, 28.0f)];
        [switchView setTag:997];
        [cell addSubview:switchView];
        [switchView release];
    }

    // recover switchView from the cell
    switchView = [cell viewWithTag:997];
    [switchView addTarget:self action:@selector(switchEm:)
    ➥forControlEvents:UIControlEventValueChanged];

    // Set up the cell
    NSArray *crayon = [[[sectionArray objectAtIndex:section] objectAtIndex:row]
    ➥componentsSeparatedByString:@"#"];
    [cell setText:[crayon objectAtIndex:0]];
```

Recipe 6-6   **Continued**

```
    // Retrieve the switch state and apply it
    NSNumber *value = [boolDict objectForKey:[crayon objectAtIndex:0]];
    if (!value) value = [NSNumber numberWithBool:NO];
    [switchView setOn:[value boolValue] animated:NO];

    return cell;
}
```

Figure 6-8   Use cell reuse to create memory-efficient
tables with custom controls.

Recipe: Building a Multiwheel Table

Sometimes you'd like your users to pick from several lists at once. That's where
UIPickerViews really excel. UIPickerViews produce tables offering individually
scrolling "wheels," as shown in Figure 6-9. Users interact with each wheel to build
their selection.

These tables, although superficially similar to standard UITableViews, use distinct data
and delegate protocols. To be specific, at the time of writing Apple has not specified a
data source protocol at all. All picker view support is handled through the
UIPickerViewDelegate protocol including the calls normally associated with data
sources. Here are some points to keep in mind about the ways picker views differ from
tables:

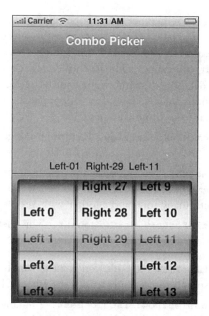

Figure 6-9   `UIPickerView` instances enable users to
select from independently scrolling wheels.

- **There are no `UIPickerViewControllers`.**

  `UIPickerView` instances act as subviews to other views. They are not intended to
  be the central focus of an application view.

- **Picker views use numbers not objects.**

  Components, that is to say the wheels, are indexed by numbers, not by
  `NSIndexPath` instances. It's altogether a much more informal class than the
  `UITableView`.

- **The view height for pickers is static.**

  You can't resize pickers the way you would a standard `UITableView` just by
  manipulating its frame. All pickers are 216 pixels high, a number you can test by
  lining the view up with the bottom of the screen. Any other frame height looks
  distorted or clipped.

Creating the UIPickerView

You can use any frame size for your `UIPickerView` as long as your height is 216 pixels
and your width is 320 pixels. That being said, you can float the table wherever you need
it on the screen. And float you'll have to. The picker does not respond well to iPhone
reorientation, so you need to center it and keep it onscreen should the user rotate his or
her unit.

When creating the picker, remember two key points. First, you want to enable the selection indicator. That is the blue bar that floats over the selected items. So set `showsSelectionIndicator` to YES. Second, don't forget to assign the delegate. Without delegate support, you cannot add data to the view or define its features.

Implement three key data source methods for your `UIPickerView` to make it function properly. These methods are as follows. Let your application control the number of columns and the rows that form those columns:

- **numberOfComponentsInPickerView.** Return an integer, the number of columns.
- **pickerView: numberOfRowsInComponent.** Return an integer, the maximum number of rows per wheel. These numbers do not need to be identical. You can have one wheel with many rows and another with very few.
- **pickerView: titleForRow: forComponent.** This method specifies the text used to label a row on a given component. Return an `NSString`.

In addition to these data source methods, you want to supply one further delegate method. This method responds to user interactions via wheel selection:

- **pickerView: didSelectRow: inComponent.** Add any application-specific behavior to this method. If needed, you can query the `pickerView` to return the `selectedRowInComponent:` for any of the wheels in your view.

Note

The undocumented `setSoundsEnabled:` controls whether your users hear the clicking effects associated with the wheels.

Recipe 6-7   Using a `UIPickerView` for Multicolumn Selection

```
@interface HelloController : UIViewController <UIPickerViewDelegate>
{
    UIPickerView *pickerView;
    UILabel *comboView;
}
@end

@implementation HelloController

- (HelloController *) init
{
    if (self = [super init]) self.title = @"Combo Picker";
    return self;
}
```

Recipe 6-7   **Continued**

```objc
// Number of wheels
- (NSInteger)numberOfComponentsInPickerView:(UIPickerView *)pickerView
{ return 3; }

// Number of rows per wheel
- (NSInteger)pickerView: (UIPickerView *)pView numberOfRowsInComponent:
➥(NSInteger) component  { return 30; }

// Return the title of each cell by row and component
- (NSString *)pickerView:(UIPickerView *)pickerView titleForRow:(NSInteger)row
➥ forComponent:(NSInteger)component
{
    return [NSString stringWithFormat:@"%@%d", (component != 1) ? @"Left" :
    ➥@"Right", row];
}

// Respond to user selection
- (void)pickerView:(UIPickerView *)aPickerView didSelectRow:(NSInteger)row
➥inComponent:(NSInteger)component
{
    printf("User selected row %d for component %d\n", row, component);

    int first = [pickerView selectedRowInComponent:0];
    int second = [pickerView selectedRowInComponent:1];
    int third = [pickerView selectedRowInComponent:2];

    NSString *results = [NSString stringWithFormat:@"Left-%@%d  Right-%@%d
    ➥Left-%@%d",
                            (first  < 10) ? @"0" : @"",
                            first,
                            (second < 10) ? @"0" : @"",
                            second,
                            (third  < 10) ? @"0" : @"",
                            third];
    [comboView setText:results];

}

- (void)loadView
{
    self.view = [[UIView alloc] initWithFrame:[[UIScreen mainScreen]
    ➥applicationFrame]];
    self.view.backgroundColor = [UIColor lightGrayColor];

    // Add the picker
    float height = 216.0f;
```

Recipe 6-7   Continued

```
    pickerView = [[UIPickerView alloc] initWithFrame:CGRectMake(0.0f,
➥416.0f - height, 320.0f, height)];
    pickerView.delegate = self;
    pickerView.showsSelectionIndicator = YES;
    [self.view addSubview:pickerView];
    [pickerView release];

    // Add a results label
    comboView = [[UILabel alloc] initWithFrame:CGRectMake(0.0f, 170.0f, 320.0f,
➥32.0f)];
    [comboView setBackgroundColor:[UIColor clearColor]];
    [comboView setTextAlignment:UITextAlignmentCenter];
    [comboView setText:@"Left-00  Right-00  Left-00"];
    [self.view addSubview:comboView];
    [comboView release];
}

-(void) dealloc
{
    [pickerView release];
    [comboView release];
    [super dealloc];
}
@end
```

Recipe: Using the `UIDatePicker`

When you want to ask your user to enter date information, Apple supplies a tidy subclass
of `UIPickerView` to handle several kinds of time entry. Figure 6-10 shows the four
built-in styles of `UIDatePickers` that you can choose from. These range from selecting a
time, to selecting a date, to selecting a combination of the two.

Creating the Date Picker

Lay out a date picker exactly as you would a `UIPickerView`. Create a frame that's
320 pixels wide by 216 pixels high. After that, things get much, much easier. You need
not set a delegate or define data source methods. Instead, you assign a date picker
mode. (Choose from `UIDatePickerModeTime`, `UIDatePickerModeDate`,
`UIDatePickerModeDateAndTime`, and `UIDatePickerModeCountDownTimer`), and
then add a target for when the selection changes (`UIControlEventValueChanged`.)

All that remains is to create the callback method you triggered with the value-
changed event. After that you're done. Implementing `UIDatePicker` objects is almost
insanely simple, as Recipe 6-8 demonstrates.

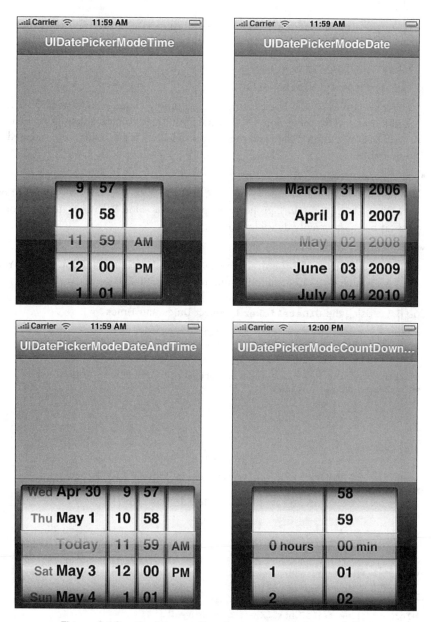

Figure 6-10 The iPhone offers four stock date picker models.
Use the datePickerMode property to select the picker you want
to use in your application.

Here are a few properties you'll want to take advantage of in the UIDatePicker class:

- date

Set the date property to initialize the picker.

- maximumDate and minimumDate

These properties set the bounds for date and time picking. Assign each one a standard NSDate. With these, you can constrain your user to pick a date from next year rather than just enter a date and then check whether it falls within an accepted time frame.

- minuteInterval

Sometimes you want to use 5-, 10-, 15-, or 30-minute intervals on your selections. Use the minuteInterval property to specify that value. Whatever number you pass, it has to be evenly divisible into 60.

- countDownDuration

Use this property to set the maximum available value for a countdown timer. You can go as high as 23 hours and 59 minutes (that is, 86,399 seconds).

Recipe 6-8   Using the UIDatePicker to Select Dates and Times

```
// Respond to a user when the date has changed
- (void) changedDate: (UIDatePicker *) picker
{
    NSString *caldate = [[[picker date] dateWithCalendarFormat:@"%B %d, %Y"
    ➥timeZone:nil] description];
    [resultsView setText:caldate];
}


- (void)loadView
{
    self.view = [[UIView alloc] initWithFrame:[[UIScreen mainScreen]
    ➥ applicationFrame]];
    self.view.backgroundColor = [UIColor lightGrayColor];

    // Add the picker
    float height = 216.0f;
    pickerView = [[UIDatePicker alloc] initWithFrame:CGRectMake(0.0f, 416.0f -
    ➥height, 320.0f, height)];
    pickerView.datePickerMode = UIDatePickerModeDate;
    [pickerView addTarget:self action:@selector(changedDate:)
    ➥forControlEvents:UIControlEventValueChanged];
    [self.view addSubview:pickerView];
    [pickerView release];

    // Add a results label
    resultsView = [[UILabel alloc] initWithFrame:CGRectMake(0.0f, 170.0f, 320.0f,
    ➥32.0f)];
```

Recipe 6-8   **Continued**

```
    [resultsView setBackgroundColor:[UIColor clearColor]];
    [resultsView setTextAlignment:UITextAlignmentCenter];
    [self.view addSubview:resultsView];
    [resultsView release];
}
```

Recipe: Creating Fully Customized Group Tables

If alphabetic section list tables are the M. C. Eschers of the iPhone table world, with each section block precisely fitting into the negative spaces provided by other sections in the list, then freeform group tables are the Marc Chagalls. Every bit is drawn as a freeform handcrafted work of art.

It's relatively easy to create all the tables you've seen so far in this chapter once you've mastered the knack. Perfecting the group table (usually called "preferences table" by iPhone devotees because that's the kind of table used in the Settings application) remains an illusion. Building group tables is all about the collage. They're all about handcrafting a look, piece by piece.

Tools like Interface Builder are meant to place layout directly in the hands of the developer instead of trying to approach things programmatically. Unfortunately, there's a problem: Interface Builder does not, at least at this time, create preferences tables. So, it's up to you to programmatically put all that material together after all. There are still standardized methods and approaches you can take to build these tables. These all involve monstrous data source methods with lots and lots of switch calls.

When you've got the basics under control, the preferences table becomes a project you can mold and shape. Figure 6-11 shows a simple preferences table that consists of two groups: a four-item checklist and a block with text and a text entry field. Recipe 6-9 demonstrates all the work that goes into providing even such a little creation.

Unfortunately, adding new items or updating old ones requires a lot of fine detail work. That work isn't centralized in any way. You must review each of the data source methods and update with your new or refined items. The next section introduces what those data source methods are and what they do.

Creating Grouped Preferences Tables

There's nothing special involved in terms of laying out a new UITableViewController for a preferences table. You allocate it. You initialize it with the grouped table style. That's pretty much the end of it. All done and dusted. It's the data source and delegate methods that provide the challenge. Here are the methods you'll need to define:

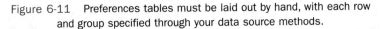

Figure 6-11   Preferences tables must be laid out by hand, with each row
and group specified through your data source methods.

- `numberOfSectionsInTableView:`

  All preferences tables contain groups of items. Each group is contained in one of
  those lovely rounded rectangles. Return the number of groups you'll be defining
  as an integer.

- `tableView: titleForHeaderInSection:`

  Add the titles for each section into this method. Return an `NSString` with the
  requested section name.

- `tableView: numberOfRowsInSection:`

  Each section may contain any number of cells. Have this method return an integer
  indicating the number of rows (that is, cells) for that group.

- `tableView: heightForRowAtIndexPath:`

  Tables that use flexible row heights cost more in terms of computational intensity.
  If you need to use variable heights (Recipe 6-9 does so), implement this optional
  method to specify what those heights will be.

- `tableView: cellForRowAtIndexPath:`

  This is the standard cell-for-row method you've seen throughout this chapter.
  What sets apart is its implementation. Instead of using one kind of cell, Recipe 6-9
  builds different kinds of reusable cells (with different reuse tags) for each cell type.
  As this recipe shows, things become much more complicated when using several
  cell types. Make sure you manage your reuse queue carefully.

- `tableView: didSelectRowAtIndexPath:`

  You provide case-by-case reactions to cell selection in this delegate method depending on the cell type selected.

Recipe 6-9   A Simple Grouped Preferences-Style Table

```
// Number of groups
- (NSInteger)numberOfSectionsInTableView:(UITableView *)tableView
{
    return 2;
}


// Section Titles
- (NSString *)tableView:(UITableView *)tableView
➡titleForHeaderInSection:(NSInteger)section
{
    switch (section)
    {
        case 0:
            return @"Civics";
        case 1:
            return @"Checked Items";
        default:
            return @"";
    }
}


// Number of rows per section
- (NSInteger)tableView:(UITableView *)tableView
➡numberOfRowsInSection:(NSInteger)section
{
    switch (section)
    {
        case 0:
            return 2;
        case 1:
            return 4;
        default:
            return 0;
    }
}


// Heights per row
- (CGFloat)tableView:(UITableView *)tableView heightForRowAtIndexPath:(NSIndex
➡Path *)indexPath
{
    int section = [indexPath section];
```

Recipe 6-9   **Continued**

```
    int row = [indexPath row];

    switch (section)
    {
        case 0:
            if (row == 0) return 80.0f;
            return 350.0f;
        case 1:
            return 44.0f;
        default:
            return 44.0f;
    }
}


// Produce cells
- (UITableViewCell *)tableView:(UITableView *)tableView
➥cellForRowAtIndexPath:(NSIndexPath *)indexPath
{
    NSInteger row = [indexPath row];
    NSInteger section = [indexPath section];
    UITableViewCell *cell;

    switch (section)
    {
        case 0:
            if (row == 0) {
                // Add a text field to the cell
                cell = [tableView dequeueReusableCellWithIdentifier:@"textCell"];
                if (!cell) {
                    cell = [[[UITableViewCell alloc] initWithFrame:CGRectZero
                    ➥reuseIdentifier:@"textCell"] autorelease];
                    UILabel *label = [[UILabel alloc]
                    ➥initWithFrame:CGRectMake(20.0f, 10.0f, 100.0f, 20.0f)];
                    [label setText:@"Name:"];
                    [cell addSubview:label];
                    [label release];
                    [cell addSubview:[[UITextField alloc]
                    ➥initWithFrame:CGRectMake(20.0f, 40.0f, 280.0f, 30.0f)]];
                }
                UITextField *tf = [[cell subviews] lastObject];
                tf.placeholder = @"Enter Your Name Here";
                tf.delegate = self;
                tf.borderStyle = UITextBorderStyleBezel;
                return cell;
            }
            if (row == 1) {
                // Create a big word-wrapped UILabel
```

Recipe 6-9   **Continued**

```objc
        cell = [tableView
        ➥dequeueReusableCellWithIdentifier:@"libertyCell"];
        if (!cell) {
            cell = [[[UITableViewCell alloc] initWithFrame:CGRectZero
            ➥reuseIdentifier:@"libertyCell"] autorelease];
            [cell addSubview:[[UILabel alloc]
            ➥initWithFrame:CGRectMake(20.0f, 10.0f, 280.0f, 330.0f)]];
        }
        UILabel *sv = [[cell subviews] lastObject];
        sv.text = @"When in the Course of human events, it becomes
necessary for one people to dissolve the political bands which have connected them
with another, and to assume among the powers of the earth, the separate and equal
station to which the Laws of Nature and of Nature's God entitle them, a decent
respect to the opinions of mankind requires that they should declare the causes
which impel them to the separation.";
        sv.textAlignment = UITextAlignmentCenter;
        sv.lineBreakMode = UILineBreakModeWordWrap;
        sv.numberOfLines = 9999;
        return cell;
    }
    break;
    case 1:
    // Create cells with accessory checking
    cell = [tableView dequeueReusableCellWithIdentifier:@"checkCell"];
    if (!cell) {
        cell = [[[UITableViewCell alloc] initWithFrame:CGRectZero
        ➥reuseIdentifier:@"checkCell"] autorelease];
        cell.accessoryType = UITableViewCellAccessoryNone;
    }
    cell.text = [NSString stringWithFormat:@"This is option #%d",
    ➥row + 1];
    return cell;
    break;
default:
    break;
}

// Return a generic cell if all else fails
cell = [tableView dequeueReusableCellWithIdentifier:@"any-cell"];
if (cell == nil) {
    cell = [[[UITableViewCell alloc] initWithFrame:CGRectZero
    ➥reuseIdentifier:@"any-cell"] autorelease];
}

return cell;
}


- (void) notify: (NSString *) aMessage
{
```

```objc
    UIAlertView *baseAlert = [[UIAlertView alloc]
                              initWithTitle:@"Alert" message:aMessage
                              delegate:self cancelButtonTitle:nil
                              otherButtonTitles:@"Okay", nil];
    [baseAlert show];
}


// TextField delegate handles return events and dismisses keyboard
- (BOOL)textFieldShouldReturn:(UITextField *)textField
{
    [textField resignFirstResponder];
    [self notify:[NSString stringWithFormat:@"Hello %@", [textField text]]];
    return YES;
}


// Respond to user selection based on the cell type
- (void)tableView:(UITableView *)tableView didSelectRowAtIndexPath:(NSIndexPath *)
➥newIndexPath
{

    int section = [newIndexPath section];
    int row = [newIndexPath row];
    UITableViewCell *cell = [self.tableView cellForRowAtIndexPath:newIndexPath];

    switch (section)
    {
        case 0:
            if (row == 0)
            {
                [self notify:[NSString stringWithFormat:@"Hello %@",
                ➥[[[cell subviews] lastObject] text]]];
            }
            case 1:
            if (cell.accessoryType == UITableViewCellAccessoryNone)
                cell.accessoryType = UITableViewCellAccessoryCheckmark;
            else
                cell.accessoryType = UITableViewCellAccessoryNone;
            break;
            break;
        default:
            break;
    }

    [self performSelector:@selector(deselect) withObject:NULL afterDelay:0.5];
}
```

Summary

This chapter has introduced advanced iPhone tables: from multirowed picker elements to indexed alphabetic listings to preferences tables. The skills covered in this chapter should enable you to build a wealth of table-based applications for the iPhone and iPod touch. Here are some key points to take away from this chapter:

- Apple has designed `UITableViews` to work in certain ways. Defy Apple. Don't constrain yourself to those design paths if they don't take you where you need to go. This chapter covered many alternative ways to gain access to cell and table subviews and manage those views as needed.

- Index controls provide a great way to navigate quickly through large ordered lists. Take advantage of their power when working with tables that would otherwise become unnavigable.

- Date pickers are highly specialized and very good at what they do: soliciting your users for dates and times. Picker views provide a less-specialized solution but require more work on your end to bring them to life.

- As complicated and annoying as preferences tables are to program, they are the single most requested feature when it comes to iPhone programming. You see them almost ubiquitously in third-party software. They allow you to combine many kinds of interactive input on a good-looking and easy-to-use scrolling page. When you've conquered all the fussy aspects, they become a powerful tool in your programming arsenal.

7

Media

As you'd expect, the iPhone can load and display media from a wide variety of formats. It does music; it does movies. It handles images and Web pages. You can present PDF documents and photo albums and more. In this chapter, you're about to discover way after way that you can import or download data into your program and display that data using the iPhone's multitouch interface. This chapter introduces recipes that let you present a rich variety of media types to your users. You'll see how to build viewers for these data types and how to load them with content both from the iPhone itself and from remote locations.

Recipe: Browsing the Documents Folder by File Type

The Documents folder does exactly what the name suggests. You store documents to and access them from this directory. Apple suggests you store file data created by or browsed from your program.

The Documents folder resides in the application sandbox. It is one of three directories automatically created in the sandbox in addition to your application bundle. The other two are Library and tmp. Library stores user defaults and other state information for your program. The tmp folder provides a place to create transient files on-the-fly. Files in Documents and Library are not transient. iTunes backs up all Documents and Library files whenever the iPhone syncs. When the iPhone reboots, it discards any tmp files.

The one standard folder that's missing from this mix is Application Support. On the Mac, the Application Support folder has a specific role. It holds files, plug-ins, and supporting data that don't belong in your application bundle, which support the application as it runs, but which are not vital for the proper execution of your application. On the iPhone, any materials like this should be stored either in the Library folder (preferable for more static material) or Documents folder (for mutable data like SQL data bases that the user will change and update).

Often, when working with media, you'll want to browse your documents folder to find files that your user has created or downloaded. Browsing this folder allows you to produce a user-selectable list of available files.

Recipe 7-1 demonstrates how to create a table and populate it with filenames from the Documents folder. These names are selected by path extension. This code collects all files that match into an array of path extensions. Figure 7-1 shows this in action, listing document files ending with txt, c, h, or m.

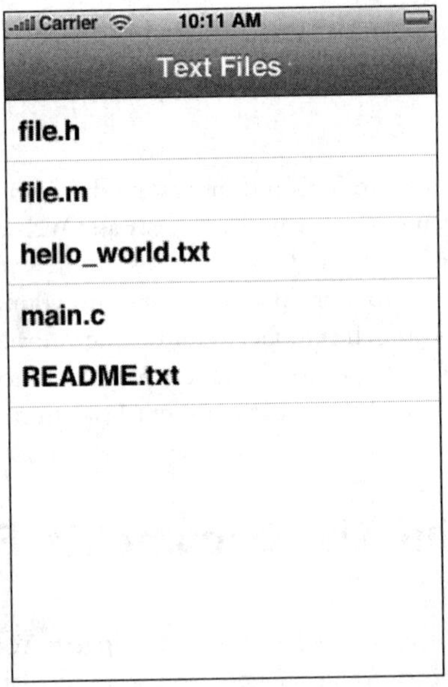

Figure 7-1   Browsing by extension type in the Documents folder enables you to present a list of matching filenames to your users.

Locating Documents

You're free to use both standard and nonstandard file locations on the Macintosh. The iPhone with its sandbox is far more structured—rigidly so by Apple's dictates. Its files appear in better-defined locations. On the Macintosh, locating the documents folder usually means searching the user domain. This is the standard way to locate documents folders:

```
NSArray *paths =
NSSearchPathForDirectoriesInDomains(NSDocumentDirectory,
     NSUserDomainMask, YES);
return [paths lastObject];
```

The iPhone is more constrained. You can reliably locate the top sandbox folder by calling the home directory function. This lets you navigate down one level to the Documents folder as a matter of course with full assurance of reaching the proper destination:

```
#define DOCUMENTS_FOLDER [NSHomeDirectory()
stringByAppendingPathComponent:@"Documents"]
```

   With the Documents folder located, pull in an array of files by calling
NSFileManager's directoryContentsAtPath:. NSArray's
pathsMatchingExtensions: method retrieves just those file types you want to work
with. Recipe 7-1 uses these methods to create a file list of text files that feed a table as
its data source.

Recipe 7-1   Building a User-Selectable Table of Documents

```
#define DOCUMENTS_FOLDER [NSHomeDirectory()
stringByAppendingPathComponent:@"Documents"]

- (HelloController *) init
{
    if (self = [super init]) self.title = @"Text Files";

    // initialize the file list with any text documents
    fileList = (NSMutableArray *) [[[[NSFileManager defaultManager]
    ➥directoryContentsAtPath:DOCUMENTS_FOLDER] pathsMatchingExtensions:[NSArray
    ➥arrayWithObjects:@"txt", @"c", @"h", @"m", nil]] retain];
    return self;
}


- (void) loadView
{

    [super loadView];

    // Reveal the documents folder — so you can pre-fill it for the simulator
    printf("Documents folder is %s\n", [DOCUMENTS_FOLDER UTF8String]);

    self.tableView.autoresizesSubviews = YES;
    self.tableView.autoresizingMask = (UIViewAutoresizingFlexibleWidth |
    ➥UIViewAutoresizingFlexibleHeight);

}


- (NSInteger)numberOfSectionsInTableView:(UITableView *)tableView
{
    return 1;
}


- (NSInteger)tableView:(UITableView *)tableView
➥numberOfRowsInSection:(NSInteger)section
{
    return [fileList count];
}
```

Recipe 7-1   **Continued**

```
// Return a cell for the ith row
- (UITableViewCell *)tableView:(UITableView *)tableView
➥cellForRowAtIndexPath:(NSIndexPath *)indexPath
{
    UITableViewCell *cell = [tableView dequeueReusableCellWithIdentifier:@"any-
    ➥cell"];
    if (cell == nil) {
        cell = [[[UITableViewCell alloc] initWithFrame:CGRectZero
        ➥reuseIdentifier:@"any-cell"] autorelease];
    }

    cell.text = [fileList objectAtIndex:[indexPath row]];
    return cell;
}
```

Loading and Viewing Images

When working with images, no single solution fits all problems. In the next few sections, you'll discover recipes that enable you to work with various kinds of images and image sources. These recipes range from local display to images downloaded live from the World Wide Web. Each recipe offers a different spin on what you might otherwise assume was a simple issue.

Image display is all about memory. Treat small and large image display as two separate problems. With small images, say less than half a megabyte in size, load them directly to UIImageView and throw them onscreen. You can even layer them onto a scroller (see Recipe 7-2) to enable user-directed resizing and placement.

With big images, a class such as UIWebView easily handles memory-intense data (as shown in Recipe 7-3). WebView objects offer a less satisfactory interface because they are optimized for PDF files and Web pages, but they won't choke when it comes to big files. You get the resizing and display power you need, but the initial presentation tends to be extremely compact. At the time of writing, Apple does not provide a "scale to screen" option to start the UIWebView image presentation at the best possible scale.

When viewing and selecting images from onboard albums, look no further than the UIImagePickerController class. It simplifies browsing through both your camera roll and your synced albums as well as picking images, cropping them, and snapping new pictures. Recipes 7-4 through 7-6 demonstrate its range of functionality.

As you'll see, each of these recipes introduces a different way to display and interact with your iPhone images.

> **Note**
>
> The iPhone supports the following image types: PNG, JPG, THM, JPEG, TIF, TIFF, GIF, BMP, BMPF, ICO, CUR, XBM, and PDF.

Recipe: Displaying Small Images

It's trivial to display small images (under about a half megabyte in size). This holds especially true when loading them from the application bundle. Use the `UIImage` `imageNamed:` method to load `UIImageView` with the contents of an application image. Results returned by `imageNamed:` are cached, so file retrieval is extremely efficient:

```
contentView = [[UIImageView alloc] initWithFrame:[[UIScreen mainScreen]
➥applicationFrame]];
[contentView setImage:[UIImage imageNamed:@"helloworld.png"]];
```

You won't always store images in the application bundle. To load pictures from other locations, use `imageWithContentsOfFile:` and pass it a path to your image. `UIImage` handles the rest, loading the image from a file:

```
NSString *path = [DOCUMENTS_FOLDER
stringByAppendingString:@"myImage.png"];
[contentView setImage:[UIImage imageWithContentsOfFile:path]];
```

You can also load image data from a live host instead of grabbing it from a file. Recipe 7-2 demonstrates how to initialize image data from the contents of a Web-based URL. In this case, the image data is an up-to-date weather map from www.weather.com. This code loads that data to a `UIImageView` object and layers that image view onto a `UIScrollView` instance. This produces the fully interactive interface shown in Figure 7-2. Users can scroll through the map and zoom in and out.

In this recipe, the scroll view matches its content size to the reported image size

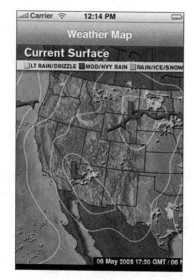

Figure 7-2   This live weather map is downloaded from a World Wide Web URL and layered onto a scroll view that enables users to scale and pan through the image.

([img size]), and the maximum and minimum zooms range between two times actual to half of actual size. These settings allow full user interaction with the image while limiting that interaction to a reasonable scope that won't unduly burden the iPhone's memory.

Note

The UIImageView class can display a single image or a moving slideshow. Recipe 4-8's butterfly shows how to animate an image display.

Recipe 7-2 Downloading Image Data to Display on a UIScrollView

```
@interface HelloController : UIViewController <UIScrollViewDelegate>
{
    UIScrollView *contentView;
    UIImageView *imgView;
}
@end

@implementation HelloController

- (id)init
{
    if (self = [super init]) self.title = @"Weather Map";
    return self;
}

// Return the UIImageView instance that gets zoomed by the scroller
- (UIView *)viewForZoomingInScrollView:(UIScrollView *)scrollView
{
    return imgView;
}

- (void)scrollViewDidEndZooming:(UIScrollView *)scrollView withView:(UIView *)view
➥atScale:(float)scale
{
    // perform any post-scaling tasks here like re-centering
}

- (void)loadView
{
    // Download the 600x405 weather map and load it into the image view
    NSURL *url = [NSURL URLWithString:@"http://image.weather.com/images/maps/
➥current/curwx_600x405.jpg"];
    UIImage *img = [UIImage imageWithData:[NSData dataWithContentsOfURL:url]];
    imgView = [[UIImageView alloc] initWithImage:img];
```

```
    [imgView setUserInteractionEnabled:NO];

    // Set up the main scroller
    contentView = [[UIScrollView alloc] initWithFrame: [[UIScreen mainScreen]
    ➥applicationFrame]];
    [contentView setScrollEnabled:YES];
    [contentView setContentSize:[img size]];
    [contentView addSubview:imgView];
    [imgView release] ;

    [contentView setMaximumZoomScale: 2.0f];
    [contentView setMinimumZoomScale: 0.5f];
    [contentView setDelegate:self];

    self.view = contentView;
    [contentView release]; // reduce retain count by one
    // Provide support for auto-rotation and resizing
    contentView.autoresizesSubviews = YES;
    contentView.autoresizingMask = (UIViewAutoresizingFlexibleWidth |
    ➥UIViewAutoresizingFlexibleHeight);
}

// Allow the view to respond to iPhone Orientation changes
-(BOOL)shouldAutorotateToInterfaceOrientation:
➥(UIInterfaceOrientation)interfaceOrientation
{
    return YES;
}

-(void) dealloc
{
    [imgView release];
    [contentView release];
    [super dealloc] ;
}
@end
```

Recipe: Using a `UIWebView` to Display Images

As image size grows, you can shift away from the scroll view/image view approach and use the `UIWebView` class instead. The `UIWebView` class is a marvel. Recipe 7-3 demonstrates how to load and display images using this class. It uses the document browser from Recipe 7-1, customized to enable selection of PNG, JPEG, TIFF, and PDF images. No further programming is necessary to support these file types. They're all built in, including the PDF paging support shown in Figure 7-3 (left) and, as you'd suppose, HTML/CSS support.

Note

Loading large PDF data files into `UIWebView` instances may trigger `applicationDidReceiveMemoryWarning:` callbacks to your application delegate. You can generally ignore these warnings as the Apple-supplied `UIWebView` class properly reduces its memory load. Use Instruments to profile your application if you have further concerns.

The drawback is, as already mentioned, that for images you don't get any immediate control over image size. Images display at an alarmingly high pixels per inc (ppi), as Figure 7-3 (right) shows. Work around this by generating HTML source to set the image width and height properties and produce the exact presentation desired.

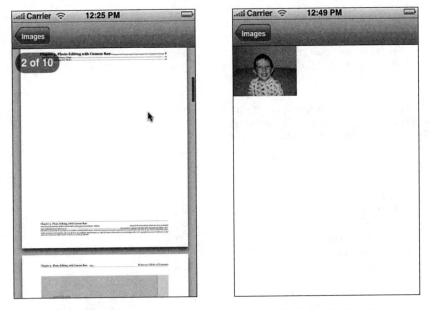

Figure 7-3   (Left) `UIWebView` objects ship with built-in PDF paging support as well as full compatibility with all iPhone-supported image types. (Right) When working with `UIWebView`, the default image display size is far from ideal.

Recipe 7-3   Displaying Images with the `UIWebView` Class

```
#define DOCUMENTS_FOLDER [NSHomeDirectory()
➥stringByAppendingPathComponent:@"Documents"]
```

Recipe 7-3   **Continued**

```objc
@interface WebController : UIViewController
{
    UIWebView *webView;
}
@end


@implementation WebController

- (id)initWithFile: filename
{

    // Initialize a URL pointing to the image file to display
    NSString *path = [DOCUMENTS_FOLDER stringByAppendingPathComponent:filename];
    NSURL *fileURL = [[NSURL alloc] initFileURLWithPath:path];
    NSURLRequest *req = [NSURLRequest requestWithURL:fileURL];
    // Initialize the Web view
    webView = [[UIWebView alloc] initWithFrame:[[UIScreen mainScreen]
    ➥applicationFrame]];
    // allow user interaction
    [webView setScalesPageToFit:YES];

    // Load the Web view with the contents of the image file URL
    [webView loadRequest:req];
    return self;
}

- (void)loadView
{
    self.view = webView;
    [webView release];
}

-(void) dealloc
{
    [webView release];
    [super dealloc];
}
@end
```

Displaying Web Pages with `UIWebView`

It takes a few small changes to modify Recipe 7-3 to display Web pages rather than images. These changes are as follows:

1. Switch the extensions to search for HTML files rather than images in your main interface.

2. Replace the `WebController`'s `initWithFile:` with the contents of Listing 7-1.

This simple two-step swap-out provides you with a rich-featured Web browser for local HTML source. You'll be able to connect to Web-based assets and navigate by tapping on links. `UIWebView` offers a full-featured Safari-esque browser in a simple-to-use class.

Listing 7-1   **Loading HTML Source into `UIWebView` Objects**

```
- (id)initWithFile: filename
{
    // Read in the HTML source
    NSString *fileText = [NSString stringWithContentsOfFile:filename
    ↪encoding:NSUTF8StringEncoding error:NULL];

    // Initialize the Web view
    webView = [[UIWebView alloc] initWithFrame:[[UIScreen mainScreen]
    ↪applicationFrame]];

    // Load it with the HTML source
    if (!fileText) [webView loadHTMLString: [error localizedDescription]
    ↪baseURL:fileURL]; else [webView loadHTMLString:fileText baseURL:fileURL];

    // Allow direct user interaction
    [webView setScalesPageToFit:YES];
    return self;
}
```

Recipe: Browsing Your Image Library

The `UIImagePickerController` class is an odd one. It's highly specialized with relatively few public methods and some moderate quirks. For example, it has its own navigation controller built in. If you push it onto an existing navigation controller–based view scheme, it adds a second navigation bar below the first. That means although you can use it with a tab bar and although you can use it as an independent view system, that you can't really push it onto an existing navigation stack and have it look right. Instead, it's meant to be used as a modal controller. You'll see this in the next recipe, while this recipe introduces a more direct method of working with its built-in navigation.

The `UIImagePickerController`'s navigation controller is integrated directly into the picker object. You don't pop back to the root view the way you do with normal view stacks (that is, [self.navigationController popToRootViewAnimated:YES]). Instead, pop the controller directly (that is, [self popToRootViewControllerAnimated:YES]). This moves control back to the albums screen. Why would you want to do this? Popping after each selection lets you set up a loop like the one used in Recipe 7-4, letting your user pick photos one after another until leaving the program.

Recipe 7-4 shows the picker in its simplest mode, pick-from-album mode, as seen in Figure 7-4. Set the picker to use any of the legal source types. The three kinds of sources are as follows:

- `UIImagePickerControllerSourceTypePhotoLibrary`, all images synced to the iPhone plus any camera roll (used here)

- `UIImagePickerControllerSourceTypeSavedPhotosAlbum`, aka just the camera roll

- `UIImagePickerControllerSourceTypeCamera`, which enables you to shoot pictures with the built-in iPhone camera

Figure 7-4   Apple supplies several prebuilt albums, including this Graduation Day one, for in-Simulator testing.

This recipe follows a basic work path. Select an album, select an image, and repeat. This simple flow works because there's no image editing involved. That's because the `allowsImageEditing` property defaults to `NO`. So, any selection (basically any image tap) redirects control to the `UIImagePickerControllerDelegate` object to the finished picking image method. When image editing is enabled, the callback flow changes, and you're much better off using the kind of modal interaction style introduced in Recipe 7-5.

> **Note**
>
> Recipe 7-4 saves a copy of the selected image to the Documents folder. It grabs the PNG representation of the image (this returns `NSData *`) and writes that to file.

Recipe 7-4 **Selecting an Image and Writing It to the Documents Folder**

```objc
@interface HelloController : UIImagePickerController
<UIImagePickerControllerDelegate>
@end

@implementation HelloController

#define SOURCETYPE UIImagePickerControllerSourceTypePhotoLibrary
#define DOCSFOLDER [NSHomeDirectory() stringByAppendingPathComponent:@"Documents"]

- (id) init
{
    if (self = [super init]) self.title = @"Hello World";
    if ([UIImagePickerController isSourceTypeAvailable:SOURCETYPE])
        self.sourceType = SOURCETYPE;
    self.delegate = self;
    return self;
}

- (void)imagePickerController:(UIImagePickerController *)picker
➥didFinishPickingImage:(UIImage *)image editingInfo:(NSDictionary *)editingInfo
{
    // Find a unique path name so files are not overwritten
    int i = 0;
    NSString *uniquePath = [DOCSFOLDER
    ➥stringByAppendingPathComponent:@"selectedImage.png"];
    while ([[NSFileManager defaultManager] fileExistsAtPath:uniquePath])
        uniquePath = [NSString stringWithFormat:@"%@/%@-%d.%@", DOCSFOLDER,
        ➥@"selectedImage", ++i, @"png"];

    printf("Writing selected image to Documents folder\n");
    [UIImagePNGRepresentation(image) writeToFile: uniquePath atomically:YES];
    [self popToRootViewControllerAnimated:YES];
}

- (void)imagePickerControllerDidCancel:(UIImagePickerController *)picker
{
    printf("User cancelled\n");
    [self popToRootViewControllerAnimated:YES];
}

@end
```

Recipe: Selecting and Customizing Images from the Camera Roll

This recipe extends image picker interaction to add image edits. Working with edits more or less mandates modal interaction. Modal presentations limit the user's interaction options to a single view, in this case one presented by the `UIImagePickerController`, for some period of time. Chapter 4, "Alerting Users," introduced modal interaction for alert view and action sheet objects. Recipe 7-5 uses modality with image pickers.

Modal presentations are built in to every `UIViewController`. They work like this. When a parent controller calls `presentModalViewController: animated:`, a child view controller slides onscreen from the bottom of the window. The user interacts with the modal controller, finishes his or her work, and then you call `dismissModalViewControllerAnimated:`. This slides the controller back away. Modal presentations let you temporarily redirect control away from your main view structure and return when the subtask completes.

To enable image editing in a `UIImagePickerController`, set the `allowsImageEditing` property to `YES`. This enables users to scale and position images after selection, or in the case of camera shots, after snapping a photo. On the iPhone, this behavior appears in the Set Wallpaper feature of Settings. Figure 7-5 shows the post-selection editor.

Figure 7-5   Use the interactive image editor to move, scale, and choose your final presentation.

This window prompts users to move and scale the image as desired. When the user taps Choose, control moves to the picker delegate. On Cancel, control bounces back to the album view.

The delegate method `imagePickerController: didFinishPickingImage: editingInfo:` returns an edited version of the image as its second argument. This image reflects the scaling and translation specified by the user. The `UIImage` returned is small, sized to fit the iPhone screen.

The third argument, the `editingInfo` dictionary, now becomes important. It contains a copy of the original image and a rectangle that represents the image cropping. These items are set as objects of the dictionary and can be recovered for use when needed.

Note

To populate the camera roll on the iPhone simulator, locate the user file system in ~/Library/Application Support/iPhone Simulator/User. Copy a 100APPLE folder from a real iPhone to the Media/DCIM folder. Make sure to copy both the JPG images and the small THM thumbnail files.

Recipe 7-5   **Adding User Editing to Image Selection**

```
@interface HelloController : UIImagePickerController
➥<UIImagePickerControllerDelegate>
@end

@implementation HelloController

#define SOURCETYPE UIImagePickerControllerSourceTypeSavedPhotosAlbum
// #define SOURCETYPE UIImagePickerControllerSourceTypePhotoLibrary
#define DOCSFOLDER [NSHomeDirectory() stringByAppendingPathComponent:@"Documents"]

- (id) init
{
    if (!(self = [super init])) return self;

    // Set up to use the photo roll aka "Saved Photos"
    if ([UIImagePickerController isSourceTypeAvailable:SOURCETYPE])
    ➥    self.sourceType = SOURCETYPE;
    self.allowsImageEditing = YES;
    self.delegate = self;

    return self;
}

- (void)imagePickerController:(UIImagePickerController *)picker
➥didFinishPickingImage:(UIImage *)image editingInfo:(NSDictionary *)editingInfo
{
```

Recipe 7-5   **Continued**

```
    // Find a unique path name so files are not overwritten
    int i = 0;
    NSString *uniquePath = [DOCSFOLDER
➥stringByAppendingPathComponent:@"selectedImage.png"];
    while ([[NSFileManager defaultManager] fileExistsAtPath:uniquePath])
        uniquePath = [NSString stringWithFormat:@"%@/%@-%d.%@", DOCSFOLDER,
➥@"selectedImage", ++i, @"png"];

    printf("Writing selected image to Documents folder\n");
    [UIImagePNGRepresentation(image)  writeToFile: uniquePath atomically:YES];
    // Show the editing changes
    printf("Dictionary: %s\n", [[editingInfo description] UTF8String]);

    // Pop after saving the edited file
    [[self parentViewController] dismissModalViewControllerAnimated:YES];
}


- (void)imagePickerControllerDidCancel:(UIImagePickerController *)picker
{
    [[self parentViewController] dismissModalViewControllerAnimated:YES];
}
-(void) dealloc
{
    [super dealloc];
}
@end


@interface PrimaryController : UIViewController
@end


@implementation PrimaryController
- (void) snap
{
    [self presentModalViewController:[[HelloController alloc] init] animated:YES];
}


- (void) loadView
{
    [super loadView];

    UIView *contentView = [[UIView alloc] initWithFrame:[[UIScreen mainScreen]
➥applicationFrame]];
    contentView.backgroundColor = [UIColor whiteColor];
    self.view = contentView;
    [contentView release];
```

Recipe 7-5   Continued

```
self.navigationItem.rightBarButtonItem = [[[UIBarButtonItem alloc]
                                          initWithTitle:@"Select"
                                          style:UIBarButtonItemStylePlain
                                          target:self
                                          action:@selector(snap)] autorelease];
}


@end
```

Recipe: Snapping Pictures with the iPhone Camera

Recipes 7-4 and 7-5 introduced two of the three `UIImagePickerController` modes: picking from the entire photo collection and picking just from the camera roll. Recipe 7-6 presents the third mode, snapping photos with the iPhone's built-in camera. Figure 7-6 shows this interface in action. As you might suppose, this feature does not work in the Simulator. You must run it from the iPhone for it to work.

As with the other modes, you can allow or disallow image editing as part of the photo–capture process. One feature the camera interaction brings that has no parallel is the Preview screen, which displays after the user taps the green camera "snap" button. The preview screen enables you to retake the photo or use the photo as is. On tapping Use Photo, control passes to the next phase. If you've enabled image editing, that takes place next. If not, control moves to the standard "did finish picking" method.

As with edits, use a modal presentation for shooting photos. If you don't, you'll have to hack your way into returning control back to your main program. Using the camera interface as a modal view controller makes it simple to both present and respond to the camera.

> **Note**
>
> Press and hold the Sleep/Wake button and tap the Home key to take screenshots, like the one shown in Figure 7-6. The screen flashes white to let you know that the shot has been added to your DCIM folder. Alternatively, use the iPhone Organizer in Xcode (Control-Command-O) to snap live pictures of your screen.

Recipe 7-6   **Accessing the iPhone Camera**

```
@implementation CameraController

#define SOURCETYPE UIImagePickerControllerSourceTypeCamera
#define DOCSFOLDER [NSHomeDirectory() stringByAppendingPathComponent:@"Documents"]

- (id) init
{
    if (!(self = [super init])) return self;

    // Set up as the camera source
    if ([UIImagePickerController isSourceTypeAvailable:SOURCETYPE])
    ➥self.sourceType = SOURCETYPE;

    // Just snap here. Although you can easily add image editing if you want
    self.allowsImageEditing = NO;

    self.delegate = self;
    return self;
}
- (void)imagePickerController:(UIImagePickerController *)picker
➥didFinishPickingImage:(UIImage *)image editingInfo:(NSDictionary *)editingInfo
{
    // Find a unique path name so files are not overwritten
    int i = 0;
    NSString *uniquePath = [DOCSFOLDER
    ➥stringByAppendingPathComponent:@"selectedImage.png"];
    while ([[NSFileManager defaultManager] fileExistsAtPath:uniquePath])
        uniquePath = [NSString stringWithFormat:@"%@/%@-%d.%@", DOCSFOLDER,
        ➥@"selectedImage", ++i, @"png"];

    printf("Writing selected image to Documents folder\n");
    [UIImagePNGRepresentation(image)  writeToFile: uniquePath atomically:YES];

    // Thread of control ends here
    [[self parentViewController] dismissModalViewControllerAnimated:YES];
    [picker release];
}

- (void)imagePickerControllerDidCancel:(UIImagePickerController *)picker
{
    [[self parentViewController] dismissModalViewControllerAnimated:YES];
    [picker release];
}
@end
```

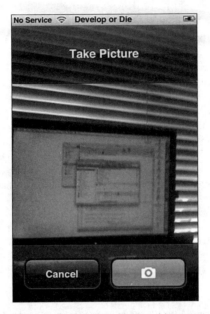

Figure 7-6   The iPhone camera interface enables you to snap photos,
resize and scale them, and reshoot if necessary.

Working with iPhone Audio

As you'd expect, the iPhone with its iPod-based roots is a powerful audio-capable device. Using iPhone audio in your programs is neither simple nor straightforward. Although Apple once had a public QuickTime-like class called Celestial, in Firmware 2.0 it moved this class into its PrivateFrameworks folder. That cut off developers from many beautiful, elegant, and easy-to-use classes and routines that made iPhone audio playback and recording a thing of beauty. Instead, with the iPhone SDK, developers are officially limited to two approaches, System Audio and Audio Queues:

- **System Audio services** enables you to play back short sounds, providing both alerts and vibration. Recipe 4-11 introduced these calls and showed you how to use them in your programs.

- **Audio Queue services** offers a C-based interface to the iPhone's Audio Toolbox framework. The iPhone SDK officially provides no simple and beautiful Objective-C classes for general audio playback. The programming samples provided by Apple are complicated and a bit buggy.

Fortunately, two elegant and general playback solutions are available if you're willing to dig enough. These solutions hide within the Media Player framework. Recipes 7-7 and 7-8 introduce each approach. The first gains behind-the-scenes access to the

Celestial framework for audio playback. The second uses the `MPMoviePlayer` class to play back audio and movies.

Note

The iPhone sandbox provides no access to your onboard iTunes Music Library. You cannot view or play back any file inside the Library or even get a listing or request playback from an "authorized" program. You can play back only those files you have access to, typically limited to those inside the application bundle or the Documents folder.

Recipe: Playing Audio with Celestial

Officially, the Celestial media framework is off limits. Unofficially, the Media Player framework offers several built-in Celestial features for audio playback. That's because the iPhone's media player is based on Celestial and exposes several of its classes. You can access these classes through undocumented API calls. The classes that enable you to play audio of nearly any type are as follows:

- **MPItem.** In Celestial, `AVItem` objects feed data from movies and audio files on the iPhone. `MPItem` offers a media player version of the standard Celestial `AVItem`. Initialize `MPItem` instances with a path that leads to the media in question.

- **MPAVController.** This class provides a centralized audio-visual controller to handle item playback and queue management. One shared instance of `MPAVController` remains available for you to use at any time.

- **MPArrayQueueFeeder.** This audio queue stores a list of pending media that's due for playback, like in a playlist. You initialize it with an array of paths that point to each item that you want played back.

- **AVController.** This class is the standard Celestial AV controller, which forms part of the `MPAVController` object. You can access this Celestial-based controller through the shared Media Player controller object and ask it to play back `MPItem` data.

Each of these classes is included in the Media Player framework and linkable. You supply the header to use them in your applications. Listing 7-2 provides that bare-bones header file (Playback.h) that exposes these classes and their most basic interface.

Note

See Chapter 1, "Introducing the iPhone SDK," for further discussion about using undocumented calls and features in your programs.

Listing 7-2   **Playback.h**

```
#import <MediaPlayer/MediaPlayer.h>

// Celestial's AV Item
@interface AVItem : NSObject
@end

// Media Player's version of AVItem
@interface MPItem : AVItem
- (id)initWithPath:(NSString *)path error:(id *)anError;
@end

// Media Player's primary playback controller
@interface MPAVController : NSObject
+ (id) sharedInstance;
- (id) avController;
@end

// Celestial's AVController
@interface AVController : NSObject
- (void) play: (id *) whatever;
- (void) pause;
- (void) setQueueFeeder:(id)fp8;
@end

// Celestial's AV Queue Feeder
@interface AVQueueFeeder : NSObject
@end

// Media Player's version of Celestial's feeder
@interface MPQueueFeeder : AVQueueFeeder
@end

// The Media Player array-based feeder
@interface MPArrayQueueFeeder : MPQueueFeeder
- (id) initWithPaths:(id)fp8;
@end
```

Recipe 7-7 presents an extremely no-frills player that loads a copy of Martin Luther King's "I have a dream" audio from the application bundle and plays it back. This method allocates a new MPItem and initializes it with the path to the audio file. The shared audio controller loads that MPItem and starts playback. In about five calls, you get functionality equaling page after page of AudioQueue programming.

The advantages to using Celestial are many. You never have to deal with complex AudioQueue calls. Celestial's AVController class handles nearly any audio format you can throw at it. You get a lot of performance for little programming.

There are drawbacks, too. Celestial playback interferes with any ongoing iPod playback. Start playing your audio and you cut into whatever song was playing. In contrast, System Audio services playback does not interrupt. It overlays any iPod audio with whatever short alert you need to play.

To stop playback, call [avc pause]. Unfortunately, you cannot "unpause" to continue playback after that.

AVController broadcasts several notifications you'll want to keep track of. The two most important are AVController_ItemReadyToPlay and AVController_ItemPlaybackDidEnd. The former tells your program when the queue has finished loading the data, which may take a second or two to do. The latter lets you know when playback has naturally ended, as opposed to when a user taps a Pause or Stop button. AVController also sends notifications about the queue selection changing and more. You can subscribe to all notifications (see Chapter 1 for details) to listen in to AVController's state broadcasts.

Recipe 7-7   **Playing Back Audio with Celestial's AVController**

```
- (void) startPlayback : (id) sender
{
    // Recover the AV Controller
    avc = [[MPAVController sharedInstance] avController];

    // Set up a queue to feed the controller
    id feeder = [[MPArrayQueueFeeder alloc] initWithPaths:[NSArray
    ➥arrayWithObject:path]];
    [avc setQueueFeeder:feeder];
    [feeder release];

    // Start playback
    [avc play:nil];
}
```

Recipe: Using the Media Player for Audio and Video Playback

As Figure 7-7 shows, the full-screen media player interface offers scrubbing, play/pause control, and more. These features are available for both audio and video playback. The difference lies in whether you supply a file URL that points to an audio file or a video file. Swap out a video URL for the audio one used in this recipe, and you end up with a full-screen movie.

Like other examples in this chapter, the MPMoviePlayerController plays by its own rules. You do not push it onto a navigation stack. You do not invoke it modally. Instead, you create it and tell it to play. It takes control of the screen, offering the playback controls shown in Figure 7-7. To regain control, subscribe your application to the

`MPMoviePlayerPlaybackDidFinishNotification` notification. This notification is
sent under two circumstances: when playback naturally ends, or when the user taps Done.

Recipe 7-8 is made up of two methods. One starts playback, the other cleans up when
playback ends. This exact code can be used to play back audio or to play back video. All
you need to provide is a movie file rather than an audio one. Supported file types include
MOV, MP4, MPV, M4V, and 3GP, as well as MP3, AIFF, M4A, and so forth.

Figure 7-7   The full-screen media player interface offers extensive
user control over audio playback.

Recipe 7-8   Using `MPMoviePlayerController` to Play Back Audio or Video

```
-(void)myMovieFinishedCallback:(NSNotification*)aNotification
{
    // Remove and release the observer
    MPMoviePlayerController* theMovie=[aNotification object];
    [[NSNotificationCenter defaultCenter] removeObserver:self
    ➥name:MPMoviePlayerPlaybackDidFinishNotification object:theMovie];
    [theMovie release];

    // restore the status bar to portrait orientation
    [[UIApplication sharedApplication]
    ➥setStatusBarOrientation:UIInterfaceOrientationPortrait animated:YES];
}

- (void) startPlayback : (id) sender
{
    // create a new player and initialize it with the path
    NSString *path = [[NSBundle mainBundle] pathForResource:@"dream"
    ➥ofType:@"m4a"];
    MPMoviePlayerController* theMovie=[[MPMoviePlayerController alloc]
    ➥initWithContentURL:[NSURL fileURLWithPath:path]];
    theMovie.scalingMode=MPMovieScalingModeAspectFill;
```

```
    // Add an observer to catch when playback ends
    [[NSNotificationCenter defaultCenter] addObserver:self
➥selector:@selector(myMovieFinishedCallback:)
➥name:MPMoviePlayerPlaybackDidFinishNotification object:theMovie];

    // Start playback
    [theMovie play];
}
```

Recipe: Recording Audio

Unfortunately, Celestial's insanely easy-to-use audio recorder object did not seem to make the transition from 1.1.4 to 2.0. That leaves developers with Audio Queue recording. Recipe 7-9 offers a bare-bones recording wrapped in an Objective-C class. Note how the class delays ending a recording for a second to fully clear out pending buffers. This sample is based entirely on Apple sample code and is indebted to the trailsinthe-sand.com Web site's excellent tutorials.

Recipe 7-9   **Basic Audio Queue Recording**

```
#import <UIKit/UIKit.h>
#import <AudioToolbox/AudioQueue.h>
#import <AudioToolbox/AudioFile.h>


#define NUM_BUFFERS 3
#define kAudioConverterPropertyMaximumOutputPacketSize        'xops'
#define DOCUMENTS_FOLDER [NSHomeDirectory()
➥stringByAppendingPathComponent:@"Documents"]

// Custom recording state storage
typedef struct
    {
        AudioFileID             audioFile;
        AudioStreamBasicDescription dataFormat;
        AudioQueueRef           queue;
        AudioQueueBufferRef     buffers[NUM_BUFFERS];
        UInt32                  bufferByteSize;
        SInt64                  currentPacket;
        BOOL                    recording;
    } RecordState;

// Objective-C wrapper for the Audio Queue functionality
@interface Recorder : NSObject {
    RecordState recordState;
    CFURLRef fileURL;
```

Recipe 7-9   **Continued**

```objc
}

- (BOOL)    isRecording;

// Automatically generate a dated file in Documents
- (void)    toggleRecording;

// Manual recording
- (void)    startRecording: (NSString *) filePath;
- (void)    stopRecording;

@end

// Derive the Buffer Size. I punt with the max buffer size.
void DeriveBufferSize (
                        AudioQueueRef                audioQueue,
                        AudioStreamBasicDescription  ASBDescription,
                        Float64                      seconds,
                        UInt32                       *outBufferSize
) {
    static const int maxBufferSize = 0x50000;

    int maxPacketSize = ASBDescription.mBytesPerPacket;
    if (maxPacketSize == 0) {
        UInt32 maxVBRPacketSize = sizeof(maxPacketSize);
        AudioQueueGetProperty (
                        audioQueue,
                        kAudioConverterPropertyMaximumOutputPacketSize,
                        &maxPacketSize,
                        &maxVBRPacketSize
                        );
    }

    Float64 numBytesForTime =
    ASBDescription.mSampleRate * maxPacketSize * seconds;
    *outBufferSize =  (UInt32) ((numBytesForTime < maxBufferSize) ?
numBytesForTime : maxBufferSize);

}

// Forward Declaration to Input Buffer Handler
static void HandleInputBuffer (
                        void                    *aqData,
                        AudioQueueRef           inAQ,
                        AudioQueueBufferRef     inBuffer,
```

Recipe 7-9   **Continued**

```
                                    const AudioTimeStamp              *inStartTime,
                                    UInt32                            inNumPackets,
                                    const AudioStreamPacketDescription *inPacketDesc
                                    );

// Assign the file metadata
OSStatus SetMagicCookieForFile (
                                    AudioQueueRef inQueue,
                                    AudioFileID   inFile
) {
    OSStatus result = noErr;
    UInt32 cookieSize;

    if (
        AudioQueueGetPropertySize (
                                    inQueue,
                                    kAudioQueueProperty_MagicCookie,
                                    &cookieSize
                                    ) == noErr
        ) {
        char* magicCookie =
        (char *) malloc (cookieSize);
        if (
            AudioQueueGetProperty (
                                    inQueue,
                                    kAudioQueueProperty_MagicCookie,
                                    magicCookie,
                                    &cookieSize
                                    ) == noErr
            )
            result =    AudioFileSetProperty (
                                            inFile,
                                            kAudioFilePropertyMagicCookieData,
                                            cookieSize,
                                            magicCookie
                                            );
        free (magicCookie);
    }
    return result;
}

// Write out current packets
static void HandleInputBuffer (
                                    void              *aqData,
                                    AudioQueueRef     inAQ,
```

Recipe 7-9   **Continued**

```
                                AudioQueueBufferRef              inBuffer,
                                const AudioTimeStamp            *inStartTime,
                                UInt32                          inNumPackets,
                                const AudioStreamPacketDescription  *inPacketDesc
) {
    RecordState *pAqData = (RecordState *) aqData;

    if (inNumPackets == 0 &&
        pAqData->dataFormat.mBytesPerPacket != 0)
        inNumPackets =
        inBuffer->mAudioDataByteSize / pAqData->dataFormat.mBytesPerPacket;

    if (AudioFileWritePackets (
                            pAqData->audioFile,
                            NO,
                            inBuffer->mAudioDataByteSize,
                            inPacketDesc,
                            pAqData->currentPacket,
                            &inNumPackets,
                            inBuffer->mAudioData
                            ) == noErr) {
        pAqData->currentPacket += inNumPackets;

        if (pAqData->recording == 0)
            return;

        AudioQueueEnqueueBuffer (
                            pAqData->queue,
                            inBuffer,
                            0,
                            NULL
                            );
    }
}


// Write the buffers out
void AudioInputCallback(
                    void *inUserData,
                    AudioQueueRef inAQ,
                    AudioQueueBufferRef inBuffer,
                    const AudioTimeStamp *inStartTime,
                    UInt32 inNumberPacketDescriptions,
                    const AudioStreamPacketDescription *inPacketDescs)
{
    RecordState* recordState = (RecordState*)inUserData;
```

Recipe 7-9 **Continued**

```
    if(!recordState->recording)  { printf("Not recording, returning\n"); return;
}

    printf("Writing buffer %d\n", recordState->currentPacket);
    OSStatus status = AudioFileWritePackets(recordState->audioFile,
                                    NO,
                                    inBuffer->mAudioDataByteSize,
                                    inPacketDescs,
                                    recordState->currentPacket,
                                    &inNumberPacketDescriptions,
                                    inBuffer->mAudioData);
    if(status == 0) // success
    {
        recordState->currentPacket += inNumberPacketDescriptions;
    }

    AudioQueueEnqueueBuffer(recordState->queue, inBuffer, 0, NULL);
}
// For use with the file naming, which is automatic
@interface NSDate (extended)
-(NSDate *) dateWithCalendarFormat:(NSString *)format timeZone: (NSTimeZone *)
➥timeZone;
@end

@implementation Recorder

// Initialize the recorder
- (id) init
{
    self = [super init];
    recordState.recording = NO;
    return self;
}

// Set up the recording format as low-quality mono AIFF
- (void)setupAudioFormat:(AudioStreamBasicDescription*)format
{
    format->mSampleRate = 8000.0;
    format->mFormatID = kAudioFormatLinearPCM;
    format->mFormatFlags = kLinearPCMFormatFlagIsBigEndian |
    ➥kLinearPCMFormatFlagIsSignedInteger | kLinearPCMFormatFlagIsPacked;

    format->mChannelsPerFrame = 1; // mono
    format->mBitsPerChannel = 16;
    format->mFramesPerPacket = 1;
    format->mBytesPerPacket = 2;
```

Recipe 7-9   **Continued**

```
    format->mBytesPerFrame = 2; // not used, apparently required
    format->mReserved = 0;
}


// Begin recording
- (void) startRecording: (NSString *) filePath
{
    [self setupAudioFormat:&recordState.dataFormat];
    fileURL =  CFURLCreateFromFileSystemRepresentation (NULL, (const UInt8 *)
    ➥[filePath UTF8String], [filePath length], NO);
    recordState.currentPacket = 0;

    OSStatus status;
    status = AudioQueueNewInput(&recordState.dataFormat,
                                HandleInputBuffer,
                                &recordState,
                                CFRunLoopGetCurrent(),
                                kCFRunLoopCommonModes,
                                0,
                                &recordState.queue);

    if (status != 0) {
        printf("Could not establish new queue\n");
        return;
    }

    status = AudioFileCreateWithURL(fileURL,
                                    kAudioFileAIFFType,
                                    &recordState.dataFormat,
                                    kAudioFileFlags_EraseFile,
                                    &recordState.audioFile);
    if (status != 0)
    {
        printf("Could not create file to record audio\n");
        return;
    }

    DeriveBufferSize (
                    recordState.queue,
                    recordState.dataFormat,
                    0.5,
                    &recordState.bufferByteSize
                    );
    // printf("0Buffer size: %d\n", recordState.bufferByteSize);
```

```
    for(int i = 0; i < NUM_BUFFERS; i++)
    {
        status = AudioQueueAllocateBuffer(recordState.queue,
                                   recordState.bufferByteSize,
                                   &recordState.buffers[i]);
        if (status) {
            printf("Error allocating buffer %d\n", i);
            return;
        }
        status = AudioQueueEnqueueBuffer(recordState.queue,
        ➥recordState.buffers[i], 0, NULL);
        if (status) {
            printf("Error enqueuing buffer %d\n", i);
            return;
        }
    }

    status = SetMagicCookieForFile(recordState.queue, recordState.audioFile);
    if (status != 0)
    {
        printf("Magic cookie failed\n");
        return;
    }

    status = AudioQueueStart(recordState.queue, NULL);
    if (status != 0)
    {
        printf("Could not start Audio Queue\n");
        return;
    }

    recordState.currentPacket = 0;
    recordState.recording = YES;
    return;
}

// There's generally about a one-second delay before the buffers fully empty
- (void) reallyStopRecording
{
    AudioQueueFlush(recordState.queue);
    AudioQueueStop(recordState.queue, NO);
    recordState.recording = NO;
    SetMagicCookieForFile(recordState.queue, recordState.audioFile);
    for(int i = 0; i < NUM_BUFFERS; i++)
    {
```

Recipe 7-9   **Continued**

```
            AudioQueueFreeBuffer(recordState.queue,
                            recordState.buffers[i]);

    }

    AudioQueueDispose(recordState.queue, YES);
    AudioFileClose(recordState.audioFile);
}

// Stop the recording after waiting just a second
- (void) stopRecording
{
    [self performSelector:@selector(reallyStopRecording) withObject:NULL
    ➥afterDelay:1.0f];
}

// Automatically create a file in Documents and start/stop recording to it
- (void) toggleRecording
{
    // Create a new dated file
    NSDate *now = [NSDate dateWithTimeIntervalSinceNow:0];
    NSString *caldate = [[now dateWithCalendarFormat:@"%b_%d_%H_%M_%S"
    ➥timeZone:nil] description]; // no :'s.
    NSString *filePath = [NSString stringWithFormat:@"%@/%@.aiff",
    ➥DOCUMENTS_FOLDER, caldate];

    if(!recordState.recording)
    {
        printf("Starting recording\n");
        [self startRecording: filePath];
    }
    else
    {
        printf("Stopping recording\n");
        [self stopRecording];
    }
}

- (BOOL) isRecording
{
    return recordState.recording;
}

@end
```

Reading in Text Data

Of all iPhone media, text data proves (unsurprisingly) the simplest to read in and write out. The NSString class easily loads text data from an iPhone file:

```
NSString *path = [[NSBundle defaultBundle] pathForResource:@"myText"
➥ofType:@"txt"];
NSString *fileText = [NSString stringWithContentsOfFile:path encoding:
NSUTF8StringEncoding error:nil];
```

After loading a string from the contents of a file, you might add it into a text view (textView.text = fileText), split it into strings for, for example, a table ([fileText componentsSeparatedByString:@"\n"]), or maybe use it as the body for a text alert (see Chapter 4).

To output text, ask the string to write itself out to a file:

```
NSError *error;
[myString writeToFile:path atomically:YES encoding:NSUTF8StringEncoding
➥error:&error];
```

Displaying Property Lists

Property lists, those files used by Apple to store defaults and other kinds of system data, aren't exactly "media." On the other hand, they are something you may want to read from disk and display onscreen in your program. In that rather generous spirit, here's how you can read in a property list (in this case, the SpringBoard preferences, which is readable despite sandbox restrictions) and produce a string description suitable for display in your favorite UITextView or UILabel. This method works for files with the strings extension as well as the plist:

```
#define PLISTPATH @"/private/var/mobile/Library/Preferences/
➥com.apple.springboard.plist"

NSDictionary *plist = [NSMutableDictionary
dictionaryWithContentsOfFile:PLISTPATH];
if (plist) textView.text = [plist description];
else textView.text = @"Could not read property list from file";
```

Most complex structures, including sets, arrays, dictionaries, and so forth, return an NSString description on demand. It's a great way to convert a property list into a viewable format. To go the other way, converting an NSString XML property list representation to a property list, use the propertyList method (e.g., id plist = [myXMLString propertyList]).

> **Note**
>
> Property lists and dictionaries can also be serialized into an XML string. Chapter 10, "Connecting to Services," shows how to do this and how to recover data from its serialized format.

Recovering Media from Backup Files

When iTunes backs up an iPhone, it stores data from each application's Documents and Library folders. These files are encoded and checksummed, and added to a central backup manifest. On the Macintosh, a backup folder for each synced iPhone appears in ~/Library/Application Support/MobileSync/Backup; on Windows, in C:\Documents and Settings*UserName*\Application Data\Apple Computer\SyncServices\Local. Inside each folder appears one Info.plist, one Manifest.plist, and many mdbackup files:

- The Info.plist file describes the device, its name, its serial number, and its iTunes preferences, along with other device-specific information.

- The Manifest.plist file stores a table of contents of all the backed-up files, along with their modification time and data hash. This does two things. It ensures that the data remains consistent with the time it was backed up, and it prevents third-party developers from loading custom data back to the iPhone on restore. The former is a good thing, the latter not so much of one.

- Mdbackup files contain serialized versions of each file backed up to your computer. My Macintosh-based mdhelper command-line utility (http://ericasadun.com/ftp/Macintosh) scans through these mobile device backup files and recovers the backed-up data from them.

Serialized data appears in an encoded block. It's simple to access this block and store it to disk in its original form. It takes just three steps:

1. Read in the mdbackup file to a dictionary:
   ```
   NSDictionary *mddict = [NSDictionary
   dictionaryWithContentsOfFile:backupPath];
   ```

2. Extract the encoded data block:
   ```
   NSData *data = [mddict objectForKey:@"Data"];
   ```

3. Store the data out to disk:
   ```
   [data writeToFile:testPath atomically:YES];
   ```

These three steps enable you to convert those otherwise impenetrable data blocks into the original files, whether for the manifest or for individually backed-up data. Recipe 7-10 shows the mdhelper routine that extracts manifests from the backup folders.

Recipe 7-10   **Recovering Manifest Data from iTunes Backups**

```
// Recover all manifests from available folders
void getManifests()
{
    for (NSString *path in backupFolders())
    {
        NSString *fullPath = [backupDirPath()
        ➥stringByAppendingPathComponent:path];

        // Get the path to the Manifest.plist file
```

Recipe 7-10   **Continued**

```
        NSString *manifestPath = [fullPath
    ➥stringByAppendingPathComponent:@"Manifest.plist"];

        // Get the path to the Info.plist file
        NSString *infoPath = [fullPath
    ➥stringByAppendingPathComponent:@"Info.plist"];

        // Read in the manifest and info dictionaries
        NSDictionary *manifestDict = [NSDictionary
    ➥dictionaryWithContentsOfFile:manifestPath];
        NSDictionary *infoDict = [NSDictionary
    ➥dictionaryWithContentsOfFile:infoPath];

        // Read in the device name from Info.plist
        NSString *deviceName = [infoDict objectForKey:@"Device Name"];

        // Read in the manifests's data glob
        NSData *data = [manifestDict objectForKey:@"Data"];

        // Output the manifest's data glob to disk
        NSString *outfile = [[recoveryFolderPath()
    ➥stringByAppendingPathComponent:deviceName] stringByAppendingString:@"-
    ➥Manifest.plist"];
        if (data) printf("Extracting manifest for device %s\n", [deviceName
    ➥UTF8String]);
        [data writeToFile:outfile atomically:YES];

        [data release];
        [outfile release];
        [deviceName release];
        [infoPath release];
        [manifestPath release];
        [fullPath release];
    }
}
```

Summary

This chapter introduced many ways to handle media, including loading, storing, select-ing, and extracting files. You've seen recipes that worked with audio, video, image, and text data. Before moving on from this chapter, here are some thoughts about the recipes you've seen here:

- Whether working with images or audio, choose a presentation method that best matches the characteristics of the file you're working with. With the iPhone, there's rarely a one-size-fits-all solution for media.

- Although Apple has not made the Celestial `AVController` class public, it's available in public frameworks. You bring the headers. Let Apple bring the functionality you need.

- Audio Queue provides powerful low-level audio routines but they're not for the faint of heart or for anyone who just wants a quick solution. If you need the kind of fine-grained audio control that Audio Queues bring, Apple supplies extensive documentation on achieving your goals.

- Many classes deliver more than advertised: Use `UIWebView` objects to display HTML, PDF files, and images. Use `MPMoviePlayerController` to play back both movies and audio files.

Controls

The UIControl class provides the basis for many iPhone interactive elements, including buttons, text fields, sliders, and switches. These controls have more in common than their ancestor class. Controls all use similar layout and target-action approaches. This chapter introduces controls and their use. You discover how to build and customize controls in a variety of ways. You read about well-documented SDK calls and about less-documented ones. You see how disassembling the UIControl view hierarchy enables you to access and modify control elements. From the prosaic to the obscure, this chapter introduces a wide range of control recipes you can reuse in your programs.

Recipe: Building Simple Buttons

The iPhone supports several kinds of buttons. The two most commonly used buttons are the freestanding UIButton instances built from scratch and the UIBarButtonItem ones that live exclusively on bars, including navigation bars, tab bars, and toolbars.

UIBarButtonItems provide an extremely simple way to add push-button functionality to your applications with a minimum of programming. Listing 8-1 shows a typical call that you'd find in a UIViewController loadView method. You create the button with a title, a style, a target, and an action. The parent view, whether a navigation bar, tab bar, or toolbar, handles placement and sizing issues for you.

Listing 8-1   **Adding a UIBarButtonItem to a Navigation Bar**

```
// Add a randomize button
UIBarButtonItem *randomButton = [[[UIBarButtonItem alloc]
                          initWithTitle:@"Randomize"
                          style:UIBarButtonItemStylePlain
                          target:self
                          action:@selector(randomize)] autorelease];
self.navigationItem.rightBarButtonItem = randomButton;
```

`UIBarButtonItems` use target-action. Like all controls, they enable you to add at least one target and callback action for when users interact with them. Bar button items do not specify the kind of event involved; the only event of interest is a button tap.

The drawback to working with bar button items is that they cannot be placed arbitrarily onscreen. They are not views. So, you cannot set their frame and add them to other views. The bars that own them both build and manage their presentation. To place buttons into arbitrary views, you need to work with the `UIButton` class instead.

> **Note**
>
> Once built by its parent, you *can* access a bar button item's actual view. Call the undocumented `UIButton view` method. You cannot remove that view from its parent and treat it as an independent object without encountering serious complications. Instead, use the view to add subviews like the (undocumented) `UIToolbarButtonBadge` class, as shown later in this chapter.

The `UIButton` class

`UIButton` instances add interactive buttons to your iPhone applications. They offer more traditional controls, complete with frames and event specification for target-action calls. When tapped, they send messages to a target you specify. The iPhone offers two ways to build `UIButtons`. You can use a precooked button type or build a custom button from scratch.

The current iPhone SDK offers the following precooked button types. As you can see, the button types are not very general. They've been added to the SDK primarily for Apple's convenience, not yours. Nonetheless, you can use these in your programs as needed:

- **Detail Disclosure.** This is the same round, blue circle with the chevron you see when you add a detail disclosure accessory to table cells.
- **Info Light and Info Dark.** These two buttons offer a small circled *i* like you see on a Macintosh's Dashboard widget. These are used in the Weather and Stocks application to flip the view from one side to the other.
- **Contact Add.** This round, blue circle has a white + in its center and can be seen in the Contacts application for adding new people to your Address Book.
- **Rounded Rectangle.** This button provides a simple onscreen rounded rectangle that surrounds the button text. It's not an especially attractive button (that is, it's not very "Apple" looking), but it is simple to program and use in your applications.

To use a precooked button, allocate it, set its frame, and add a target. Don't worry about adding custom art or creating the overall look of the button. The SDK takes care of all that. Listing 8-2 illustrates how to build a simple, rounded, rectangle button. To build one of the other standard button types, omit the title line. Rounded rectangles are the only precooked button type that use a title.

> **Note**
>
> Use the `UIControlEventTouchUpInside` event to catch user taps on buttons.

Listing 8-2   **Building a "Precooked" Rounded Rectangle Button**

```
UIButton *button = [UIButton buttonWithType:UIButtonTypeRoundedRect];
[button setFrame:CGRectMake(0.0f, 0.0f, 80.0f, 30.0f)];
[button setCenter:CGPointMake(160.0f, 208.0f)];
[button setTitle:@"Beep" forState:UIControlStateNormal];
[button addTarget:self action:@selector(playSound:)
➥forControlEvents:UIControlEventTouchUpInside];
[contentView addSubview:button];
```

Building Custom Buttons

When using the `UIButtonTypeCustom` style, you supply all button art. The number of images depends on how you want the button to work. For a simple push button, you might add a single background image and vary the label color to highlight when the button is pushed. For a toggle-style button, you might use four images: for the "off" state in a normal presentation, the "off" state when highlighted (that is, pressed), and two more for the "on" state. You choose and design the interaction details.

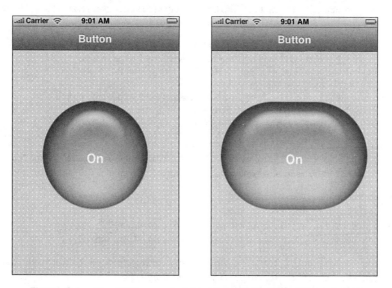

Figure 8-1   Use `UIImage` stretching to resize art for arbitrary button widths. Set the left cap width to specify where the stretching can take place.

Recipe 8-1 builds a button that toggles on and off, demonstrating the detail that goes into building custom buttons. When tapped, the button switches its art from green to red, or red to green. This allows your (noncolorblind) users to instantly identify a current state. Figure 8-1 (left) shows the button created by this recipe.

The UIImage stretchable image calls in this recipe play an important role in button creation. Stretchable images enable you to create buttons of arbitrary width, turning circular art into lozenge-shaped buttons. You specify the caps at either end (that is, the art that should not be stretched). In this case, the cap is 110 pixels wide. If you were to change the button width from the 220 pixels used in this recipe to 300, the button stretches from the middle at the point where the cap ends, as shown in Figure 8-1 (right).

Recipe 8-1   **Building a UIButton That Toggles On and Off**

```
@interface HelloController : UIViewController
{
    UIImageView          *contentView;
    BOOL             isOn;
}
@end

@implementation HelloController
- (UIButton *) buildButton: (NSString *) aTitle
{
    // Create a button sized to our art
    UIButton *button = [[UIButton alloc] initWithFrame:CGRectMake(0.0f, 0.0f,
220.0f, 233.0f)];

    // The cap width indicates the location where the stretch occurs
    [button setBackgroundImage:[[UIImage imageNamed:@"green.png"]
➥stretchableImageWithLeftCapWidth:110.0 topCapHeight:0.0]
➥forState:UIControlStateNormal];
    [button setBackgroundImage:[[UIImage imageNamed:@"green2.png"]
➥stretchableImageWithLeftCapWidth:110.0 topCapHeight:0.0]
➥forState:UIControlStateHighlighted];

    // Set up the button aligment properties
    button.contentVerticalAlignment = UIControlContentVerticalAlignmentCenter;
    button.contentHorizontalAlignment = UIControlContentHorizontalAlignmentCenter;

    // Set the title, font and color. The color switches from
    // white to gray for highlights
    [button setTitle:aTitle forState:UIControlStateNormal];
    [button setTitle:aTitle forState:UIControlStateHighlighted];

    [button setTitleColor:[UIColor whiteColor] forState:UIControlStateNormal];
    [button setTitleColor:[UIColor lightGrayColor]
➥forState:UIControlStateHighlighted];

    [button setFont:[UIFont boldSystemFontOfSize:24.0f]];

    isOn = NO;
```

Recipe 8-1   **Continued**

```objc
    return [button autorelease];
}

- (void) toggleButton: (UIButton *) button
{
    // Swap the art when the state changes
    if (isOn = !isOn)
    {
        [button setTitle:@"On" forState:UIControlStateNormal];
        [button setTitle:@"On" forState:UIControlStateHighlighted];
        [button setBackgroundImage:[[UIImage imageNamed:@"green.png"]
        ➥stretchableImageWithLeftCapWidth:110.0 topCapHeight:0.0]
        ➥forState:UIControlStateNormal];
        [button setBackgroundImage:[[UIImage imageNamed:@"green2.png"]
        ➥stretchableImageWithLeftCapWidth:110.0 topCapHeight:0.0]
        ➥forState:UIControlStateHighlighted];
    }
    else
    {
        [button setTitle:@"Off" forState:UIControlStateNormal];
        [button setTitle:@"Off" forState:UIControlStateHighlighted];
        [button setBackgroundImage:[[UIImage imageNamed:@"red.png"]
        ➥stretchableImageWithLeftCapWidth:110.0 topCapHeight:0.0]
        ➥forState:UIControlStateNormal];
        [button setBackgroundImage:[[UIImage imageNamed:@"red2.png"]
        ➥stretchableImageWithLeftCapWidth:110.0 topCapHeight:0.0]
        ➥forState:UIControlStateHighlighted];
    }
}
- (void)loadView
{
    // Load an application image and set it as the primary view
    contentView = [[UIImageView alloc] initWithFrame:[[UIScreen mainScreen]
    ➥applicationFrame]];
    [contentView setImage:[UIImage imageNamed:@"bluedots.png"]];
    [contentView setUserInteractionEnabled:YES];
    self.view = contentView;
    [contentView release];

    // Add the button
    UIButton *button = [self buildButton:@"On"];
    [button setCenter:CGPointMake(160.0f, 200.0f)];
    [contentView addSubview: button];
[button addTarget:self action:@selector(toggleButton:)
➥forControlEvents: UIControlEventTouchUpInside];

    isOn = YES;
}
- (void) dealloc
{
```

```
    [contentView release];
    [super dealloc];
}
@end
```

Glass Buttons

During the SDK beta period, Apple dropped official support for its simple
`UIGlassButton` class. This class offered a much better-looking alternative to the rounded
rectangle and supported control tinting, too. At the time of writing, the `UIGlassButton`
class still exists in the simulator's `UIKit` framework, but Apple does not fully implement
it in the iPhone's `UIKit` framework.

Recipe: Adding Animated Elements to Buttons

You cannot add subviews to buttons, but you can certainly creatively layer art in front
of or behind them. Use the standard `UIView` hierarchy to do this, making sure to
disable user interaction for any view that might otherwise obscure your button
(`setUserInteractionEnabled:NO`). Figure 8-2 shows what happens when you
combine semitranslucent button art with an animated `UIImageView` behind it. The
image view contents "leak" through to the viewer, enabling you to add live animation
elements to the button.

Recipe 8-2   **Adding Animated Elements Behind a `UIButton`**

```
- (void)loadView
{
    // Load an application image and set it as the primary view
    contentView = [[UIImageView alloc] initWithFrame:[[UIScreen mainScreen]
➥applicationFrame]];
    [contentView setImage:[UIImage imageNamed:@"bluedots.png"]];
    [contentView setUserInteractionEnabled:YES];
    self.view = contentView;
    [contentView release];

    // load in the animation cells for the butterfly
    NSMutableArray *bflies = [[NSMutableArray alloc] init];
    for (int i = 1; i <= 17; i++) {
        NSString *cname = [NSString stringWithFormat:@"bf_%d.png", i];
        UIImage *img = [UIImage imageNamed:cname];
        if (img) [bflies addObject:img];
    }

    // create the image view and add it
```

```
UIImageView *imageView = [[UIImageView alloc] initWithFrame:CGRectMake(0.0f,
➥0.0f, 80.0f, 80.0f)];
[imageView setAnimationImages:bflies];
[imageView setAnimationDuration:1.2f];
[imageView startAnimating];
[bflies release];

[contentView addSubview:imageView];
[imageView release];
[imageView setCenter:CGPointMake(160.0f, 200.0f)];
[imageView setUserInteractionEnabled:NO];

// Add the button and set it to play the sound
UIButton *button = [self buildButton:@"PushMe"];
[button setCenter:CGPointMake(160.0f, 200.0f)];
[contentView addSubview: button];
[button addTarget:self action:@selector(playSound:) forControlEvents:
➥UIControlEventTouchDown];
}
```

Figure 8-2   Combine semitranslucent button art with animated
UIImageViews to build eye-catching UI elements. In this recipe, the
butterfly flaps "within" the button.

Recipe: Animating Button Responses

There's more to UIControls than frames and target-action. All controls inherit from the UIView class. This means you can use UIView animation blocks when working with controls just as you would with standard views. Recipe 8-3 builds a toggle switch that flips around using UIViewAnimationTransitionFlipFromLeft to spin the button while changing states.

Unlike Recipe 8-1, this code doesn't switch art. Instead, it switches buttons. There are two: an on button and an off button, both of which rest on a clear UIView. Giving the two buttons a see-through parent enables you to apply the flip to just those buttons without involving the rest of the user interface. Skip the clear background, and you end up spinning the entire window—not a good UI choice.

As this recipe uses the same semitranslucent art as the previous recipes, it's important that only one button appears onscreen at any time. To make this happen, the current button removes itself from that clear superview while in the animation block. The button with the opposite state takes its place. Figure 8-3 shows the flipping button in midflip.

Figure 8-3   Use UIView animation blocks to flip between control states. Here, a button twirls around to move between Off and On.

Recipe 8-3   Adding UIView Animation Blocks to Controls

```
- (void) toggleButton: (UIButton *) button
{
    [UIView beginAnimations:nil context:NULL];
```

Recipe 8-3   **Continued**

```
[UIView setAnimationDuration:1.0f];
[UIView setAnimationTransition:
 UIViewAnimationTransitionFlipFromLeft forView:clearView cache:YES];

// swap out the button views during the flip
[button removeFromSuperview];
if (isOn = !isOn)[clearView addSubview:onButton];
else [clearView addSubview:offButton];

[UIView commitAnimations];
}
```

Recipe: Customizing Switches

Nontrivial `UIControl` objects are usually built from a series of subviews. By navigating a control's subview tree, you can expose and customize objects that normally would not be accessible from the standard SDK. Take switches, for example. The SDK offers just one type of switch: an On/Off button. It takes just a few lines of code to edit that button to transform it to the Yes/No button shown in Figure 8-4 (left).

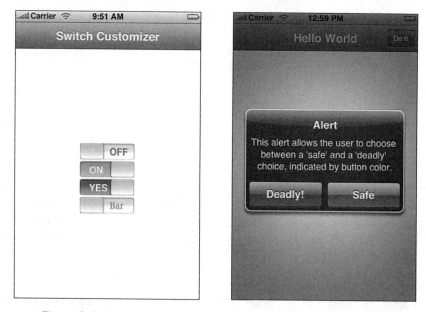

Figure 8-4   (Left) A bit of object dumpster diving allows you to expose and customize underlying `UISwitch` views. (Right) Color `UIAlertView` buttons by accessing the alert's subviews.

This kind of customization relies on understanding a control's view tree. Listing 8-3 shows how you might explore that hierarchy. Send a control object to explode: level: with an initial level of 0. The method recursively descends the tree, presenting each subview in turn.

Listing 8-3   **Exploring UIControl View Hierarchy**

```
#define outstring(anObject) [[anObject description] UTF8String]

- (void) explode: (id) aView level: (int) aLevel
{
    // indent to show the current level
    for (int i = 0;  i < aLevel; i++) printf("—", aLevel);

    // show the class and superclass for the current object
    printf("%s:%s\n", outstring([aView class]), outstring([aView superclass]));

    // recurse for all subviews
    for (UIView *subview in [aView subviews])
        [self explode:subview level:(aLevel + 1)];
}
```

When sent a switch, explode creates the following results in the Xcode console. As you can see, a switch has a single subview, a custom UISwitchSlider object. This has four subviews. Three images create the backgrounds and the switch art. One view owns the two labels used on the switch. Because these labels are standard UILabel instances, you can tell them to use whatever text you supply:

```
UISwitch:UIControl
 --_UISwitchSlider:UISlider
 ----UIImageView:UIView
 ----UIImageView:UIView
 ----UIView:UIResponder
 ------UILabel:UIView
 ------UILabel:UIView
 ----UIImageView:UIView
```

Knowing how the views are set up enables you to build a UISwitch subclass that accesses these items. Recipe 8-4 shows the UICustomSwitch class implementation that adds label text customization.

> **Note**
>
> The extended UISwitch class definition in Recipe 8-4 also exposes the undocumented setAlternateColors: call that enables you to use an orange background rather than a blue one. See Chapter 1, "Introducing the iPhone SDK," for a discussion about using undocumented features in your applications.

Recipe 8-4   **Adding Text Customization to iPhone Switches**

```
// Add the undocumented alternate colors
@interface UISwitch (extended)
- (void) setAlternateColors:(BOOL) boolean;
@end

// Expose the _UISwitchSlider class
@interface _UISwitchSlider : UIView
@end

// UICustomSwitch allows you to set the left and right label text
@interface UICustomSwitch : UISwitch
- (void) setLeftLabelText: (NSString *) labelText;
- (void) setRightLabelText: (NSString *) labelText;
@end

@implementation UICustomSwitch
- (_UISwitchSlider *) slider {
    return [[self subviews] lastObject];
}
- (UIView *) textHolder {
    return [[[self slider] subviews] objectAtIndex:2];
}
- (UILabel *) leftLabel {
    return [[[self textHolder] subviews] objectAtIndex:0];
}
- (UILabel *) rightLabel {
    return [[[self textHolder] subviews] objectAtIndex:1];
}
- (void) setLeftLabelText: (NSString *) labelText {
    [[self leftLabel] setText:labelText];
}
- (void) setRightLabelText: (NSString *) labelText {
    [[self rightLabel] setText:labelText];
}
@end
```

Customizing `UIAlertView` Buttons

Accessing subviews enables you to customize to any number of classes. Figure 8-4 (right) shows a UIAlertView with a customized button. Colored red, it indicates the same kind of danger that's found in UIActionSheet destructive buttons. This is a hack.

The coloring is not consistent. Because UIAlertView is an undocumented button class, it does not respond to the standard tintColor calls. Instead, you must set the background color for the button. This means the color bleeds past the button edges. Fortunately, the bleeding is slight and only pendants need avoid this method. The lesson here is caution when working with nonstandard SDK classes. Many of them present using `drawRect:` calls and do not lend themselves perfectly to customization.

To work, Listing 8-4 uses the `willPresentAlertView:` delegate method. This approach enables the alert to finish building itself before customizing the button. Alert views and action sheets (along with most of the bar classes) don't completely build their component views until just before they appear onscreen. Waiting lets the subviews establish themselves before you modify them and before they appear onscreen to your user.

Listing 8-4   Coloring `UIActionSheet` Buttons

```
- (void)willPresentAlertView:(UIAlertView *)alertView
{
    [[[alertView subviews] objectAtIndex:2] setBackgroundColor:[UIColor
    ➥colorWithRed:0.5 green:0.0f blue:0.0f alpha:1.0f]];
}
```

Recipe: Adding Custom Slider Thumbs

Keeping with the modifying control elements theme, be aware that many controls offer public customization. You don't have to hack your way to the prize. The `UISlider` class, for example, enables you to change the look of its thumb component without searching through a subview hierarchy. Set this thumb to whatever image you like by calling `setThumbImage: forState:`. This next recipe changes the focus away from searching for the right view to dynamic customization. It builds the thumb art on-the-fly.

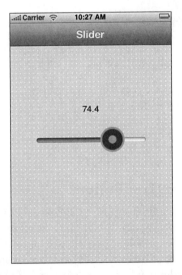

Figure 8-5   Core Graphics calls enable this slider's thumb image to dim or brighten based on the current slider value.

Recipe 8-5 builds a slider whose thumb image dynamically varies. In this case, the brightness of the thumb image correlates directly with the current slider value. A `createImage` routine builds the thumbs at runtime, as the user manipulates the slider. Core Graphics calls build the target-like image shown in Figure 8-5. The inner circle brightness is set to the slider value.

This kind of feedback could be based on any kind of data. You might grab values from onboard sensors or make calls out to the Internet. No matter what live update scheme you use, dynamic updates are certainly graphics intensive—but it's not as expensive as you might fear. The Core Graphics calls are fast, and the memory requirements for the thumb-sized images are minimal. Recipe 8-5 uses Apple sample code to create customizable bitmap contexts. It then fills that context with target-style art based on a floating-point value (`percentage`) passed to the `createImage` function. This function returns a new thumb image whenever the user interacts with the slider.

Recipe 8-5   **Building Dynamic Slider Thumbs**

```
// MyCreateBitmapContext: Source based on Apple Sample Code
CGContextRef MyCreateBitmapContext (int pixelsWide,
                                    int pixelsHigh)
{
    CGContextRef    context = NULL;
    CGColorSpaceRef colorSpace;
    void *          bitmapData;
    int             bitmapByteCount;
    int             bitmapBytesPerRow;

    bitmapBytesPerRow   = (pixelsWide * 4);
    bitmapByteCount     = (bitmapBytesPerRow * pixelsHigh);

    colorSpace = CGColorSpaceCreateDeviceRGB();
    bitmapData = malloc( bitmapByteCount );
    if (bitmapData == NULL)
    {
        fprintf (stderr, "Memory not allocated!");
        return NULL;
    }
    context = CGBitmapContextCreate (bitmapData,
                                     pixelsWide,
                                     pixelsHigh,
                                     8,
                                     bitmapBytesPerRow,
                                     colorSpace,
                                     kCGImageAlphaPremultipliedLast);
    if (context== NULL)
    {
        free (bitmapData);
```

Recipe 8-5   **Continued**

```
            fprintf (stderr, "Context not created!");
            return NULL;
        }
    CGColorSpaceRelease( colorSpace );

    return context;
}

// Build a thumb image based on the grayscale percentage
id createImage(float percentage)
{
    CGRect aRect = CGRectMake(0.0f, 0.0f, 48.0f, 48.0f);
    CGContextRef context = MyCreateBitmapContext(48, 48);
    CGContextClearRect(context, aRect);

    // Outer gray circle
    CGContextSetFillColorWithColor(context, [[UIColor lightGrayColor] CGColor]);
    CGContextFillEllipseInRect(context, aRect);

    // Inner circle with feedback levels
    CGContextSetFillColorWithColor(context, [[UIColor colorWithRed:percentage
    ➥green:0.0f blue:0.0f alpha:1.0f] CGColor]);
    CGContextFillEllipseInRect(context, CGRectInset(aRect, 4.0f, 4.0f));

    // Inner gray circle
    CGContextSetFillColorWithColor(context, [[UIColor lightGrayColor] CGColor]);
    CGContextFillEllipseInRect(context, CGRectInset(aRect, 16.0f, 16.0f));

    CGImageRef myRef = CGBitmapContextCreateImage (context);
    free(CGBitmapContextGetData(context));
    CGContextRelease(context);

    return [UIImage imageWithCGImage:myRef];
}

@interface HelloController : UIViewController
{
    UIImageView *contentView;
    UILabel *valueLabel;
    UIImage *knob;
}
@end

@implementation HelloController
- (void) updateValue: (UISlider *) slider
{
```

```
    [valueLabel setText:[NSString stringWithFormat:@"%3.1f", [slider value]]];

    CGImageRef oldknobref = [knob CGImage];
    UIImage *knob = createImage([slider value] / 100.0f);
    [slider setThumbImage:knob forState:UIControlStateNormal];
    [slider setThumbImage:knob forState:UIControlStateHighlighted];
    CFRelease(oldknobref);
}

- (void)loadView
{
    contentView = [[UIView alloc] initWithFrame:[[UIScreen mainScreen]
    ➥applicationFrame]];
    [contentView setImage:[UIImage imageNamed:@"bluedots.png"]];
    [contentView setUserInteractionEnabled:YES];
    self.view = contentView;
    [contentView release];

    // Add a text label to show the current slider scale
    valueLabel = [[UILabel alloc] initWithFrame:CGRectMake(50.0f, 100.0f, 220.0f,
    ➥40.0f)];
    valueLabel.textAlignment = UITextAlignmentCenter;
    valueLabel.text = @"50.0";
    valueLabel.backgroundColor = [UIColor clearColor];
    [contentView addSubview:valueLabel];
    [valueLabel release];

    // Build the slider
    UISlider *slider = [[UISlider alloc] initWithFrame:CGRectMake(50.0f, 160.0f,
    ➥220.0f, 40.0f)];
    slider.backgroundColor = [UIColor clearColor];
    slider.minimumValue = 0.0f;
    slider.maximumValue = 100.0f;
    slider.continuous = YES;
    slider.value = 50.0f;

    // Add the custom knob
    knob = createImage(0.5);
    [slider setThumbImage:knob forState:UIControlStateNormal];
    [slider setThumbImage:knob forState:UIControlStateHighlighted];

    [slider addTarget:self action:@selector(updateValue:)
    ➥forControlEvents:UIControlEventValueChanged];

    [contentView addSubview: slider];
    [slider release];
}
@end
```

Adding Text to the Slider

Unfortunately, text is computationally expensive. You can add text to the slider, as in Listing 8-5, but at a huge cost to normal interaction. This listing demonstrates how to put labels into a core graphics context. You'll be better off precomputing these thumb images and loading them from those precomputed images rather than generating them on-the-fly. Although this routine simulates well on a Macintosh, the iPhone's chip is too underpowered to handle the extra burden that text processing adds to live image creation. In contrast, precomputed images are cheap, both computationally and in terms of memory storage.

Keep in mind that the Quartz coordinate system starts at the bottom left, not the top left. Adding text to a point in the image uses the Quartz system.

Listing 8-5   **Adding Thumb Text**

```
id createImage(float percentage)
{
    CGRect aRect = CGRectMake(0.0f, 0.0f, 48.0f, 48.0f);
    CGContextRef context = MyCreateBitmapContext(48, 48);
    CGContextClearRect(context, aRect);

    CGContextSetFillColorWithColor(context, [[UIColor lightGrayColor] CGColor]);
    CGContextFillEllipseInRect(context, aRect);

    CGContextSetFillColorWithColor(context, [[UIColor colorWithRed:percentage
    ➥green:0.0f blue:0.0f alpha:1.0f] CGColor]);
    CGContextFillEllipseInRect(context, CGRectInset(aRect, 4.0f, 4.0f));

    CGContextSetFillColorWithColor(context, [[UIColor whiteColor] CGColor]);
    CGContextSelectFont(context, "Georgia", 14.0f, kCGEncodingMacRoman);
    CGContextSetTextDrawingMode(context, kCGTextFill);
    CGContextSetShouldAntialias(context, true);
    NSString *outString = [NSString stringWithFormat:@"%4.2f", percentage];
    CGContextShowTextAtPoint(context, 10, 20, [outString UTF8String], [outString
    ➥length]);

    CGImageRef myRef = CGBitmapContextCreateImage (context);
    free(CGBitmapContextGetData(context));
    CGContextRelease(context);

    return [UIImage imageWithCGImage:myRef];
}
```

Recipe: Dismissing a `UITextField` Keyboard

The most commonly asked question about the UITextField control is, "How do I dismiss the keyboard?" There's no built-in way to automatically detect this. When users finish editing the contents of a UITextField, the keyboard should go away.

Fortunately, it takes little work to respond to the end of edits. By watching for the Return key, you can resign first-responder status. This moves the keyboard out of sight, as Recipe 8-6 shows. Here are a few key points about doing this:

- Set the Return key type to `UIReturnKeyDone`. Using a "Done"-style Return key tells the user how to finish editing. Figure 8-6 shows a keyboard using the Done key style.

- Implement `textFieldShouldReturn:`. This method catches all return key presses—no matter how they are named. Use the method to resign first responder. This hides the keyboard until the user touches another text field or text view.

- Make sure your view controller implements the `UITextFieldDelegate` protocol and that you set the field delegate to point to your controller.

Your code needs to handle each of these points to create a smooth interaction process for your `UITextField` instances. Figure 8-6 shows `UITextField` controls in action, with the keyboard in place during a field edit.

Figure 8-6   Catch Return key presses to know when your user has finished editing a text field so you can dismiss the keyboard.

Recipe 8-6   **Using the Done Key to Dismiss a Text Field Keyboard**

```
// This method catches the Return action
- (BOOL)textFieldShouldReturn:(UITextField *)textField
{
```

Recipe 8-6   **Continued**

```
    [textField resignFirstResponder];
    return YES;
}
- (void)loadView
{
    contentView = [[UIView alloc] initWithFrame:[[UIScreen mainScreen]
    ➥applicationFrame]];
    contentView.backgroundColor = [UIColor whiteColor];
    self.view = contentView;
    [contentView release];

    // Create a field with a Done return key
    namefield = [[[UITextField alloc] initWithFrame:CGRectMake(120.0f, 40.0f,
    ➥150.0f, 30.0f)] retain];
    [namefield setBorderStyle:UITextBorderStyleRoundedRect];

    namefield.placeholder = @"name";
    namefield.returnKeyType = UIReturnKeyDone;
    namefield.clearButtonMode = UITextFieldViewModeWhileEditing;
    namefield.delegate = self;
    [contentView addSubview:namefield];
    [namefield release];
}
```

Recipe: Dismissing **UITextView** Keyboards

When dismissing keyboards, UITextView instances require a slightly different approach than UITextField ones. Users should be able to tap Return in the text view, adding carriage returns without dismissing the keyboard. Instead, add a Done button to the general interface when the text view becomes active, as Figure 8-7 shows. Use this key to resign first-responder status when the user finishes his or her edits.

To sense text view activity, your view controller must implement the UITextViewDelegate protocol, and it must be set as the text view's delegate. The textViewDidBeginEditing: delegate method triggers whenever a user taps the view. Detecting this enables you to either add or enable the Done button. Users can then tap on Done after they've finished editing. The Done button offers an obvious way to finish editing and dismiss the keyboard.

Recipe 8-7 demonstrates how to add the navigation item button in the delegate method call and how to remove it when the user is done editing. Reveal the Done button when the view becomes active. Hide it when resigning the view's first-responder status.

Figure 8-7   Add a Done key to the navigation bar when users start
interacting with a text view. This offers users an obvious way to finish
editing and dismiss the keyboard.

Recipe 8-7   Adding a Done Button to Active `UITextView` Sessions

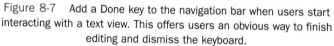

```
@interface HelloController : UIViewController <UITextViewDelegate>
{
    UITextView *contentView;
}
@end


@implementation HelloController

// Reveal a done button when editing starts
- (void) textViewDidBeginEditing: (UITextView *) textView
{
    self.navigationItem.rightBarButtonItem = [[[UIBarButtonItem alloc]
                                    initWithTitle:@"Done"
                                    style:UIBarButtonItemStyleDone
                                    target:self
                                    action:@selector(doneEditing:)]
                                    autorelease];
}

// The done button forces the text view to resign its first-responder status
- (void) doneEditing: (id) sender
```

Recipe 8-7   **Continued**

```
{
    [contentView resignFirstResponder];
    self.navigationItem.rightBarButtonItem = NULL;
}
- (void)loadView
{
    // Load an application image and set it as the primary view
    contentView = [[UITextView alloc] initWithFrame:[[UIScreen mainScreen]
    ➥applicationFrame]];
    [contentView setDelegate:self];
    self.view = contentView;
    [contentView release];
}

-(void) dealloc
{
    [contentView release];
    [super dealloc];
}
@end
```

Recipe: Adding an Undo Button to Text Views

Recipe 8-7 showed how to catch user interactions within a text view. The UITextViewDelegate protocol can also sense user-generated changes to the displayed text. The textView: shouldChangeTextInRange: replacementText: method triggers whenever the user types or deletes text within the view. By returning YES and revealing an undo button, you create the basic structure that supports reverting to the most recently saved state.

Recipe 8-8 adds persistent data to the basic structure built in Recipe 8-7. The application now saves a copy of the text to a file when users tap Done to dismiss the keyboard. During edits, if the user taps Undo, the program replaces the text view contents with the contents of that file and hides the Undo button again.

These changes ensure that the Undo button appears only when the visual text has changed from the stored text. Figure 8-8 shows the interface built by this recipe when the Undo button has been triggered by user text changes.

Figure 8-8   The Undo button at the top-left corner of the screen appears only
after the user has changed text in the text view from the most recently stored
state. Tapping Done saves any changes to the file (and hides Undo). Tapping
Undo reverts the view contents to the most recently stored version.

Recipe 8-8   **Adding Undo Support to Text Views**

```
@interface HelloController : UIViewController <UITextViewDelegate>
{
    UITextView *contentView;
    BOOL readyToUndo;
}
@end


@implementation HelloController

#define FILEPATH [NSHomeDirectory()
➥stringByAppendingPathComponent:@"Documents/MyText.txt"]
// Reveal a Done button when starting to edit
- (void) textViewDidBeginEditing: (UITextView *) textView
{
    self.navigationItem.rightBarButtonItem = [[[UIBarButtonItem alloc]
                                    initWithTitle:@"Done"
                                    style:UIBarButtonItemStyleDone
                                    target:self
                                    action:@selector(doneEditing:)]
                                    autorelease];
    readyToUndo = YES;
```

Recipe 8-8   **Continued**

```
}

// Only reveal the undo after text has actually been typed or deleted
- (BOOL)textView:(UITextView *)textView shouldChangeTextInRange:(NSRange)range
➥replacementText:(NSString *)text
{
    if (readyToUndo)
        self.navigationItem.leftBarButtonItem = [[[UIBarButtonItem alloc]
                                                 initWithTitle:@"Undo"
                                                 style:UIBarButtonItemStylePlain
                                                 target:self
                                                 action:@selector(undoEditing:)]
                                                 autorelease];

    readyToUndo = NO;
    return YES;
}

// The Done button forces the text view to resign its first-responder status and
➥saves changes
- (void) doneEditing: (id) sender
{
    NSError *error;

    [contentView resignFirstResponder];
    self.navigationItem.rightBarButtonItem = NULL;
    self.navigationItem.leftBarButtonItem = NULL;
    [[contentView text] writeToFile:FILEPATH atomically: YES
    ➥encoding:NSUTF8StringEncoding error: &error];
}

// Undo means revert to last saved state
- (void) undoEditing: (id) sender
{
    if ([[NSFileManager defaultManager] fileExistsAtPath:FILEPATH])
        [contentView setText:[NSString stringWithContentsOfFile:FILEPATH]];
    else
        [contentView setText:@""];

    readyToUndo = YES;
    self.navigationItem.leftBarButtonItem = NULL;
}

- (void)loadView
{
    // Load an application image and set it as the primary view
    contentView = [[UITextView alloc] initWithFrame:[[UIScreen mainScreen]
    ➥applicationFrame]];
    [contentView setDelegate:self];
    self.view = contentView;
```

```
    [contentView release];

    // Preload with text if any has been saved
    if ([[NSFileManager defaultManager] fileExistsAtPath:FILEPATH])
        [contentView setText:[NSString stringWithContentsOfFile:FILEPATH]];
}
@end
```

Recipe: Creating a Text View–Based HTML Editor

Although Apple officially removed HTML support from the UITextView class, it remains hidden in the UIKit framework. Access this undocumented feature when you want to add simple rich text extensions. Obviously, Apple intends you to use UIWebView rather than UITextView for HTML display, but UITextView offers an appealing alternative for low-rent markup.

To access this HTML display, declare setContentToHTMLString: as shown in Recipe 8-9. This undocumented UITextView method tells the text view to interpret a string as HTML source. Using UITextView offers a couple of small benefits:

- First, UITextViews can be edited. You can initialize the view with HTML text and then allow your user to edit the results. Text picks up the properties of the surrounding elements. If you add text to a bold headline, for example, the new text remains bolded.

- Second, UITextViews can easily be reloaded. If you allow your user to edit text in text-based source mode, for example, you can then reload those changes into the same view in HTML mode.

Recipe 8-9 shows how to build a simple HTML editor. Figure 8-9 shows both the text source and HTML presentation in the same UITextView. This is not a common (or, really, practical) use of the technology, but it highlights a feature that you may have a reason to use some day. More often, you'll just want to initialize text with a few rich text features (like a bolded headline) and then allow users to edit that text directly.

> **Note**
>
> Use NSLocalizedString to internationalize text. Pass it any key from your language folder's Localizable.strings files (for example, from French.lproj or English.lproj). NSLocalizedString(@"Title", nil) looks for the Title key in a strings file and returns the localized string that matches that key. The iPhone knows which language to use, thus which lproj folder to look in, via General, International Settings. To internationalize an application name, add an InfoPlist.strings file to each lproj folder. Set your CFBundleDisplayName key in those files. Consult Apple documents for up-to-date details after the SDK is released.

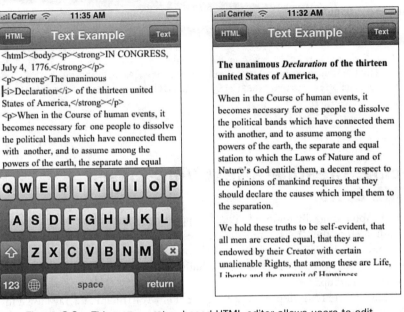

Figure 8-9   This `UITextView`-based HTML editor allows users to edit
source and see the results in the same view.

Recipe 8-9   Using Undocumented `UITextView` HTML Features

```
- (void) presentText: (id) sender
{
    // dismiss keyboard if it exists
    [contentView resignFirstResponder];
    // Store text only if previous editor was text-based
    if ([contentView tag]) self.sourceText = [contentView text];

    // Text-based Editor
    [contentView setText:self.sourceText];
    [contentView setEditable:YES];
    [contentView setTag:YES];
}

- (void) presentHTML: (id) sender
{
    // dismiss keyboard if it exists
    [contentView resignFirstResponder];

    // Store text only if previous editor was text-based
    if ([contentView tag]) self.sourceText = [contentView text];

    // HTML-based Presentation-only
```

Recipe 8-9   **Continued**

```
[contentView setContentToHTMLString:self.sourceText];
[contentView setEditable:NO];
[contentView setTag:NO];
}


- (void)loadView
{
    // Load an application image and set it as the primary view
    contentView = [[UITextView alloc] initWithFrame:[[UIScreen mainScreen]
    ➥applicationFrame]];
    [contentView setAutocorrectionType:UITextAutocorrectionTypeNo];
    [contentView setTag:NO];
    [contentView setEditable:NO];
    self.view = contentView;
    [contentView release];

    // Load the HTML source
    self.sourceText = [NSString stringWithContentsOfFile:[[NSBundle mainBundle]
    ➥pathForResource:@"decl" ofType:@"html"]];
    [contentView setContentToHTMLString:self.sourceText];

    // Add Text and HTML buttons
    self.navigationItem.rightBarButtonItem = [[[UIBarButtonItem alloc]
                                    initWithTitle:@"Text"
                                    style:UIBarButtonItemStylePlain
                                    target:self
                                    action:@selector(presentText:)]
                                    autorelease];
    self.navigationItem.leftBarButtonItem = [[[UIBarButtonItem alloc]
                                    initWithTitle:@"HTML"
                                    style:UIBarButtonItemStylePlain
                                    target:self
                                    action:@selector(presentHTML:)]
                                    autorelease];

}
```

Recipe: Building an Interactive Search Bar

The UISearchBar class offers a simple search-themed text field that's well suited for display in an application's navigation bar. Figure 8-10 shows a search bar in action, hunting among crayon names for colors that match the search term. The search is live. As users tap in text, the table automatically updates.

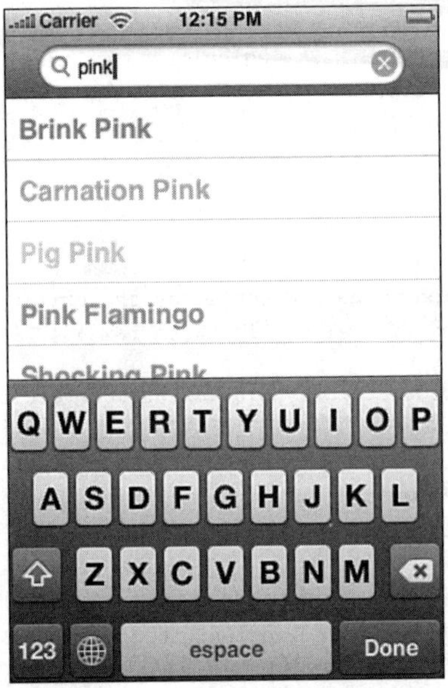

Figure 8-10   Search bars offer excellent interactive controls for
locating items in long lists.

Recipe 8-10 uses `searchBar: textDidChange:` to catch search bar text changes.
This method rebuilds the array that feeds the onscreen table as the user taps new characters.
It matches the text in the search field to items in the array.

Notice the Return key swap-out used in Figure 8-10. Normally, search bars delay
searches until the user finishes typing in a term. That's why they display Search for their
default Return key. Recipe 8-10's live interaction doesn't use that search model. Instead,
the Done key lets the user examine the results of the live search he or she has already
performed upon dismissing the keyboard.

To replace the Return key, access the `UISearchBar` instance's search field subview
and set the text traits for that field. At this time, the text view is the frontmost (that is,
last) view. Should this change in future SDK releases, adjust the recipe code accordingly.

Recipe 8-10   **Using a Search Bar with Live Feedback**

```
// create an array by matching to the search string
- (void) buildSearchArrayFrom: (NSString *) matchString
{
    NSString *upString = [[matchString uppercaseString] autorelease];
    if (searchArray) [searchArray release];

    searchArray = [[NSMutableArray alloc] init];
    for (NSString *word in colorArray)
    {
```

Recipe 8-10 **Continued**

```
        if ([matchString length] == 0)
        {
            [searchArray addObject:word];
            continue;
        }

        NSRange range = [[[[word componentsSeparatedByString:@" #"]
    ➥objectAtIndex:0] uppercaseString] rangeOfString:upString];
        if (range.location != NSNotFound) [searchArray addObject:word];
    }

    [self.tableView reloadData];
}

// When the search text changes, update the array
- (void)searchBar:(UISearchBar *)searchBar textDidChange:(NSString *)searchText
{
    [self buildSearchArrayFrom:searchText];
    if ([searchText length] == 0) [searchBar resignFirstResponder];
}

// When the search ("done") button is clicked, hide the keyboard
- (void)searchBarSearchButtonClicked:(UISearchBar *)searchBar
{
    [searchBar resignFirstResponder];
}
// Prepare the Table View
- (void)loadView
{
    [super loadView];

    // Retrieve the text and colors from file
    NSString *pathname = [[NSBundle mainBundle]  pathForResource:@"crayons"
    ➥ofType:@"txt" inDirectory:@"/"];
    NSString *wordstring = [NSString stringWithContentsOfFile:pathname];
    colorArray = [[wordstring componentsSeparatedByString:@"\n"] retain];
    [self buildSearchArrayFrom:@""];

    search = [[UISearchBar alloc] initWithFrame:CGRectMake(0.0f, 0.0f, 280.0f,
    ➥44.0f)];
    search.delegate = self;
    search.placeholder = @"color match text";
    search.autocorrectionType = UITextAutocorrectionTypeNo;
    search.autocapitalizationType = UITextAutocapitalizationTypeNone;
    self.navigationItem.titleView = search;
    [search release];

    // "Search" is the wrong key usage here. Replacing it with "Done"
```

Recipe 8-10   **Continued**

```
    UITextField *searchField = [[search subviews] lastObject];
    [searchField setReturnKeyType:UIReturnKeyDone];
}
```

Recipe: Adding Callout Views

If you've used Google Maps on the iPhone, you've likely seen UICalloutView instances in action. They are, despite their name, a kind of UIControl instance. They are undocumented but available in the UIKit framework.

Callout views point to something onscreen. They can display a temporary message before moving to another message with an attached disclosure button. Figure 8-11 shows a screen with several callout views displayed, some showing their original (temporary) message, others showing the final one. Recipe 8-11 provides the code that built this screen.

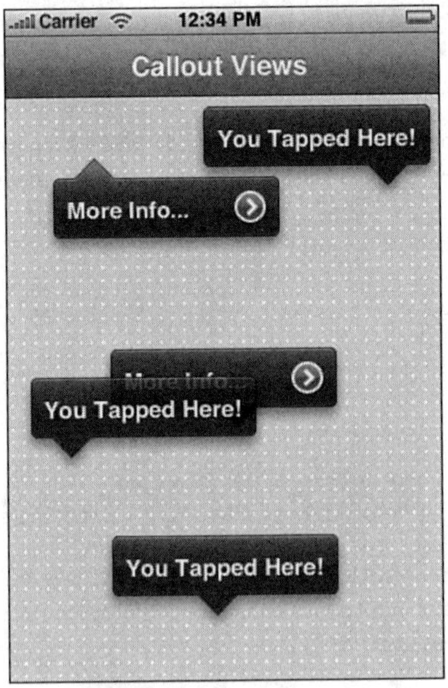

Figure 8-11   UICalloutView instances point to things. They can display an initial message (here, "You Tapped Here!") and a final message ("More Info ... " in this case) with an attached disclosure button. Callouts are used in Apple's Google Maps application.

Because the class is undocumented, you need to define headers. Listing 8-6 shows a UICalloutView class definition. It's incomplete, but it offers enough functionality that you can effectively use the class in your programs.

Listing 8-6   **Defining the `UICalloutView` Interface**

```
@class UIImageView, UILabel, UIPushButton;

@interface UICalloutView : UIControl
- (UICalloutView *)initWithFrame:(struct CGRect)aFrame;
- (void)fadeOutWithDuration:(float)duration;
- (void)setTemporaryTitle:(NSString *)fp8;
- (NSString *)temporaryTitle;
- (void)setTitle:(NSString *)fp8;
- (NSString *)title;
- (void)addTarget:(id)target action:(SEL)selector;
- (void)removeTarget:(id)target;
- (void)setAnchorPoint:(struct CGPoint)aPoint boundaryRect:(struct CGRect)aRect
➥animate:(BOOL)yorn;
@end
```

To create a callout, pass an anchor point—that's the coordinates that the callout points to—plus a generalized boundary rectangle. These bounds are, as far as I can tell, completely ignored.

The callout uses two titles: a temporary one and a normal one. When you add a temporary title, this title displays for a second or so before fading to the normal title, the one with the disclosure. You can also add subtitles to the callout, but they look horrible and I don't recommend using them.

Set the target for the disclosure by calling `addTarget: action:`. The selector you pass gets called when the disclosure is tapped. User taps on the callout don't count; they are ignored by the iPhone. So if you want to get rid of a callout when a new one appears, it's up to you to dismiss it. Use `fadeOutWithDuration:` and specify the fadeout time in seconds.

Recipe 8-11   **Using `UICalloutViews`**

```
@interface TapView : UIImageView
@end

@implementation TapView
- (void) hideDisclosure: (UIPushButton *) calloutButton
{
    UICalloutView *callout = (UICalloutView *)[calloutButton superview];
    [callout fadeOutWithDuration:1.0f];
}

- (UICalloutView *) buildDisclosure
{
    UICalloutView *callout = [[[UICalloutView alloc] initWithFrame:CGRectZero]
    ➥autorelease];
    callout.contentVerticalAlignment = UIControlContentVerticalAlignmentCenter;
```

Recipe 8-11   **Continued**

```
    callout.contentHorizontalAlignment =
UIControlContentHorizontalAlignmentCenter;

    [callout setTemporaryTitle:@"You Tapped Here!"];
    [callout setTitle:@"More Info..."];
    [callout addTarget:self action:@selector(hideDisclosure:)];

    return callout;
}


- (void) showDisclosureAt:(CGPoint) aPoint
{
    UICalloutView *callout = [self buildDisclosure];
    [self addSubview:callout];
    [callout setAnchorPoint:aPoint boundaryRect:CGRectMake(0.0f, 0.0f, 320.0f,
    ➥100.0f) animate:YES];
}


- (void) touchesBegan:(NSSet*)touches withEvent:(UIEvent*)event
{
    [self showDisclosureAt:[[touches anyObject] locationInView:self]];
}


@end
```

Adding a Page Indicator Control

Sadly, the UIPageControl class does not live up to expectations. It does not belong to the same class as the excellent version seen in SpringBoard. They look the same; they perform differently. The UIPageControl class available in the official SDK is awkward to handle, hard to tap, and will generally annoy your users. So when using it, make sure you add alternative navigation options (such as the swiping covered in Chapter 2, "Views") so that the page control acts more as an indicator and less as a control.

Figure 8-12 shows a page control in action. Taps to the left or right of the bright-colored current page indicator trigger UIControlEventValueChanged events, launching whatever method you set as the control's action. You can query the control for its new value by calling currentPage and set the available page count by adjusting the numberOfPages property.

Recipe 8-12 displays five unique pages of images, but in fact, it uses only two image views. At any given time, one view is displayed, and the other view is ready to load with the next image—regardless of whether that image is numerically before or after the current one. When the user moves to a new page, the view controller loads the new image into the unused image view and calls a UIViewAnimation block to swap between the two image views. The numeric relation between the two "pages" determine whether the swap pushes the images from right to left, or left to right.

Figure 8-12   The `UIPageControl` class offers an interactive indicator for multipage presentations. Taps to the left or right of the active dot enable users to select new pages. At least they do in theory. The page control is hard to tap and offers poor response performance.

Recipe 8-12   **Using the `UIPageControl` Indicator**

```
@interface HelloController : UIViewController
{
    SwipeView *contentView;
    int currentPage;
}
@end

@implementation HelloController
- (id)init
{
    if (!(self = [super init])) return self;
    self.title = @"Page Control";
    return self;
}

// Build and return an  animation with the given direction
```

Recipe 8-12 **Continued**

```objc
- (CATransition *) getAnimation:(NSString *) direction
{
    CATransition *animation = [CATransition animation];
    [animation setDelegate:self];
    [animation setType:kCATransitionPush];
    [animation setSubtype:direction];
    [animation setDuration:1.0f];
    [animation setTimingFunction:[CAMediaTimingFunction
    ➥functionWithName:kCAMediaTimingFunctionEaseInEaseOut]];
    return animation;
}

// Perform the page turn animation, in this case a push
- (void) pageTurn: (UIPageControl *) pageControl
{
    CATransition *transition;
    int secondPage = [pageControl currentPage];
    if ((secondPage - currentPage) > 0)
        transition = [self getAnimation:@"fromRight"];
    else
        transition = [self getAnimation:@"fromLeft"];
    UIImageView *newView = (UIImageView *)[[contentView subviews]
    ➥objectAtIndex:0];
    [newView setImage:[UIImage imageNamed:[NSString stringWithFormat:@"f%d.png",
    ➥secondPage + 1]]];
    [contentView exchangeSubviewAtIndex:0 withSubviewAtIndex:1];
    [[contentView layer] addAnimation:transition
    ➥forKey:@"transitionViewAnimation"];

    currentPage = [pageControl currentPage];
}

- (void)loadView
{
    UIView *baseView = [[[UIView alloc] initWithFrame:[[UIScreen mainScreen]
    ➥applicationFrame]] autorelease];

    // Add the content view with its two images
    contentView = [[[SwipeView alloc] initWithFrame:[[UIScreen mainScreen]
    ➥applicationFrame]] autorelease];
    [contentView setHost:self];

    [contentView addSubview:[[UIImageView alloc] initWithFrame:[[UIScreen
    ➥mainScreen] applicationFrame]]];
    [contentView addSubview:[[UIImageView alloc] initWithFrame:[[UIScreen
    ➥mainScreen] applicationFrame]]];
```

Recipe 8-12   **Continued**

```
    for (UIView *view in [contentView subviews])   [view
➥setUserInteractionEnabled:NO];

    // initialize with "page" 3
    [[[contentView subviews] lastObject] setImage:[UIImage imageNamed:@"f3.png"]];

    [baseView addSubview:contentView];

    // Add the page control
    UIPageControl *pageControl = [[UIPageControl alloc]
➥initWithFrame:CGRectMake(0.0f, 10.0f, 320.0f, 20.0f)];
    [pageControl setNumberOfPages:5];
    [pageControl setCurrentPage:(currentPage = 2)];
    [pageControl addTarget:self action:@selector(pageTurn:)
➥forControlEvents:UIControlEventValueChanged];
    [baseView addSubview:pageControl];
    self.view = baseView;
}

-(void) dealloc
{
    [contentView release];
    [super dealloc];
}
@end
```

Recipe: Customizing Toolbars

The UITabBar class officially supports customization. The UIToolbar class does not. You
can drag view controller buttons into and out of a tab bar from its More screen. With
the toolbar, you cannot. At least you cannot do so officially.

Unofficially, the UIToolbar offers a similar (but undocumented) interaction style.
Although you can't add new items or switch items out, you can reorder the toolbar. It's
not an especially flexible interaction style, but you might be able to use it to enable users
to customize how they want your toolbar to appear or let them rearrange Scrabble letters.
The use is up to you. As with all undocumented calls in public frameworks, you are free
to use them in your program, but they can change without notice. Figure 8-13 shows
the toolbar customization screen in action.

All objects in the toolbar appear in the customization screen. That means if you
include fixed or flexible spaces, they'll show up there as well as your icons. You must add
an external way to finish editing the toolbar because once you enter the customization
mode, triggered actions stop working from the toolbar buttons. That's the role of the
Done button at the top right of the screen.

Recipe 8-13 shows how to add toolbar customization. It extends the UIToolbar class to reveal the undocumented begin and end customizing methods.

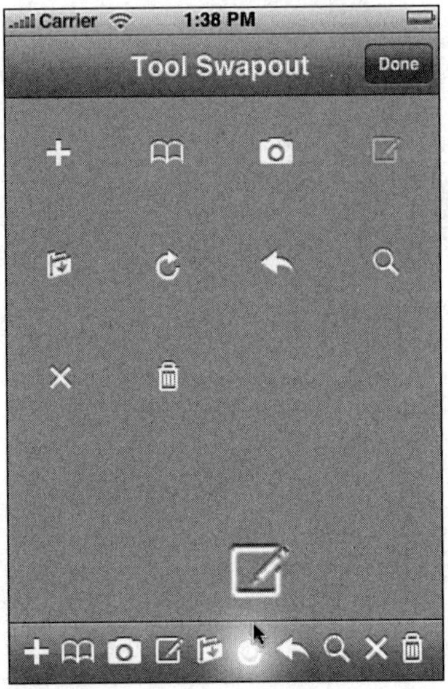

Figure 8-13   The undocumented UIToolbar customization screen allows users to reorder toolbar items.

Recipe 8-13   **Customizing Toolbars**

```
// Expose the customizing calls
@interface UIToolbar (extended)
- (void)beginCustomizingItems:(id)fp8;
- (BOOL)endCustomizingAnimated:(BOOL)fp8;
@end;

@interface HelloController : UIViewController
{
    UIImageView *contentView;
    UIToolbar *toolbar;
    NSMutableArray *allitems;
}
@end

@implementation HelloController

// When finished customizing, remove the Done button
- (void) endEditing
```

Recipe 8-13 **Continued**

```
{
    [toolbar endCustomizingAnimated:YES];
    self.navigationItem.rightBarButtonItem = NULL;
}


// Reveal the Done button and begin customizing
- (void) doAction: (id) sender
{
    [toolbar beginCustomizingItems:allitems];
    self.navigationItem.rightBarButtonItem = [[[UIBarButtonItem alloc]
                                     initWithTitle:@"Done"
                                     style:UIBarButtonItemStylePlain
                                     target:self
                                     action:@selector(endEditing)]
                                     autorelease];
}


- (void)loadView
{

    // Load an application image and set it as the primary view
    contentView = [[UIView alloc] initWithFrame:[[UIScreen mainScreen]
    ➥applicationFrame]];
    [contentView setImage:[UIImage imageNamed:@"bluedots.png"]];
    [contentView setUserInteractionEnabled:YES];
    self.view = contentView;
    [contentView release];

    toolbar = [[UIToolbar alloc] initWithFrame:CGRectMake(0.0f, 416.0f - 44.0f,
    ➥320.0f, 44.0f)];

    // Add a whole bunch of arbitrary system items with icons
    allitems = [[NSMutableArray alloc] init];
    [allitems addObject:[[[UIBarButtonItem alloc]
initWithBarButtonSystemItem:UIBarButtonSystemItemAdd target:self action:@
➥selector(doAction:)] autorelease]];
    [allitems addObject:[[[UIBarButtonItem alloc]
initWithBarButtonSystemItem:UIBarButtonSystemItemBookmarks target:self
➥action:@selector(doAction:)] autorelease]];
    [allitems addObject:[[[UIBarButtonItem alloc]
initWithBarButtonSystemItem:UIBarButtonSystemItemCamera target:self action:@
➥selector(doAction:)] autorelease]];
    [allitems addObject:[[[UIBarButtonItem alloc]
initWithBarButtonSystemItem:UIBarButtonSystemItemCompose target:self
➥action:@selector(doAction:)] autorelease]];
    [allitems addObject:[[[UIBarButtonItem alloc]
initWithBarButtonSystemItem:UIBarButtonSystemItemOrganize target:self
➥action:@selector(doAction:)] autorelease]];
```

```
    [allitems addObject:[[[UIBarButtonItem alloc]
initWithBarButtonSystemItem:UIBarButtonSystemItemRefresh target:self
➥action:@selector(doAction:)] autorelease]];
    [allitems addObject:[[[UIBarButtonItem alloc]
initWithBarButtonSystemItem:UIBarButtonSystemItemReply target:self action:@
➥selector(doAction:)] autorelease]];
    [allitems addObject:[[[UIBarButtonItem alloc]
initWithBarButtonSystemItem:UIBarButtonSystemItemSearch target:self action:@
➥selector(doAction:)] autorelease]];
    [allitems addObject:[[[UIBarButtonItem alloc]
initWithBarButtonSystemItem:UIBarButtonSystemItemStop target:self action:@
➥selector(doAction:)] autorelease]];
    [allitems addObject:[[[UIBarButtonItem alloc]
initWithBarButtonSystemItem:UIBarButtonSystemItemTrash target:self action:@
➥selector(doAction:)] autorelease]];

    [toolbar setItems:allitems];
    [contentView addSubview:toolbar];
    [toolbar release];
}

-(void) dealloc
{
    [toolbar release];
    [allitems release];
    [contentView release];
    [super dealloc];
}
@end
```

Toolbar Tips

When working with toolbars, here are a few tricks of the trade that might come in handy:

- **Fixed spaces can have widths.**

    Of all UIBarButtonItems, only UIBarButtonSystemItemFixedSpace items can be assigned a width. So create the spacer item, set its width, and only then add it to your items array.

    ```
    UIBarButtonItem *spacer = [[[UIBarButtonItem alloc]
    initWithBarButtonSystemItem:UIBarButtonSystemItemFixedSpace
    target:NULL action:NULL] autorelease];
    spacer.width = 20;
    [items addObject:spacer];
    ```

- **Use a single flexible space for left or right alignment.**

  Adding a single `UIBarButtonSystemItemFlexibleSpace` at the start of an items list right-aligns all the remaining items. Adding one to the end, left-aligns. Use two, one at the start and one at the end to create center alignments.

- **Take missing items into account.**

  When hiding bar button items due to context, don't just use flexible spacing to get rid of the item. Instead, replace the item with a fixed-width space that matches the item's original size. That preserves the layout and leaves all the other icons in the same position both before and after the item disappears.

- **Bar button items aren't views.**

  If you ever need to add a subview to one, give it a proper parent and let that parent (whether it's a toolbar, tab bar, or navigation bar) build it onscreen. You can then use the undocumented `view` call to recover the bar button item's view.

Summary

This chapter introduced many nonstandard (and in some cases nonofficial and undocumented) ways to interact with and get the most from the controls in your applications. Before you move on to the next chapter, here are a few thoughts for you to ponder:

- Don't be afraid to peek into controls and discover how they're put together. Once you have exposed standard SDK classes like labels or buttons, customize them to your specifications and desires.

- Just because an item belongs to the `UIControl` class doesn't mean you can't treat it like a `UIView`. Give it subviews, resize it, animate it, move it around the screen, or tag it for later.

- Core Graphics lets you build visual elements as needed. Combine the comfort of the SDK classes with a little real-time wow to add punch to your presentation.

- As with the search bar keyboard example, don't let Apple's preconceived notions about how a control should be used stand in the way of using it the way you think you should. If "search" doesn't describe what users need to do at the end of an interaction, switch the Return button to a better phrase that does.

- Callout views are just one of many undocumented classes that ship with `UIKit` and add richness to your applications.

- This chapter covered a lot of undocumented classes and calls. As with all undocumented and unofficial material, use with due care in your production software.

People, Places, and Things

In addition to standard user interface controls and media components that you'd see on any computer, the iPhone SDK provides a number of tightly focused developer solutions specific to iPhone and iPod touch delivery. These classes and routines access narrow iPhone core functionality. The most useful of these include Address Book access ("people"), Core Location ("places"), and sensors ("things"). Each of these personalizes the iPhone: where you are, who you know, and how you hold the phone. This chapter presents recipes that show you how to use these technologies in your own development work.

Address Book Frameworks

The iPhone SDK provides two address book frameworks: AddressBook.framework and AddressBookUI.framework. As their names suggest, they occupy two distinct niches in the iPhone SDK. Address Book contains low-level C-based structures and routines for accessing contact information from the iPhone's onboard SQLite databases. Address Book UI provides high-level Objective-C based `UIViewController` browser objects to present to users. Both frameworks are small. They provide just a few classes and data types.

On the iPhone, contact data resides in the home Library folder. On the Macintosh simulator, you can freely access these files in ~/Library/Application Support/iPhone Simulator/User/Library. The two files, AddressBook/AddressBook.sqlitedb and AddressBook/AddressBookImages.sqlitedb use standard SQLite3 to store contact information and optional contact images. On the iPhone, you cannot access these directly. The files live in /var/mobile/Library/AddressBook. You must either use the two Address Book frameworks or break out of the sandbox. The latter may invalidate any application's App Store eligibility.

Address Book UI

The Address Book UI framework provides a few precooked views that interact with the onboard contacts database. These include a general people picker, a one-contact display, and a contact editor. You set a delegate and then push these controllers onto your navigation stack or display them modally, as shown in the recipes in this chapter.

Like the Image Picker and Camera controllers you saw in Chapter 7, "Media," the Address Book UI controllers are not very flexible. Apple intends you to use them as provided, with little or no customization from the developer. What's more, they require a certain degree of low-level programming prowess. As you'll see, these classes interact with the underlying Address Book in circuitous ways.

Address Book

In the C-based Address Book framework, the ABPerson type provides the core contact structure. This record stores all information for each contact, including name, e-mail, phone numbers, and so forth. Because each person may have multiple e-mails, phone numbers, and important dates associated with his or her contact, ABPerson uses a convoluted "multivalue" structure to store that information. In normal programming terms, this means an array. In Address Book terms, this involves a little extra programming.

Handling People Picker Calls

Because dates, strings, and numbers all use different typing, Address Book provides functions to help you store and recover mixed type data to and from the contact data files. If you're looking for clean Objective-C or Core Foundation calls, look again.

When responding to GUI interactions via the AddressBookUI people picker, you generally recover untyped multivalued properties. That is, you copy a value from the ABPerson record without knowing exactly what it is you have copied. You must request the property type and then provide separate handling for each type, extracting the actual value from its array. For example

```
id theProperty = [(id)ABRecordCopyValue(person, property) autorelease];
int propertyType = ABPersonGetTypeOfProperty(property);
if (propertyType == kABMultiStringPropertyType)
    NSString *result = [(NSString *)[(NSArray
➥*)ABMultiValueCopyArrayOfAllValues(theProperty) objectAtIndex:identifier]
➥autorelease];
```

Here, the copy value function extracts a property, which is handed off to get a property type. Testing this property type against all known kinds lets you identify a class for the extracted property and provide a typed result object.

Fortunately, this kind of complex untyped handling is limited to interactively selecting properties like a phone number, e-mail address, or street address. It's much easier to let users select an entire contact at once and recover general information from that contact.

Querying the Address Book and Its Records

Direct database searches are definitely simpler than responding to the GUI. To request a list of all available contacts (businesses as well as individuals), call the "all people" function. This returns an array of all available ABPersons. The badly named create function seen here returns an Address Book reference populated with data from your entire Contacts database. You're not actually creating a new Address Book. You're just supplying the copy array function with a link to the existing one:

```
peopleArray = (NSMutableArray
➥*)ABAddressBookCopyArrayOfAllPeople(ABAddressBookCreate());
```

Query `ABPerson` records to pull out any and all properties. There are quite a number of them, about 17 if I counted correctly. They range from birthdays and middle names to e-mail addresses and job titles. Some of these return a string or an integer, others a dictionary or a date. Some return a single value (people rarely have multiple first names), others return arrays (people often have many e-mail addresses).

Here are ways to pull out a contact's first name, last name, and organization from an `ABPerson` record. Each of these returns a string. Notice how the `ABRecordCopyValue` function returns an untyped value. Know these property types in advance or call `ABPersonGetTypeOfProperty()` to request the type:

```
NSString *firstName = [(NSString *)ABRecordCopyValue(person,
➥kABPersonFirstNameProperty) autorelease];
NSString *lastName = [(NSString *)ABRecordCopyValue(person,
➥kABPersonLastNameProperty) autorelease];
NSString *biz = [(NSString *)ABRecordCopyValue(person,
➥kABPersonOrganizationProperty) autorelease];
```

Recipe: Accessing Address Book Image Data

Some Address Book contacts may use photo data. Others may not. Associated images offer an elegant way to match people to faces and enhance the iPhone experience. When used, pictures are stored in the AddressBookImages.sqlitedb database. To check whether a photo is available, call `ABPersonHasImageData(person)`, where `person` is an `ABPerson` record. This returns `YES` or `NO`, indicating whether you can request image data.

When `YES`, call `ABPersonCopyImageData(person)` to provide the `NSData` reference that you can use to fill a `UIImage` object. Here's a typical call to add image data to a `UITableCell`:

```
if (ABPersonHasImageData(person)) {
    UIImage *img = [UIImage imageWithData:(NSData
    ➥*)ABPersonCopyImageData(person)];
    [cell setImage:img];
} else { [cell setImage:NULL]; }
```

Unfortunately, photos do not conform to any native sizing. One image may be thumbnail sized, whereas another is full screen. Recipe 9-1 demonstrates how to access and resize contact images to fit a standard thumbnail size that you specify, in this case 60 by 60 pixels. This recipe returns table cells populated with address information and (where possible) a 60x60 contact image. To do this, it creates a custom bitmap context and fills that context with the scaled image.

Note
This code calls the `MyCreateBitmapContext` function, which can be found in Recipe 8-5.

Recipe 9-1   **Accessing and Resizing Contact Images**

```
#define IMG_SIZE    60

// Draw the image into a 60x60 bitmap and use that bitmap to
// create a new UIImage
id createImage(CGImageRef image)
{
    // Set the size of the output image
    CGRect aRect = CGRectMake(0.0f, 0.0f, IMG_SIZE, IMG_SIZE);

    // Create a bitmap context to store the new thumbnail
    CGContextRef context = MyCreateBitmapContext(IMG_SIZE, IMG_SIZE);

    // Clear the context and draw the image into the rectangle
    CGContextClearRect(context, aRect);
    CGContextDrawImage(context, aRect, image);

    // Return a UIImage populated with the new thumbnail
    CGImageRef myRef = CGBitmapContextCreateImage (context);
    free(CGBitmapContextGetData(context));
    CGContextRelease(context);

    return [UIImage imageWithCGImage:myRef];
}

// Return the string that best represents the contact name
// or organization
- (NSString *) getName: (ABRecordRef) person
{
    NSString *firstName = [(NSString *)ABRecordCopyValue(person,
    ➥kABPersonFirstNameProperty) autorelease];
    NSString *lastName = [(NSString *)ABRecordCopyValue(person,
    ➥kABPersonLastNameProperty) autorelease];
    NSString *biz = [(NSString *)ABRecordCopyValue(person,
    ➥kABPersonOrganizationProperty) autorelease];

    if ((!firstName) && !(lastName))
    {
        if (biz) return biz;
```

```
        return @"[No name supplied]";
    }

    if (!lastName) lastName = @"";
    if (!firstName) firstName = @"";

    return [NSString stringWithFormat:@"%@ %@", firstName, lastName];
}

// Provide a table cell that contains the contact name and,
// where possible, a contact image
- (UITableViewCell *)tableView:(UITableView *)tableView
➥cellForRowAtIndexPath:(NSIndexPath *)indexPath
{
    NSInteger row = [indexPath row];
    UITableViewCell *cell = [self.tableView
    ➥dequeueReusableCellWithIdentifier:@"any-cell"];
    if (cell == nil)
        cell = [[[UITableViewCell alloc] initWithFrame:CGRectZero
        ➥reuseIdentifier:@"any-cell"] autorelease];

    id person = [searchArray objectAtIndex:row];
    cell.text = [self getName:person];

    // Set the cell image when image data is available
    if (ABPersonHasImageData(person))
    {
        UIImage *img = createImage([[UIImage imageWithData:(NSData *)
        ➥ABPersonCopyImageData(person)] CGImage]);
        [cell setImage:img];
    }
    else [cell setImage:NULL];

    return cell;
}
```

Recipe: Displaying Address Book Information

The AddressBookUI framework simplifies contact information display. Use an
ABPersonViewController instance to present the data stored in an ABPerson record,
as shown in Figure 9-1. AddressBookUI takes all the design details out of the equation,
creating a perfect layout. As Recipe 9-2 shows, just allocate the controller, set the
displayedPerson to an ABPerson record, and then push the view controller into
place.

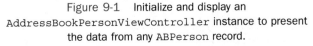

Figure 9-1   Initialize and display an
AddressBookPersonViewController instance to present
the data from any ABPerson record.

Recipe 9-2   **Using the ABPersonViewController**

```
- (void)tableView:(UITableView *)tableView didSelectRowAtIndexPath:(NSIndexPath
➥*)newIndexPath
{
    ABPersonViewController *pvc = [[ABPersonViewController alloc] init];
    pvc.displayedPerson = [searchArray objectAtIndex:[newIndexPath row]];
    [[self navigationController] pushViewController:pvc animated:YES];
}
```

Recipe: Browsing the Address Book

The AddressBookUI framework offers several launchable controllers. Browsing your
entire Contacts list turns out to be just as easily accomplished as displaying an individual
contact screen. Use the ABPeoplePickerNavigationController class to present an
interactive browser, as shown in Figure 9-2. Here's the code that created that figure:

```
ABPeoplePickerNavigationController *ab = [[ABPeoplePickerNavigationController
➥alloc] init];
[ab setPeoplePickerDelegate:self];
[self presentModalViewController:ab animated:YES];
```

What remains tricky is deciding when to navigate away and how to recover any selected data. Three delegate methods control how your picker reacts to user interactions. You specify how to react after users tap a contact, or any of a contact's properties, or when the user taps Cancel:

- `peoplePickerNavigationController:`
  `➥shouldContinueAfterSelectingPerson:`

  When users tap a contact, you have two choices. You can accept the person as the final selection and dismiss the modal view controller, or you can navigate to the individual display seen in Figure 9-1. To pick just the person, this method must return NO. To continue to the individual screen, return YES. The second argument contains the selected person, in case you want to stop after selecting any ABPerson record.

- `peoplePickerNavigationController:`
  `➥shouldContinueAfterSelectingPerson: property: identifier:`

  This optional method does not get called until the user has progressed to an individual contact display screen, like the one shown in Figure 9-1. Then, it's up to you whether to return control to your program (return NO) or to continue (return YES). Recipe 9-3 demonstrates how to determine which property has been tapped and to recover its value. This is, unfortunately, both ugly and complicated.

Figure 9-2   The iPhone people picker navigation
control enables users to search through the contacts
database and select a person or organization.

- `peoplePickerNavigationControllerDidCancel:`

  After a user taps Cancel, you'll want to dismiss the modal view. Catch the cancel event by implementing this delegate method and use it to perform the dismissal.

Recipe 9-3   Handling People Picker Events

```
// Handle the tap on a username

- (BOOL) peoplePickerNavigationController:(ABPeoplePickerNavigationController
➡*)peoplePicker shouldContinueAfterSelectingPerson:(ABRecordRef)person
{
    self.title = [self getName:person];
    return YES; // continue to secondary screen
}


// Handle the tap on a user property
- (BOOL) peoplePickerNavigationController:(ABPeoplePickerNavigationController
➡*)peoplePicker shouldContinueAfterSelectingPerson:(ABRecordRef)person
➡property:(ABPropertyID)property identifier:(ABMultiValueIdentifier)identifier
{
    // Get the selected property and its property type
    id theProperty = (id)ABRecordCopyValue(person, property);
    int propertyType = ABPersonGetTypeOfProperty(property);

    // determine the kind of property passed and
    // print out its value to the debugging console
    if (propertyType == kABStringPropertyType) {
        printf("%s\n", [theProperty UTF8String]);
     } else if (propertyType == kABIntegerPropertyType) {
        printf("%d\n", [theProperty integerValue]);
     } else if (propertyType == kABRealPropertyType) {
        printf("%d\n", [theProperty floatValue]);
     } else if (propertyType == kABDateTimePropertyType) {
        printf("%s\n", [[theProperty description] UTF8String]);
     } else if (propertyType == kABMultiStringPropertyType) {
        printf("%s\n",
                  [[(NSArray *)ABMultiValueCopyArrayOfAllValues(theProperty)
                  ➡objectAtIndex:identifier] UTF8String]);
     } else if (propertyType == kABMultiIntegerPropertyType) {
        printf("%d\n",   [[(NSArray
➡*)ABMultiValueCopyArrayOfAllValues(theProperty) objectAtIndex:identifier]
➡integerValue]);
      } else if (propertyType == kABMultiRealPropertyType) {
        printf("%f\n",   [[(NSArray
➡*)ABMultiValueCopyArrayOfAllValues(theProperty) objectAtIndex:identifier]
➡floatValue]);
      } else if (propertyType == kABMultiDateTimePropertyType) {
        printf("%s\n",   [[[(NSArray
➡*)ABMultiValueCopyArrayOfAllValues(theProperty) objectAtIndex:identifier]
➡description] UTF8String]);
```

Recipe 9-3 **Continued**

```
    } else if (propertyType == kABMultiDictionaryPropertyType) {
        printf("%s\n",    [[[(NSArray
➡*)ABMultiValueCopyArrayOfAllValues(theProperty) objectAtIndex:identifier]
➡description] UTF8String]);
    }

    [self dismissModalViewControllerAnimated:YES];
    CFRelease(theProperty);
    [peoplePicker release];
    return NO; // leave the picker after printing property
}

// Handle a user's Cancel tap
- (void) peoplePickerNavigationControllerDidCancel:
➡(ABPeoplePickerNavigationController *)peoplePicker
{
    [self dismissModalViewControllerAnimated:YES];
    [peoplePicker release];
}
```

Browsing for (Only) E-Mail Addresses

When you want users to pick, for example, an e-mail address, you won't want to present them with a person's street address or fax number. Instead, you can limit the people picker's displayed properties to show just those items you want the users to select from. To make this happen, choose the displayed properties by submitting an array of property types to the controller:

```
ABPeoplePickerNavigationController *ab = [[ABPeoplePickerNavigationController
➡alloc] init];
[ab setDisplayedProperties:[NSArray arrayWithObject:[NSNumber
➡numberWithInt:kABPersonEmailProperty]]];
```

Adding New Contacts

The ABNewPersonViewController class provides an interactive way to add new contacts to your Address Book. Unfortunately, at the time of writing, this class was not fully implemented by Apple. At some future point, here's how the class will work. The method shown here presets the person's first and last name, but that's not mandatory:

```
- (void) presentSheet
{
    ABNewPersonViewController *np = [[ABNewPersonViewController
➡alloc] init];
    np.addressBook = ABAddressBookCreate();
```

```
ABRecordRef aRecord = ABPersonCreate();
CFErrorRef anError;

ABRecordSetValue(aRecord, kABPersonFirstNameProperty,
➥CFSTR("Katie"), &anError);
ABRecordSetValue(aRecord, kABPersonLastNameProperty,
➥CFSTR("Bell"), &anError);
np.displayedPerson = aRecord;
CFRelease(aRecord);

np.newPersonViewDelegate = self;
[self presentModalViewController:np animated:YES];
}
```

Core Location

Core Location powers one of the nicest iPhone SDK features. This service returns (approximate) on-demand geopositioning with latitude and longitude data for iPhones and iPod touch units without built-in GPS and (pinpoint-precise) positioning for those units with GPS. Adding location to applications opens up a whole new programming arena where your computer becomes as important as what you compute. You can meet up with friends, search for local resources, or provide location-based streams of personal information.

Core Location enables applications to hook into location-aware social networking and data storage sites like fireeagle.com, outside.in, upcoming.org, twitter.com, and flickr.com. It lets you provide geotagged content or request local resources such as restaurant and events listings. With on-demand geolocation, mobile computing takes on new meaning and opens a wide range of Web 2.0 options.

How Core Location Works

The iPhone uses three (or possibly four) methods to locate you. These technologies depend on several providers including Skyhook Wireless (http://skyhookwireless.com, aka http://loki.com), Google Maps (http://maps.google.com/) and the U.S. Department of Defense Global Positioning System (http://tycho.usno.navy.mil/gpsinfo.html).

GPS Positioning

If you own a newer-model 3G iPhone, the onboard GPS system tracks your movement courtesy of a series of medium Earth orbit satellites provided by the U.S. Department of Defense. These satellites emit microwave signals, which your iPhone picks up and uses to triangulate your position to a high level of accuracy. Like any GPS system, this requires a clear path between you and the satellites, so it works best outdoors and away from trees.

GPS positioning is not currently available for the first generation 2.5G iPhone or the iPod touch line.

SkyHook WiFi Positioning

Core Location's preferred pseudo-GPS geopositioning method calls on SkyHook Wireless. SkyHook offers extremely accurate WiFi placement. When an iPhone knows the WiFi and WiMax routers you are near, it uses their MAC addresses to search SkyHook's databases, positioning you from that data.

SkyHook WiFi data collection works like this. SkyHook sends drivers down city streets throughout its covered territories, which includes most U.S. metropolitan areas. The cars scan for WiFi hotspots and when found, they record the location using traditional GPS positioning matched to the WiFi MAC address.

This works great when WiFi routers stay still. This works terribly when people pack up their WiFi routers and move with them to, say, Kentucky. That having been said, SkyHook data does get updated. It provides pretty accurate positioning and can usually locate you within a few hundred feet of your actual location, even though people and their routers will continue to move to Kentucky and other places.

Google Maps Cell Tower Positioning

A less-accurate approach involves Google Maps and cell tower positioning. Here, the iPhone uses its antenna to find the nearest four or five cell towers and then triangulates your position based on the cell tower signal strength. You've probably seen cell tower location in action; it's the kind that shows you about a half mile away from where you are standing—assuming you're not standing right next to an actual cell tower.

Curiously enough, SkyHook also offers cell tower positioning, but when I last explored the iPhone frameworks, the calls went out to Google. This may change based on Apple licensing agreements. Yahoo! ZoneTag also offers a free cell tower positioning API, which is newer and less accurate than Google's, but it is open, with a public API.

iPod touch units cannot use cell tower positioning, although both first- and second-generation iPhones can.

SkyHook Internet Provider Positioning

SkyHook actually offers a third positioning approach, but it is one I've never seen the iPhone use. Then again, I live in a major metropolitan area; I haven't given it a very good try. This last-ditch approach uses an Internet provider location to find the nearest mapped Internet provider's central office. This is a solution of last resort. The returned data is typically up to several miles off your actual location—unless you happen to be visiting your Internet provider.

Hybridizing the Approaches

The iPhone approaches location in stages. Based on the accuracy level you request, it uses a fallback method. If it cannot accurately locate you with GPS or SkyHook WiFi mapping, it falls back to the cell tower location of Google Maps. If that doesn't work, it presumably falls back further to SkyHook Internet provider location. And if that doesn't work, it finally fails. The latest releases of the SDK actually provide multiple (asynchronous!) success callbacks for each of these fallback methods. You may receive three or four results at any time.

Knowing how the iPhone does this is important. That's because any ten attempts to grab your location on a first generation iPhone may result in maybe three or four WiFi successes, the remainder falling back to cell tower hits. Although you can set your desired location accuracy to the highest possible settings (this is kCLLocationAccuracyBest, and I always do so), unless you make multiple requests, you might miss out on catching the best possible location.

The cost to this is time. A location request may take 10 or 15 seconds. Working with multiple requests, averaging and best-results repetition is best done in the background away from the GUI. When possible, avoid making your user wait for your program to finish its location queries.

Note

Apple requires that users authorize all location requests. Also, you cannot create turn-by-turn applications according to App Store terms. Keep these limitations in mind when developing your applications.

Recipe: Core Location in a Nutshell

Core Location is easy to use. Get started by following these simple steps. They walk you through the process of setting up your program to request latitude and longitude:

1. **Add the Core Location framework.** Drag it into your Xcode project and add it to the Frameworks folder in the Groups & Files column.

2. **Use the proper include files.** You need to include both CoreLocation.h and CLLocationManagerDelegate.h:

   ```
   #import <CoreLocation/CoreLocation.h>

   #import <CoreLocation/CLLocationManagerDelegate.h>
   ```

3. **Allocate a location manager.** Set its delegate to your primary view controller and set it to use the best accuracy available.

   ```
   locmanager = [[CLLocationManager alloc] init];

   [locmanager setDelegate:self];

   [locmanager setDesiredAccuracy:kCLLocationAccuracyBest];
   ```

4. **Start locating.** Tell the location manager to start updating the location. Delegate callbacks will let you know when the location has been found. This can take many seconds or up to a minute:

   ```
   [locmanager startUpdatingLocation];
   ```

5. **Handle the location events.** You'll deal with two types of callbacks: successes that return CLLocation data and failures that do not. Add the delegate methods that handle each situation. In Recipe 9-4, the success callback recovers the latitude and longitude information and launches Google Maps to display that position. Depending on your requested accuracy, you may get three or four location callbacks based on the various location methods used and the requested accuracy, so take this nonlinearity into account.

6. **Repeat.** If you can afford the time—location requests can take 10 or 20 seconds each—consider repeating the location several times to recover the best possible accuracy. The location information returns both horizontal and vertical accuracy measures that you can use to evaluate how accurate the positioning was.

Recipe 9-4   **Using Core Location to Retrieve Latitude and Longitude**

```
#import <CoreLocation/CoreLocation.h>
#import <CoreLocation/CLLocationManagerDelegate.h>

@interface HelloController : UIViewController <CLLocationManagerDelegate>
{
    UITextView          *contentView;
    CLLocationManager   *locmanager;
    BOOL                isLocating;
    BOOL                wasFound;
}
@end

@implementation HelloController

// Perform a location request - either start or stop locating
- (void) doIt
{
    if (isLocating)
    {
        [contentView setText:@"Scanning ended by request."];
        [locmanager stopUpdatingLocation];
        self.navigationItem.rightBarButtonItem = [[[UIBarButtonItem alloc]
                                                  initWithTitle:@"Find Me"
                                                  style:UIBarButtonItemStylePlain
                                                  target:self
                                                  action:@selector(doIt)]
                                                  autorelease];
    } else {
        wasFound = NO;
        [contentView setText:@"Scanning for location..."];
        self.navigationItem.rightBarButtonItem = [[[UIBarButtonItem alloc]
                                                  initWithTitle:@"Stop"
                                                  style:UIBarButtonItemStylePlain
                                                  target:self
                                                  action:@selector(doIt)]
                                                  autorelease];
        [locmanager startUpdatingLocation];
    }
    isLocating = !isLocating;
}
```

Recipe 9-4   **Continued**

```
- (void)locationManager:(CLLocationManager *)manager
➥didUpdateToLocation:(CLLocation *)newLocation fromLocation:(CLLocation
➥*)oldLocation
{
    // respond to the first location callback only
    if (wasFound) return;
    wasFound = YES;

    // Log the accuracy
    NSLog(@"%f %f", [newLocation horizontalAccuracy], [newLocation
    ➥verticalAccuracy]);

    // Location has been found. Create Google Maps URL
    CLLocationCoordinate2D loc = [newLocation coordinate];

    NSString *mapString = [NSString stringWithFormat:
    ➥ @"http://maps.google.com/maps?q=%f,%f", loc.latitude, loc.longitude];
    NSURL *url = [NSURL URLWithString:mapString];

    // Switch to Safari and display that map
    [[UIApplication sharedApplication] openURL:url];
}

- (void)locationManager:(CLLocationManager *)manager didFailWithError:(NSError
➥*)error
{
    self.navigationItem.rightBarButtonItem = [[[UIBarButtonItem alloc]
                                           initWithTitle:@"Find Me"
                                           style:UIBarButtonItemStylePlain
                                           target:self
                                           action:@selector(doIt)]
                                           autorelease];
    [contentView setText:@"Location search failed"];
    isLocating = NO;
}

- (void)loadView
{
    contentView = [[UITextView alloc] initWithFrame:[[UIScreen mainScreen]
    ➥applicationFrame]];
    [contentView setEditable:NO];
    self.view = contentView;
    [contentView release];

    locmanager = [[CLLocationManager alloc] init];
    [locmanager setDelegate:self];
    [locmanager setDesiredAccuracy:kCLLocationAccuracyBest];
```

Recipe 9-4 **Continued**

```
    isLocating = NO;

    if (!locmanager.locationServicesEnabled)
    {
        [contentView setText:@"Location Services Are Not Enabled"];
        return;
    }

    self.navigationItem.rightBarButtonItem = [[[UIBarButtonItem alloc]
                                              initWithTitle:@"Find Me"
                                              style:UIBarButtonItemStylePlain
                                              target:self
                                              action:@selector(doIt)]
                                              autorelease];

}

-(void) dealloc
{
    [contentView release];
    [super dealloc];
}
@end
```

Recipe: Reverse Geocoding to an Address

The phrase *reverse geocoding* means transforming latitude and longitude information into human-recognizable address information. Yahoo's ZoneTag service provides free, limited reverse geocoding for noncommercial use. To get started, sign up for a developer ID at http://developer.yahoo.com/yrb/zonetag/.

Once you have your ID (aka application token), you can call Yahoo! with the latitude and longitude and recover the country, state, neighborhood, and Zip Code for that location. The information is not highly accurate (you won't get a street-level address), but it's a free and open API. Recipe 9-5 demonstrates how to download ZoneTag XML data and use the iPhone's NSXMLParser class to recover location information.

Bear in mind that the Yahoo! API is subject to change. So keep checking in with ZoneTag to see whether any details have been updated over time. During the writing of this book, ZoneTag started returning the developer ID before the XML text. As you can see in Recipe 9-5, this forced the client to skip ahead the length of the ID tag before reaching actual XML.

Note

ZoneTag also returns "tags," information about local events, restaurants, and so forth. I've found these tags to be of limited use, because the service is still quite new and sparsely populated. As this book went to press, Yahoo! announced major changes in the Developer APIs. ZoneTag will be incorporated into Yahoo!'s new FireEagle service and the API will change accordingly.

Recipe 9-5 **Reverse Geocoding with ZoneTag**

```objc
@interface XMLParser : NSObject
{
    NSString          *current; // the current tag
    NSMutableString   *outstring; // results
}
@end

@implementation XMLParser

// Entry point for requesting the data from the URL
- (NSString *)parseXMLFile: (NSURL *) url
{
    outstring = [[NSMutableString alloc] init];

    NSXMLParser *parser = [[NSXMLParser alloc] initWithContentsOfURL:url];
    [parser setDelegate:self];
    [parser parse];
    [parser release];

    return [outstring autorelease];
}

// Entry point for parsing XML data directly
- (NSString *)parseXMLData: (NSData *) data
{
    outstring = [[NSMutableString alloc] init];

    NSXMLParser *parser = [[NSXMLParser alloc] initWithData:data];
    [parser setDelegate:self];
    [parser parse];
    [parser release];

    return [outstring autorelease];
}

// Parse an open XML Tag
- (void)parser:(NSXMLParser *)parser didStartElement:(NSString *)elementName
➥namespaceURI:(NSString *)namespaceURI qualifiedName:(NSString *)qName
➥attributes:(NSDictionary *)attributeDict
```

Recipe 9-5 **Continued**

```
{
    if (elementName)
        current = [NSString stringWithString:elementName];
}


// Parse the close XML tag
- (void)parser:(NSXMLParser *)parser didEndElement:(NSString *)elementName
➥namespaceURI:(NSString *)namespaceURI qualifiedName:(NSString *)qName
{
    if (current) [current release];
    current = NULL;
}


// On finding data, test to see if the container is recognized
- (void)parser:(NSXMLParser *)parser foundCharacters:(NSString *)string
{
    if (!current) return;
    if ([current isEqualToString:@"country"] ||
        [current isEqualToString:@"state"] ||
        [current isEqualToString:@"zipcode"] ||
        [current isEqualToString:@"neighbourhood"])
        [outstring appendFormat:@"%@: %@\n", current, string];
}
- (void) dealloc
{
    [current release];
    [outstring release];
    [super dealloc];
}
@end


#define APPTOKEN @"YOUR ZONE TAG DEVELOPER ID HERE"

// ZoneTag method from the calling view controller
- (void)locationManager:(CLLocationManager *)manager
➥didUpdateToLocation:(CLLocation *)newLocation fromLocation:(CLLocation
➥*)oldLocation
{
    // Respond only to the first location
    if (wasFound) return;
    wasFound = YES;
    self.navigationItem.rightBarButtonItem = NULL;

    CLLocationCoordinate2D loc = [newLocation coordinate];
    [contentView setText:@"Location found. Looking up information via Yahoo."];
```

Recipe 9-5   **Continued**

```
// Please use your own Yahoo Developer Token
if ([APPTOKEN isEqualToString:@"YOUR TOKEN HERE"])
{
    [contentView setText:@"You need to supply an application token to use
    ➥Yahoo services"];
    return;
}

// Contact Yahoo! and make a local info request
NSString *requestString = [NSString
➥stringWithFormat:@"http://zonetag.research.yahooapis.com/services/rest/V1/
➥suggestedTags.php?apptoken=%@&latitude=%f&longitude=%f&output=xml",
➥APPTOKEN, loc.latitude, loc.longitude];
NSURL *url = [NSURL URLWithString:requestString];
NSString *string = [[NSString stringWithContentsOfURL:url]
➥substringFromIndex:[APPTOKEN length]];
[contentView setText:[[XMLParser sharedInstance] parseXMLData:[string
➥dataUsingEncoding:NSUTF8StringEncoding]]];
}
```

Recipe: Accessing Maps Using Core Location Data

In addition to ZoneTag's reverse geocoding, Yahoo! provides developer-friendly ways to generate and download maps for use in your applications. Recipe 9-6 uses Yahoo's Maps service to download a map centered on the coordinates returned by Core Location. It then loads that image onto a Web view and displays it, enabling users to interactively scroll and zoom into the map, as shown in Figure 9-3.

This code uses a two-level approach. The first request returns XML containing a URL for the requested map. An `NSScanner` instance helps navigate through that simple XML to locate the map URL.

A second request downloads the map data into an `NSData` object, which is stored to file and then used to feed a `UIWebView`.

If you'd rather save the data to your iPhone photo album instead of displaying it in a Web view, first create an image with `[UIImage imageWithData:imgData]` and then call `UIImageWriteToSavedPhotosAlbum(image, NULL, NULL, NULL)`. If you want to write the data out as a JPEG image rather than your Documents folder, use `UIImageJPEGRepresentation(image, 1.0f)` to create a version of the `NSData` in JPEG format and then save the `NSData` to file.

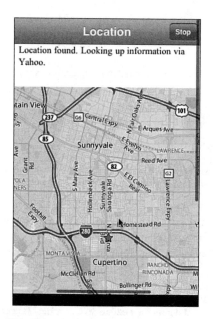

Figure 9-3   This Yahoo! map was generated from the latitude and longitude values returned by Core Location. On the Simulator, your location always defaults to 1 Infinite Loop, in Apple's headquarters in Cupertino, CA.

Note

The NSScanner class provides an expedient way to scan through strings. Although not as elegant as Perl-based solutions, it enables you to recover data by matching your string against substrings.

Recipe 9-6   **Downloading Map Data from Yahoo**

```
#define APPTOKEN @"YOUR ZONE TAG DEVELOPER ID HERE"
- (void)locationManager:(CLLocationManager *)manager
➥didUpdateToLocation:(CLLocation *)newLocation fromLocation:(CLLocation
➥*)oldLocation
{
    // Respond only to the first location
    if (wasFound) return;
    wasFound = YES;
    self.navigationItem.rightBarButtonItem = NULL;

    CLLocationCoordinate2D loc = [newLocation coordinate];
    [contentView setText:@"Location found. Looking up information via Yahoo."];
```

```
if ([APPTOKEN isEqualToString:@"YOUR TOKEN HERE"])
{
    [contentView setText:@"You need to supply an application token to use
    ➥Yahoo services"];
    return;
}


// Contact Yahoo! and make a local info request
NSString *requestString = [NSString
➥stringWithFormat:@"http://local.yahooapis.com/MapsService/V1/
➥mapImage?appid=%@&latitude=%f&longitude=%f", APPTOKEN,  loc.latitude,
➥loc.longitude];

// Retrieve the direct map location from the request URL
NSURL *url = [NSURL URLWithString:requestString];
NSString *directLocation = [NSString stringWithContentsOfURL:url];

// Scan through XML for the map URL
NSMutableString *mapURLString;
NSScanner *scanner = [NSScanner scannerWithString:directLocation];
[scanner scanUpToString:@">http://" intoString:NULL]; // first
[scanner scanUpToString:@"http://" intoString:NULL]; // second
[scanner scanUpToString:@"<" intoString:&mapURLString];

// Retrieve the image
url = [NSURL URLWithString:mapURLString];
UIImage *img = [UIImage imageWithData:[NSData dataWithContentsOfURL:url]];
NSData *imgData = UIImageJPEGRepresentation(img, 1.0f);

 // Display it on a Web view
UIWebView *wv = [[UIWebView alloc] initWithFrame:[[UIScreen mainScreen]
➥applicationFrame]];
[contentView addSubview:wv];
[wv loadData:imgData MIMEType:@"image/jpeg" textEncodingName:NULL
➥baseURL:NULL];
[wv setScalesPageToFit:YES];
self.view = wv;
}
```

Recipe: Accessing Core Device Information

The UIDevice class enables you to recover key device-specific values, including the iPhone or iPod touch model being used, the device name, and the OS name and version. As Recipe 9-7 shows, it's a one-stop solution for pulling out system details. Unfortunately, it's not a complete or exhaustive list, and Apple has disabled direct access to your iPhone's `IORegistry` even though `IOKit` remains a "public" (rather than private) framework. This keeps you from accessing what Apple would probably consider more sensitive information, such as an iPhone's IMEI, the international mobile equipment identifier used to identify the phone to its carrier network.

> **Note**
>
> Use the iPhone's unique identifier to register devices for Ad Hoc application distribution.

Recipe 9-7   Using the `UIDevice` Class

```
- (void) getDeviceInfo
{
    results = [[NSMutableString alloc] init];

    [results appendFormat:@"Identifier:\n %@\n", [[UIDevice currentDevice]
    ➥uniqueIdentifier]];
    [results appendFormat:@"Model: %@\n", [[UIDevice currentDevice] model]];
    [results appendFormat:@"Localized Model: %@\n", [[UIDevice currentDevice]
    ➥localizedModel]];
    [results appendFormat:@"Name: %@\n", [[UIDevice currentDevice] name]];
    [results appendFormat:@"System Name: %@\n", [[UIDevice currentDevice]
    ➥systemName]];
    [results appendFormat:@"System Version: %@\n", [[UIDevice currentDevice]
    ➥systemVersion]];

    [contentView setText:results];
}
```

Recipe: Enabling and Disabling the Proximity Sensor

Unless you have some pressing reason to hold an iPhone against body parts (or vice versa), enabling the proximity sensor accomplishes little. When enabled, it does one thing. It detects if there's a large object right in front of it. If so, it switches the screen off. Move the blocking object away and the screen switches back on.

Recipe 9-8 demonstrates how to enable proximity sensing on the iPhone. It sends a `setProximitySensingEnabled:` message to the shared `UIApplication` instance. Set `YES` to enable this feature, `NO` to disable it.

Recipe 9-8   Enabling Proximity Sensing

```
- (void) enable
{
    [[UIApplication sharedApplication] setProximitySensingEnabled:YES];
    self.navigationItem.rightBarButtonItem = [[[UIBarButtonItem alloc]
                                      initWithTitle:@"Disable Proximity"
```

```
                                        style:UIBarButtonItemStylePlain
                                        target:self
                                        action:@selector(disable)]
                                        autorelease];
}
```

Recipe: Using Acceleration to Locate "Up"

The iPhone provides three onboard sensors that measure acceleration along the iPhone's perpendicular axes; that is, left/right (X), up/down (Y), and front/back (Z). These values indicate the forces affecting the iPhone, from both gravity and user movement.

> **Note**
>
> You can get some really neat force feedback by swinging the iPhone around your head (centripetal force) or dropping it from a tall building (freefall). Unfortunately, you might not be able to recover that data after your iPhone becomes an expensive bit of scrap metal.

To subscribe an application to iPhone orientation notification, call `[[UIAccelerometer sharedAccelerometer] setDelegate:self]` from one of your view controllers. After, your delegate will receive `accelerometer:didAccelerate:` messages, which you can track and respond to.

Figure 9-4   A little math recovers the "up" direction by performing an arctan function using the x and y force vectors. In this sample, the arrow always points up, no matter how the user reorients the iPhone.

The UIAcceleration object sent to this method returns a floating-point value for the X, Y, and Z axes. This value ranges from -1.0 to 1.0. Recipe 9-9 uses these values to determine which way is "up," by returning the arctangent of the x and y vectors. As new acceleration messages are handled, the method rotates a UIImageView with its picture of an arrow, which you can see in Figure 9-4, to point up. The real-time response to user actions ensures that the arrow continues pointing upward, no matter how the user reorients the phone.

Recipe 9-9   Catching Acceleration Events

```
#import <math.h>

@interface HelloController : UIViewController <UIAccelerometerDelegate>
{
    UIImageView *contentView;
    UIImageView *arrowView;
}
@end

@implementation HelloController
- (void)accelerometer:(UIAccelerometer *)accelerometer
➥didAccelerate:(UIAcceleration *)acceleration
{
    float xx = -[acceleration x];
    float yy = [acceleration y];
    float angle = atan2(yy, xx);

    [arrowView setTransform:CGAffineTransformMakeRotation(angle)];
}

- (void)loadView
{
    contentView = [[UIImageView alloc] initWithFrame:[[UIScreen mainScreen]
    ➥applicationFrame]];
    [contentView setImage:[UIImage imageNamed:@"bluedots.png"]];
    self.view = contentView;
    [contentView release];

    arrowView = [[UIImageView alloc] initWithImage:[UIImage
    ➥imageNamed:@"arrow.png"]];
    [arrowView setCenter:CGPointMake(160.0f, 208.0f)];
    [contentView addSubview:arrowView];
    [arrowView release];

    [[UIAccelerometer sharedAccelerometer] setDelegate:self];
}
```

Recipe 9-9   **Continued**

```
-(void) dealloc
{
    [contentView release];
    [super dealloc];
}
@end
```

Recipe: Using Acceleration to Move Onscreen Objects

With a bit of clever programming, the iPhone's onboard accelerometer can make objects "move" around the screen, responding in real time to the way the user tilts the phone. Recipe 9-10 builds an animated butterfly that users can slide across the screen.

Figure 9-5 shows what the screen looks like as the application runs and the user interactively controls the butterfly's location.

Figure 9-5   Recipe 9-10 enables you to slide this butterfly around the screen by tilting the iPhone up, down, and sideways.

The secret to making this work lies in adding what I call a "physics timer" to the program. Instead of responding to changes in acceleration, the way Recipe 9-9 did, the accelerometer callback does nothing more than measure the current forces. It's up to the timer routine to apply those forces to the butterfly:

- As long as the direction of force remains the same, the butterfly accelerates. Its velocity increases, scaled according to the degree of acceleration force in the X or Y direction.

- The `tick` routine, called by the timer, moves the butterfly by adding the velocity vector to the butterfly's origin.

- The butterfly's range is bounded. So when it hits an edge, it stops moving in that direction. This keeps the butterfly onscreen at all times.

Recipe 9-10   Sliding an Object Based on Accelerometer Feedback

```
#import <math.h>
@interface HelloController : UIViewController <UIAccelerometerDelegate>
{
    UIImageView *contentView;
    UIImageView *butterfly;
    float xaccel, yaccel, xvelocity, yvelocity;
}
@end

@implementation HelloController
- (void) tick
{
    // Move the butterfly according to the current velocity vector
    CGRect rect = [butterfly frame];
    rect.origin.x += xvelocity;
    rect.origin.y += yvelocity;

    // Check for boundary conditions so the butterfly stays on-screen
    if (rect.origin.x > 260.0f) rect.origin.x = 260.0f;
    if (rect.origin.x < 0.0f) rect.origin.x = 0.0f;
    if (rect.origin.y > 356.0f)  rect.origin.y = 356.0f;
    if (rect.origin.y < 0.0f) rect.origin.y = 0.0f;

    [butterfly setFrame:rect];
}

#define SIGN(x)    ((x < 0.0f) ? -1.0f : 1.0f)

- (void)accelerometer:(UIAccelerometer *)accelerometer
➥didAccelerate:(UIAcceleration *)acceleration
{
```

Recipe 9-10   **Continued**

```
    // extract the acceleration components
    float xx = -[acceleration x];
    float yy = [acceleration y];

    // Has the direction changed?
    float accelDirX = SIGN(xvelocity) * -1.0f;
    float newDirX = SIGN(xx);
    float accelDirY = SIGN(yvelocity) * -1.0f;
    float newDirY = SIGN(yy);

    // Accelerate. To increase viscosity, lower the values below 1.0f
    if (accelDirX == newDirX)
        xaccel = (abs(xaccel) + 0.85f) * SIGN(xaccel);
    if (accelDirY == newDirY)
        yaccel = (abs(yaccel) + 0.85f) * SIGN(yaccel);

    // Apply acceleration changes to the current velocity
    xvelocity = -xaccel * xx;
    yvelocity = -yaccel * yy;
}

- (void)loadView
{
    contentView = [[UIImageView alloc] initWithFrame:[[UIScreen mainScreen]
    ➥applicationFrame]];
    [contentView setImage:[UIImage imageNamed:@"bluedots.png"]];
    self.view = contentView;
    [contentView release];

    // Create the butterfly
    butterfly = [[UIImageView alloc] initWithFrame:CGRectMake(40.0f, 300.0f,
    ➥60.0f, 60.0f)];
    [contentView addSubview:butterfly];
    [butterfly release];

    // Load the animation cells
    NSMutableArray *bflies = [[NSMutableArray alloc] init];
    for (int i = 1; i <= 17; i++) {
        NSString *cname = [NSString stringWithFormat:@"bf_%d.png", i];
        UIImage *img = [UIImage imageNamed:cname];
        if (img) [bflies addObject:img];
        [cname release];
    }

    // Begin the animation
    [butterfly setAnimationImages:bflies];
```

Recipe 9-10   **Continued**

```
    butterfly.animationDuration = 0.75f;
    [butterfly startAnimating];
    [bflies release];

    // Center the butterfly
    [butterfly setCenter:CGPointMake(160.0f, 208.0f)];

    // Set the butterfly's initial speed and acceleration
    xaccel = 2.0f;
    yaccel = 2.0f;
    xvelocity = 0.0f;
    yvelocity = 0.0f;

    // Activate the accelerometer
    [[UIAccelerometer sharedAccelerometer] setDelegate:self];

    // Start the physics timer
    [NSTimer scheduledTimerWithTimeInterval: 0.03f
                                    target: self
                                  selector: @selector(tick)
                                  userInfo: nil
                                   repeats: YES];
}

-(void) dealloc
{
    [contentView release];
    [super dealloc];
}
@end
```

Summary

This chapter introduced core functionality including the Address Book, Core Location, and onboard sensors. These features differentiate the iPhone and iPod touch from most other handheld platforms currently available on the market. Here are a few parting thoughts about the frameworks you just encountered:

- Although extremely useful, the low-level Address Book functions can prove frustrating to work with because of Apple's poor documentation and the complex way they approach that "multivalued" data. It helps to take these routines slowly and refer directly to the framework headers to supplement your knowledge about how the various types and records work.

- While keeping your iPhone absolutely still, you can still get varying results when calling Core Location based on the success or failure of its various positioning algorithms. Checking your location is not like checking the time. There's more variability involved.

- Compared to Google, Yahoo! is new to the social networking and geolocation world, and its developer resources reflect its commitment to building in that area. Don't overlook its developer APIs and its new location-aware services such as FireEagle and Upcoming.org.

- The iPhone's accelerometer provides a novel way to complement its touch-based interface. Use acceleration data to expand user interactions beyond the "touch here" basics and to introduce tilt-aware feedback.

Connecting to Services

As an Internet-connected device, the iPhone is particularly suited to subscribing to Web-based services. Apple has lavished the platform with a solid grounding in all kinds of network computing and its supporting technologies. The iPhone SDK handles sockets, password keychains, SQL access, XML processing, and more. This chapter surveys common techniques for network computing, offering recipes that simplify day-to-day tasks.

Recipe: Adding Custom Settings Bundles

Any iPhone application can add preferences into the main Settings screen (see Figure 10-1). Custom settings are listed after system settings, but otherwise look and act like the ones that Apple preloaded into your system. As these screenshots show, custom preferences provide a variety of data interaction styles, including text fields, switches, and sliders.

Application-based settings create standard `NSUserDefaults` entries, which you can query from your program. Use settings to store nonsensitive account preferences such as usernames and option toggles. Although passwords are visually obscured with dots, they're stored in clear text in your application sandbox. When working with more sensitive information, consider using your iPhone's secure keychain. Keychain recipes appear later in this chapter.

Declaring Application Settings

A copy of the settings schema resides in your Developer folder at /Developer/Platforms/ iPhoneOS.platform/Developer/Library/Xcode/Plug-ins/ iPhoneSettingsPlistStructDefs. xcodeplugin. Xcode uses this file to check property list syntax. In it, you can see all the definitions and the required and optional attributes used to specify custom preferences.

Each settings pane corresponds to one property list file. Recipe 10-1 shows the source for the pane in Figure 10-1 (right). It demonstrates each SDK settings type and its definition. Types include text fields (strings), sliders (floating-point numbers), switches (Boolean values), and multiple selection (one-of-n choices). In addition, you can group items and link to child panes.

Figure 10-1   (Left) Custom settings bundles appear on the Settings screen after the built-in settings, at the end of the list. On the iPhone, you may have to scroll down a bit to find them. (Right) Developer-defined preferences elements can include text fields (both regular and secure), switches, sliders, multivalue choices, group titles, and child panes.

To add new settings, build a dictionary and add it to the `PreferencesSpecifiers` array. Each individual preference dictionary needs, at a minimum, a type and a title. Some settings, like the `PSGroupSpecifier` group item, require nothing more to work. Others, such as text fields, use quite a few properties. You'll want to specify capitalization and autocorrection behaviors as well as the keyboard type and whether the password security feature obscures text, as you can see in Recipe 10-1.

To add a settings bundle to your program, follow these steps:

1. Create each of the property lists, one for each screen. The primary plist must be named Root.plist.

2. Create a new folder and add your property lists.

3. Rename the folder to **Settings.bundle**. OS X warns you about the name; go ahead and confirm the rename. The folder transforms into a bundle. (To view the contents of your new bundle, right-click [Control-click] and choose Show Package Contents from the contextual pop-up.)

4. Drag the bundle into the Groups & File column of your Xcode project (see Figure 10-2).

When you next run your program, the settings bundle installs and makes itself available to the Settings application. Should your source have any syntax errors, you'll find a blank screen rather than the settings you expect. It helps to build your settings in stages to avoid this.

Xcode offers a limited interactive syntactically aware editing window. Open the property list and then choose View, Property List Type, iPhone Settings plist. I find it easier to edit by hand in TextEdit or the stand-alone Property List Editor. Your tool comfort may differ from this.

Figure 10-2   Add the Settings.bundle into your project's Groups & Files list. Double-click the property lists to edit them further in Xcode.

Note

In Recipe 10-1, the `File` property uses no extension; the .plist extension is understood.

Recipe 10-1   **Creating a Custom Settings Pane**

```
<?xml version="1.0" encoding="UTF-8"?>
<!DOCTYPE plist PUBLIC "-//Apple//DTD PLIST 1.0//EN"
"http://www.apple.com/DTDs/PropertyList-1.0.dtd">
<plist version="1.0">
<dict>
    <key>Title</key>
    <string>YOUR_PROJECT_NAME</string>
    <key>StringsTable</key>
```

Recipe 10-1   **Continued**

```
<string>Root</string>
<key>PreferenceSpecifiers</key>
<array>
    <dict>
        <key>Type</key>
        <string>PSGroupSpecifier</string>
        <key>Title</key>
        <string>Group</string>
    </dict>
    <dict>
        <key>Type</key>
        <string>PSTextFieldSpecifier</string>
        <key>Title</key>
        <string>Name</string>
        <key>Key</key>
        <string>name_preference</string>
        <key>DefaultValue</key>
        <string></string>
        <key>IsSecure</key>
        <false/>
        <key>KeyboardType</key>
        <string>Alphabet</string>
        <key>AutocapitalizationType</key>
        <string>None</string>
        <key>AutocorrectionType</key>
        <string>No</string>
    </dict>
    <dict>
        <key>Type</key>
        <string>PSTextFieldSpecifier</string>
        <key>Title</key>
        <string>Password</string>
        <key>Key</key>
        <string>prefs_preference</string>
        <key>DefaultValue</key>
        <string></string>
        <key>IsSecure</key>
        <true/>
        <key>KeyboardType</key>
        <string>Alphabet</string>
        <key>AutocapitalizationType</key>
        <string>None</string>
        <key>AutocorrectionType</key>
        <string>No</string>
    </dict>
```

Recipe 10-1 **Continued**

```
<dict>
    <key>Type</key>
    <string>PSToggleSwitchSpecifier</string>
    <key>Title</key>
    <string>Enabled</string>
    <key>Key</key>
    <string>enabled_preference</string>
    <key>DefaultValue</key>
    <true/>
    <key>TrueValue</key>
    <string>YES</string>
    <key>FalseValue</key>
    <string>NO</string>
</dict>
<dict>
    <key>Type</key>
    <string>PSSliderSpecifier</string>
    <key>Key</key>
    <string>slider_preference</string>
    <key>DefaultValue</key>
    <real>0.5</real>
    <key>MinimumValue</key>
    <integer>0</integer>
    <key>MaximumValue</key>
    <integer>1</integer>
    <key>MinimumValueImage</key>
    <string></string>
    <key>MaximumValueImage</key>
    <string></string>
</dict>

<dict>
    <key>Type</key>
    <string>PSMultiValueSpecifier</string>
    <key>Key</key>
    <string>multi_preference</string>
    <key>DefaultValue</key>
    <string>One</string>
    <key>Title</key>
    <string>MultiValue</string>
    <key>Titles</key>
    <array>
        <string>one</string>
        <string>two</string>
        <string>three</string>
```

Recipe 10-1   **Continued**

```
            <string>four</string>
        </array>
        <key>Values</key>
        <array>
            <string>one</string>
            <string>two</string>
            <string>three</string>
            <string>four</string>
        </array>
    </dict>

    <dict>
        <key>Type</key>
        <string>PSGroupSpecifier</string>
        <key>Title</key>
        <string>Info</string>
    </dict>
    <dict>
        <key>Type</key>
        <string>PSChildPaneSpecifier</string>
        <key>Title</key>
        <string>Legal</string>
        <key>File</key>
        <string>Legal</string>
    </dict>
  </array>
</dict>
</plist>
```

Recipe: Subscribing Applications to Custom URL Schemes

Custom schemes enable applications to launch whenever Mobile Safari (or another application) opens a URL of that type. A URL scheme refers to the first part of the URL that appears before the colon, such as http or ftp. For example, should your application register xyz, any `xyz://` links go directly to your application for handling, where they're passed to the optional `application: handleOpenURL:` method.

Custom schemes launch applications whether you've defined a handler method. If all you want to do is run an application, adding the scheme and opening the URL enables cross-application launching.

Handlers extend launching to allow applications to do something with the URL that's been passed to it. They might open a specific data file, retrieve a particular name, display a certain image, or otherwise process information included in the call.

Listing 10-1 shows a simple handler that stores the passed URL into the application's preferences, presumably to be retrieved by one of the application's view controllers at a later time.

Listing 10-1   Defining a Typical URL Handler Routine

```
- (BOOL)application:(UIApplication *)application handleOpenURL:(NSURL *)url
{
    if (!url) { return NO; }

    NSString *URLString = [url absoluteString];
    [[NSUserDefaults standardUserDefaults] setObject:URLString forKey:@"url"];
    [[NSUserDefaults standardUserDefaults] synchronize];
    return YES;
}
```

Define custom URL schemes in your application's Info.plist file. Recipe 10-2 shows a property list that registers the xyz scheme. It does this by specifying two items in the CFBundleURLTypes array. The first is the CFBundleURLName, which contains an arbitrary identifier typically using Apple's standard reversed domain name style. The second consists of an array of CFBundleURLSchemes, declared as strings. This array contains one item, the xyz scheme.

When the iPhone installs the application, the Info.plist list tells SpringBoard to associate that application with the xyz scheme. Thereafter, whenever SpringBoard encounters a matching scheme, the proper application launches to handle the URL.

Recipe 10-2   Registering Custom URL Schemes

```
<?xml version="1.0" encoding="UTF-8"?>
<!DOCTYPE plist PUBLIC "-//Apple//DTD PLIST 1.0//EN"
"http://www.apple.com/DTDs/PropertyList-1.0.dtd">
<plist version="1.0">
<dict>
    <key>CFBundleDevelopmentRegion</key>
    <string>en</string>
    <key>CFBundleDisplayName</key>
    <string>${PRODUCT_NAME}</string>
    <key>CFBundleExecutable</key>
    <string>${EXECUTABLE_NAME}</string>
    <key>CFBundleIconFile</key>
    <string>Icon.png</string>
    <key>CFBundleIdentifier</key>
    <string>com.sadun.${PRODUCT_NAME:identifier}</string>
    <key>CFBundleInfoDictionaryVersion</key>
    <string>6.0</string>
    <key>CFBundleName</key>
```

Recipe 10-2   **Continued**

```
    <string>${PRODUCT_NAME}</string>
    <key>CFBundlePackageType</key>
    <string>APPL</string>
    <key>CFBundleSignature</key>
    <string>????</string>
    <key>CFBundleVersion</key>
    <string>1.0</string>
    <key>CFBundleURLTypes</key>
    <array>
        <dict>
            <key>CFBundleURLName</key>
            <string>com.sadun.demonstration</string>
            <key>CFBundleURLSchemes</key>
            <array>
                <string>xyz</string>
            </array>
        </dict>
    </array>
</dict>
</plist>
```

Recipe: Checking Your Network Status

When working with networks, you can check your connection status and recover information about your iPhone's role in that network. The next few listings demonstrate how to test network status, recover the iPhone's IP address, look up a site's IP address, and determine whether a site is reachable.

Testing the Network Status

The System Configuration framework offers many networking aware functions. Among these, SCNetworkReachabilityCreateWithAddress enables you to check whether an IP address is reachable. Pass a zeroed out address (for example, 0.0.0.0) to query your network status. Listing 10-2 shows this test in action. This method, courtesy of Apple sample code, returns YES when the network is available and NO otherwise. The returned flags must indicate both that the network is reachable (kSCNetworkFlagsReachable) and that no further connection is required (kSCNetworkFlagsConnectionRequired). Other flags you may use are as follows:

- kSCNetworkReachabilityFlagsIsWWAN tests whether your user is using the carrier's network or local WiFi. When set to YES, the network can be reached via EDGE, GPRS, or another cell connection.

- kSCNetworkReachabilityFlagsIsDirect tells you whether the network traffic goes through a gateway or arrives directly.

Note

Toggle airplane mode off and on to test this code with your network enabled and disabled.

Listing 10-2   **Checking the iPhone's Network Connection Status**

```
- (BOOL) connectedToNetwork
{
    // Create zero addy
    struct sockaddr_in zeroAddress;
    bzero(&zeroAddress, sizeof(zeroAddress));
    zeroAddress.sin_len = sizeof(zeroAddress);
    zeroAddress.sin_family = AF_INET;

    // Recover reachability flags
    SCNetworkReachabilityRef defaultRouteReachability =
➥SCNetworkReachabilityCreateWithAddress(NULL, (struct sockaddr
*)&zeroAddress);
    SCNetworkReachabilityFlags flags;

    BOOL didRetrieveFlags =
➥SCNetworkReachabilityGetFlags(defaultRouteReachability, &flags);
    CFRelease(defaultRouteReachability);

    if (!didRetrieveFlags)
    {
        printf("Error. Could not recover network reachability flags\n");
        return 0;
    }

    BOOL isReachable = flags & kSCNetworkFlagsReachable;
    BOOL needsConnection = flags & kSCNetworkFlagsConnectionRequired;
    return (isReachable && !needsConnection) ? YES : NO;
}
```

Recovering a Local IP Address

Early on, developers James "core" Cuff and Jay "saurik" Freeman discovered that the iPhone's hostname lookup features were irregular. Although newer iPhone firmware releases have fixed many bugs, the iPhone remains quirky when it comes to recovering the iPhone's hostname. Unlike the simulator and its Mac OS X host, the iPhone does not automatically add a local suffix to the iPhone's hostname.

Listing 10-3 demonstrates how to retrieve the local IP address for your iPhone. This is a handy routine to have on hand when you're establishing networked services from the iPhone, such as an FTP server or HTTP daemon. This code appends the missing-in-action local suffix, and, once the name is corrected, uses gethostbyname to return a valid host entity. After, inet_ntoa() extracts the IP address from that host.

> **Note**
>
> This code does not work on the Simulator. (The Simulator correctly adds the .local suffix automatically.) Run it only in iPhone- and iPod touch-specific code.

Listing 10-3   **Obtaining the iPhone's Local IP Address**

```
// Return the localized IP address
- (NSString *) localIPAddress
{
    char baseHostName[255];
    gethostname(baseHostName, 255);

    char hn[255];
    // This adjusts for iPhone by adding .local to the host name
    sprintf(hn, "%s.local", baseHostName);
    struct hostent *host = gethostbyname(hn);
    if (host == NULL)
    {
        herror("resolv");
        return NULL;
    }
    else {
        struct in_addr **list = host->h_addr_list;
        return [NSString stringWithCString:inet_ntoa(*list[0])];
    }

    return NULL;
}
```

Querying Site IP Addresses

The iPhone supports standard gethostbyname calls to look up IP addresses for remote sites. The method shown in Listing 10-4 accepts a site name (for example, yahoo.com or www.google.com) and returns the first available IP address for that site. As you can see, the routine to do this is standard. There are no iPhone-specific quirks to work around.

Listing 10-4   **Looking Up IP Address by Hostname**

```
- (NSString *) getIPAddressForHost: (NSString *) theHost
{
    struct hostent *host = gethostbyname([theHost UTF8String]);

    if (host == NULL) {
        herror("resolv");
        return NULL;
    }

    struct in_addr **list = (struct in_addr **)host->h_addr_list;
    NSString *addressString = [NSString stringWithCString:inet_ntoa(*list[0])];
    return addressString;
}
```

Checking Site Availability

After recovering a site's IP address, use the same
SCNetworkReachabilityCreateWithAddress function to check its availability that
you use to check whether a site can be reached. Pass a sockaddr record populated
with the site's IP address (thank you, Apple, for providing the method that does this),
and then check for the kSCNetworkFlagsReachable flag when the function returns.
Recipe 10-3 shows the site checking hostAvailable: method. It returns YES or NO.

Recipe 10-3   **Checking Whether a Site Is Reachable**

```
- (BOOL) hostAvailable: (NSString *) theHost
{

    NSString *addressString = [self getIPAddressForHost:theHost];
    if (!addressString)
    {
        printf("Error recovering IP address from host name\n");
        return NO;
    }

    struct sockaddr_in address;
    BOOL gotAddress = [self addressFromString:addressString address:&address];

    if (!gotAddress)
    {
        printf("Error recovering sockaddr address from %s\n", [addressString
        ➥UTF8String]);
        return NO;
    }
```

Recipe 10-3 **Continued**

```
SCNetworkReachabilityRef defaultRouteReachability =
➥SCNetworkReachabilityCreateWithAddress(NULL, (struct sockaddr *)&address);
SCNetworkReachabilityFlags flags;

BOOL didRetrieveFlags =
➥SCNetworkReachabilityGetFlags(defaultRouteReachability, &flags);
CFRelease(defaultRouteReachability);

if (!didRetrieveFlags)
{
    printf("Error. Could not recover network reachability flags\n");
    return NO;
}

BOOL isReachable = flags & kSCNetworkFlagsReachable;
return isReachable ? YES : NO;;
}

// Populating a sockaddr_in record.
// Direct from Apple. Thank you Apple
- (BOOL)addressFromString:(NSString *)IPAddress address:(struct sockaddr_in *)
➥address
{
    if (!IPAddress || ![IPAddress length]) {
        return NO;
    }

    memset((char *) address, sizeof(struct sockaddr_in), 0);
    address->sin_family = AF_INET;
    address->sin_len = sizeof(struct sockaddr_in);

    int conversionResult = inet_aton([IPAddress UTF8String], &address->sin_addr);
    if (conversionResult == 0) {
        NSAssert1(conversionResult != 1, @"Failed to convert the IP address string
➥into a sockaddr_in: %@", IPAddress);
        return NO;
    }

    return YES;
}
```

Recipe: Interacting with iPhone Databases

Database storage provides another support mechanism for network access. Although the iPhone offers full sqlite3 interactions, I find the Apple-provided libraries cumbersome. Listing 10-5 shows a sample SQLite access routine from Apple's SQLiteBooks code. This is a pretty typical method. Note the routines that are used. They're centered on C-based libsql calls, with little Cocoa feel to them. This routine queries SELECT author, copyright FROM book WHERE pk=? against its database.

Listing 10-5   **Sample SQL Access from Apple's SQLiteBooks Example**

```
// Brings the rest of the object data into memory. If already in memory, no action
➥is taken (harmless no-op).
- (void)hydrate {
    // Check if action is necessary.
    if (hydrated) return;
    // Compile the hydration statement, if needed.
    if (hydrate_statement == nil) {
        const char *sql = "SELECT author, copyright FROM book WHERE pk=?";
        if (sqlite3_prepare_v2(database, sql, -1, &hydrate_statement, NULL) !=
        ➥SQLITE_OK) {
            NSAssert1(0, @"Error: failed to prepare statement with message '%s'.",
            ➥sqlite3_errmsg(database));
        }
    }
    // Bind the primary key variable.
    sqlite3_bind_int(hydrate_statement, 1, primaryKey);
    // Execute the query.
    int success =sqlite3_step(hydrate_statement);
    if (success == SQLITE_ROW) {
        char *str = (char *)sqlite3_column_text(hydrate_statement, 0);
        self.author = (str) ? [NSString stringWithUTF8String:str] : @"";
        self.copyright = [NSDate dateWithTimeIntervalSince1970:sqlite3_column_
        ➥double(hydrate_statement, 1)];
    } else {
        // The query did not return
        self.author = @"Unknown";
        self.copyright = [NSDate date];
    }
    // Reset the query for the next use.
    sqlite3_reset(hydrate_statement);
    // Update object state with respect to hydration.
    hydrated = YES;
}
```

I much prefer to use Gus Mueller's FMDB Cocoa wrappers for my database needs (http://gusmueller.com/x/fmdb.zip). FMDB provides sqlite bindings that simplify iPhone database creation, access, and updates. Recipe 10-3 shows FMDB in action, sending a simple SQLite call as an NSString query ([db executeQuery:@"select * from call"]).

The method shown in Recipe 10-4 lists your recent call history. Compare the relative simplicity of this code with Listing 10-5, which shows a similar database read-through.

In Recipe 10-4, the focus remains on the high-level data rather than low-level access calls, providing an Objective-C approach to SQL access.

To use FMDB in your programs, download the code from Mueller's site, add the classes to your program, and drag the iPhone version of libsqlite3.0.dylib into your Xcode project. The dylib file is located at /Developer/Platforms/iPhoneOS.platform/ Developer/SDKs/iPhoneOS2.0.sdk/usr/lib/libsqlite3.0.dylib, along with other linkable iPhone libraries.

Note

At the time of this writing, the iPhone does not sandbox you from reading your call history. Should this policy change, use this same FMDB approach to access any other readable SQL database.

Recipe 10-4 **Accessing the iPhone Call History Using FMDB**

```
- (void) fetchCalls
{
    // Open the iPhone call history database
    NSString *dbpath = @"/private/var/mobile/Library/CallHistory/call_history.db";
    FMDatabase* db = [FMDatabase databaseWithPath:dbpath];
    if (![db open]) {
        printf("Could not open db.\n");
        return;
    }

    FMResultSet *rs = [db executeQuery:@"select * from call"];

    int i = 1; // counter
    NSMutableString *outstring = [[NSMutableString alloc] init];

    while ([rs next]) {

        // Recover the call time
        int calltime = [rs intForColumn:@"date"];
        NSDate *cdate = [NSDate dateWithTimeIntervalSince1970:calltime];
        NSString *caldate = [[cdate dateWithCalendarFormat:@"%Y-%m-%d %H:%M:%S"
        ➥timeZone:nil] description];

        // Duration in seconds
        int secs = [[rs stringForColumn:@"duration"] intValue];
        int minutes = (secs / 60) + 1;

        // Phone number
        NSString *phoneNumber = [rs stringForColumn:@"address"];
```

Recipe 10-4   **Continued**

```
        [outstring appendFormat:@"%3d: %@ %@ - %3d minutes\n", i++, caldate,
        ➥phoneNumber, minutes];

    }

    [db close];
    [contentView setText:outstring];
    [outstring release];
}
```

Recipe: Converting XML into Trees

The NSXMLParser class provided in the iPhone SDK enables you to scan through XML, creating callbacks as new elements are processed and finished. In Chapter 9, "People, Places, and Things," Recipe 9-5 introduced NSXMLParser in its simplest form: looking for leaves and keeping track of the current element. The class is terrific for when you're downloading simple data feeds and want to scrape just a bit or two of relevant information. It's not so great when you're doing production-type work that relies on error checking, status information, and back-and-forth handshaking.

Unfortunately, the iPhone SDK relies on NSXMLParser for its core XML handling. So it's up to you to bridge the gap between NSXMLParser and tree-based parse results. Fortunately, you can easily build an NSXMLParser-based class to return more standard tree-based data. This requires the kind of simple, standard tree node shown in Listing 10-6. A simple double-linked tree node offers a pointer to its parent node, an array of its children, a key value for the element container and, for leaves, a leaf value that stores XML text data from inside the container.

Listing 10-6   **Defining a Simple Tree Node for XML Support**

```
@interface TreeNode : NSObject
{
    TreeNode        *parent;
    NSMutableArray  *children;
    NSString        *key;
    NSString        *leafvalue;
}
@property (nonatomic, retain)    TreeNode        *parent;
@property (nonatomic, retain)    NSMutableArray  *children;
@property (nonatomic, retain)    NSString        *key;
@property (nonatomic, retain)    NSString        *leafvalue;

@end
```

Use this tree node data type to build a parse tree as the NSXMLParser class works its way through XML source. The three standard NSXML routines (start element, finish element, and found characters) perform a recursive depth-first descent through the tree.

Add new nodes when reaching new elements (parser: didStartElement: qualifiedName: attributes:) and add leaf values when encountering text (parser: foundCharacters:). Because XML allows siblings at the same tree depth, this code uses a stack to keep track of the current path to the tree root. Siblings always pop back to the same parent in parser: didEndElement:, so they are added at the proper level.

After finishing the XML scan, the parseXMLFile: method returns the root node.

Recipe 10-5   **Converting XML into a Parse Tree**

```
@implementation XMLParser

static XMLParser *sharedInstance = nil;

// Use just one parser instance at any time
+(XMLParser *) sharedInstance
{
    if(!sharedInstance) {
        sharedInstance = [[self alloc] init];
    }
    return sharedInstance;
}


// Public parser returns the tree root
- (TreeNode *)parseXMLFile: (NSURL *) url
{
    stack = [[NSMutableArray alloc] init];

    root = [[TreeNode alloc] init];
    root.parent = NULL;
    root.leafvalue = NULL;
    root.children = [[NSMutableArray alloc] init];

    [stack addObject:root];
    [root release];

    NSXMLParser *parser = [[NSXMLParser alloc] initWithContentsOfURL:url];
    [parser setDelegate:self];
    [parser parse];
    [parser release];

    // pop down to real root
    return [[root children] lastObject];
}
```

Recipe 10-5   **Continued**

```
// Descend to a new element
- (void)parser:(NSXMLParser *)parser didStartElement:(NSString *)elementName
➥namespaceURI:(NSString *)namespaceURI qualifiedName:(NSString *)qName
➥attributes:(NSDictionary *)attributeDict
{
    if (qName) elementName = qName;

    TreeNode *leaf = [[TreeNode alloc] init];
    leaf.parent = [stack lastObject];
    [(NSMutableArray *)[[stack lastObject] children] addObject:leaf];

    leaf.key = [NSString stringWithString:elementName];
    leaf.leafvalue = NULL;
    leaf.children = [[NSMutableArray alloc] init];

    [stack addObject:leaf];
    [leaf release];
}

// Pop after finishing element
- (void)parser:(NSXMLParser *)parser didEndElement:(NSString *)elementName
➥namespaceURI:(NSString *)namespaceURI qualifiedName:(NSString *)qName
{
    [stack removeLastObject];
}

// Reached a leaf
- (void)parser:(NSXMLParser *)parser foundCharacters:(NSString *)string
{
    [[stack lastObject] setLeafvalue:[NSString stringWithString:string]];
}
@end
```

Recipe: Storing and Retrieving Keychain Items

As mentioned earlier in this chapter, "secure" password text fields are not particularly secure. Although the text is obscured onscreen, it's stored in the preferences file in clear text. Apple provides a highly secure keychain-based password service with its Security framework.

Recipe 10-6 shows how to use this technology, using the four available Security calls. These calls allow you to add, update, query, and remove passwords from your keychain. They are as follows:

- **methodSecItemAdd().** Use SecItemAdd to create new items in your keychain. Once added, you cannot overwrite them directly. You must either update items or remove them from the keychain before adding them again.

- **SecItemUpdate() method.** Update calls allow you to modify existing keychain items. You cannot update an item that does not yet exist, so always check to see if an item can be found before attempting to change it.

- **SecItemCopyMatching() method.** Copy-matching provides the essential "find" function. It enables you to query the keychain to discover whether matching items can be found.

- **SecItemDelete() method.** The delete function does exactly what you'd guess. It removes items from the keychain.

What makes the keychain so tricky to use is its reliance on creating dictionaries to fuel all your requests. All four function calls use dictionaries to pass data, attributes, and other parameters back and forth between your program and the keychain. Search queries, update requests, and data storage each demand a slightly different set of dictionary settings.

The code in Recipe 10-6 provides a simple working one-password keychain wrapper. With it, you can set a password (`setPassword:`) or you can retrieve a password (`fetchPassword`). All the remaining work is abstracted out. Internal methods build the dictionaries and call the Security functions.

> **Note**
>
> The Security framework is available only for the iPhone device. You cannot compile or test its features in the Simulator.

Recipe 10-6   Creating a Secure Keychain Password Keeper Wrapper

```
#import <Security/Security.h>

// Password Keeper securely saves just one password
@interface PasswordKeeper: NSObject
+ (PasswordKeeper *) sharedInstance;
- (void) setPassword: (NSString *) password;
- (NSString *) fetchPassword;
@end

@implementation PasswordKeeper

static PasswordKeeper *sharedInstance = nil;

+(PasswordKeeper *) sharedInstance {
    if(!sharedInstance) {
        sharedInstance = [[self alloc] init];
    }
    return sharedInstance;
}
```

Recipe 10-6   **Continued**

```
// Translate status messages into return strings
- (NSString *) fetchStatus : (OSStatus) status
{
    if         (status == 0) return(@"Success!");
    else if (status == errSecNotAvailable) return(@"No trust results are
    ➥available.");
    else if (status == errSecItemNotFound) return(@"The item cannot be found.");
    else if (status == errSecParam) return(@"Parameter error.");
    else if (status == errSecAllocate) return(@"Memory allocation error. Failed to
    ➥allocate memory.");
    else if (status == errSecInteractionNotAllowed) return(@"User interaction is
    ➥not allowed.");
    else if (status == errSecUnimplemented) return(@"Function is not implemented");
    else if (status == errSecDuplicateItem) return(@"The item already exists.");
    else if (status == errSecDecode) return(@"Unable to decode the provided
    ➥data.");
    else
        return([NSString stringWithFormat:@"Function returned: %d", status]);
}


#define    ACCOUNT    @"iPhone Developer Cookbook Test Account"
#define    SERVICE    @"iPhone Developer Cookbook Test Service"
#define    PWKEY      @"iPhone Developer Cookbook Test Password Data"
#define    DEBUG      YES

// Return a base dictionary
- (NSMutableDictionary *) baseDictionary
{
    NSMutableDictionary *md = [[NSMutableDictionary alloc] init];

    // Password identification keys
    NSData *identifier = [PWKEY dataUsingEncoding:NSUTF8StringEncoding];
    [md setObject:identifier forKey:(id)kSecAttrGeneric];
    [md setObject:ACCOUNT forKey:(id)kSecAttrAccount];
    [md setObject:SERVICE forKey:(id)kSecAttrService];
    [md setObject:(id)kSecClassGenericPassword forKey:(id)kSecClass];

    return [md autorelease];
}

// Return a keychain-style dictionary populated with the password
- (NSMutableDictionary *) buildDictForPassword:(NSString *) password
{

    NSMutableDictionary *passwordDict = [self baseDictionary];
```

Recipe 10-6   **Continued**

```objc
    // Add the password
    NSData *passwordData = [password dataUsingEncoding:NSUTF8StringEncoding];
    [passwordDict setObject:passwordData forKey:(id)kSecValueData]; // password

    return passwordDict;
}


// Build a search query based
- (NSMutableDictionary *) buildSearchQuery
{
    NSMutableDictionary *genericPasswordQuery = [self baseDictionary];

    // Add the search constraints: One match returning both
    // data and attributes
    [genericPasswordQuery setObject:(id)kSecMatchLimitOne
                             forKey:(id)kSecMatchLimit];
    [genericPasswordQuery setObject:(id)kCFBooleanTrue
                             forKey:(id)kSecReturnAttributes];
    [genericPasswordQuery setObject:(id)kCFBooleanTrue
                             forKey:(id)kSecReturnData];

    return genericPasswordQuery;
}


// retrieve data dictionary from the keychain
- (NSMutableDictionary *) fetchDictionary
{
    NSMutableDictionary *genericPasswordQuery = [self buildSearchQuery];

    NSMutableDictionary *outDictionary = nil;
    OSStatus status = SecItemCopyMatching((CFDictionaryRef)genericPasswordQuery,
    ➥(CFTypeRef *)&outDictionary);
    if (DEBUG) printf("FETCH: %s\n", [[self fetchStatus:status] UTF8String]);

    if (status == errSecItemNotFound) return NULL;
    return outDictionary;
}


// create a new keychain entry
- (BOOL) createKeychainValue:(NSString *) password
{
    NSMutableDictionary *md = [self buildDictForPassword:password];
    OSStatus status = SecItemAdd((CFDictionaryRef)md, NULL);
    if (DEBUG) printf("CREATE: %s\n", [[self fetchStatus:status] UTF8String]);

    if (status == noErr) return YES; else return NO;
}
```

```objc
// remove a keychain entry
- (void) clearKeychain
{
    NSMutableDictionary *genericPasswordQuery = [self baseDictionary];

    OSStatus status = SecItemDelete((CFDictionaryRef) genericPasswordQuery);
    if (DEBUG) printf("DELETE: %s\n", [[self fetchStatus:status] UTF8String]);
}


// update a keychaing entry
- (BOOL) updateKeychainValue:(NSString *)password
{
    NSMutableDictionary *genericPasswordQuery = [self baseDictionary];

    NSMutableDictionary *attributesToUpdate = [[NSMutableDictionary alloc] init];
    NSData *passwordData = [password dataUsingEncoding:NSUTF8StringEncoding];
    [attributesToUpdate setObject:passwordData forKey:(id)kSecValueData];

    OSStatus status = SecItemUpdate((CFDictionaryRef)genericPasswordQuery,
    ➥(CFDictionaryRef)attributesToUpdate);
    if (DEBUG) printf("UPDATE: %s\n", [[self fetchStatus:status] UTF8String]);

    if (status == 0) return YES; else return NO;
}


// fetch a keychain value
- (NSString *) fetchPassword
{
    NSMutableDictionary *outDictionary = [self fetchDictionary];

    if (outDictionary)
    {
        NSString *password = [[NSString alloc] initWithData:[outDictionary
        ➥objectForKey:(id)kSecValueData] encoding:NSUTF8StringEncoding];
        return [password autorelease];
    } else return NULL;
}

- (void) setPassword: (NSString *) thePassword
{
    if (![self createKeychainValue:thePassword])
        [self updateKeychainValue:thePassword];
}
@end
```

Storing Multiple Keychain Values

When working with keychains, I've found that it's easiest to keep to the single-entry approach even when working with multiple passwords. To accomplish this, store serialized dictionaries rather than NSStrings. Serialization turns a dictionary into a single NSData object. You can recover your dictionary from that data by deserializing it. Listing 10-7 shows how to convert a dictionary to and from data.

Listing 10-7   Using Serialization to Convert Dictionaries to and from Data

```
// Serialize to data
- (NSData *) dataFromDictionary: (NSMutableDictionary *) dict
{

    NSString *errorString;
    NSData *outData = [NSPropertyListSerialization dataFromPropertyList:dict
➥format:NSPropertyListBinaryFormat_v1_0 errorDescription:&errorString];
    return outData;
}


// Deserialize from data
- (NSMutableDictionary *) dictionaryFromData: (NSData *) data
{

    NSString *errorString;
    NSMutableDictionary *outDict = [NSPropertyListSerialization
➥propertyListFromData:data
➥mutabilityOption:kCFPropertyListMutableContainersAndLeaves format:NULL
➥errorDescription:&errorString];
    return outDict;
}
```

Serialization keeps your keychain methods simple. You can use the same storage and retrieval calls from Recipe 10-6. At the same time, using a dictionary allows you to expand your password keeper interface to provide multiple key-value storage. Listing 10-8 shows the interface and object calls for a multipassword keychain wrapper. It's built on the same single data entry code used in Recipe 10-6.

Listing 10-8   Expanding a Single-Entry Keychain to Support Multiple Passwords

```
@interface PasswordKeeper: NSObject
+ (PasswordKeeper *) sharedInstance;
- (void) setObject: (id) anObject forKey: (NSString *) aKey;
- (void) removeObjectForKey: (NSString *) aKey;
- (id) objectForKey: (NSString *) aKey;
- (NSMutableDictionary *) passwordDict;
@end


// Simple Keychain Access Protocol Methods
```

Listing 10-7   **Continued**

```objc
- (void) setObject: (id) anObject forKey: (NSString *) aKey
{
    NSMutableDictionary *dict = [self fetchKeychainValue];
    if (dict)
    {
        // Keychain already has object
        [dict setObject:anObject forKey:aKey];
        [self updateKeychainValue:dict];
        return;
    }

    // Dictionary not found so create it
    dict = [[NSMutableDictionary alloc] init];
    [dict setObject:anObject forKey:aKey];
    if (![self createKeychainValue:dict]) [self updateKeychainValue:dict];
}

- (void) removeObjectForKey: (NSString *) aKey
{
    NSMutableDictionary *dict = [self fetchKeychainValue];
    if (dict)
    {
        // Keychain has object
        [dict removeObjectForKey:aKey];
        [self updateKeychainValue:dict];
        return;
    }
}

- (id) objectForKey: (NSString *) aKey
{
    NSMutableDictionary *dict = [self fetchKeychainValue];
    return [dict objectForKey:aKey];
}

- (NSMutableDictionary *) passwordDict
{
    return [self fetchKeychainValue];
}
```

Keychain Persistence

Keychain data persists even after de-installing your application. Maurice Cusseaux of Apple's developer relations writes, "Keychain items created by any application will be persistent across uninstalls because of the mere fact that the keychain store isn't located inside of the application bundle and there is no facility by which the system can be notified of when something is uninstalled to then also uninstall all associated keychain items. It is also a policy issue between the trade-offs of losing sensitive passwords through malicious uninstalling and keeping sensitive passwords intact and potentially secured away for the user(s)."

This behavior allows you to use the keychain to maintain persistent iPhone information. You might keep track of user registration or limit demo mode usage. The persistence means that nothing short of firmware reinstall (without a backup restore) will wipe the data.

Sending and Receiving Files

Sending files back and forth between your iPhone and another host can be challenging. At the time of this writing, Apple provided no standard way to openly sync data to and from the iPhone. (Chapter 7, "Media," discussed recovering data from iTune's mdbackup files.) Here are technologies you may want to consider adding to your applications:

- **Bonjour.** The iPhone's CFNetwork framework allows you to use Bonjour zero-configuration networking to send data between computers. Bonjour allows automatic service discovery, making it simple to connect two systems on the same network to transfer data. Apple's WiTap sample code demonstrates how to use Bonjour messaging in your application. With Bonjour, you can send short messages or entire files from one host to another.

- **FTP.** The File Transfer Protocol is especially nice to use because it's standard across so many platforms. Apple's Core Foundation FTP sample code is easy to work with. You can find source at http://developer.apple.com/samplecode/ CFFTPSample/listing1.html. There's little you have to do to get the upload and download functionality working. Once you have a user's name, password, and host information stored, FTP data transfer can be easily automated.

- **E-mail.** Apple no longer allows you to attach local files to outgoing e-mail using attachments. Because of this, if you want to use e-mail, you'll have to build your own client. A little sockets programming is all it takes to build an outgoing SMTP or SMTPAUTH utility. Google for sample code. There's quite a lot out there, mostly in standard C.

- **Web services.** You can use the iPhone's onboard Internet connection to send and receive data from the World Wide Web. You've seen how to download data from URLs in this chapter and in recipes scattered through this book. You can also upload data from the iPhone to the Web using the NSURLConnection class to handle synchronous and asynchronous requests for both GET and POST. Sean Heber's iAppADay source at Google Code (http://code.google.com/p/iappaday/) provides an excellent starting point for learning about data posting.

- **Web server.** You don't need to implement an entire Web server to serve data from your iPhone to a browser. Just a few functions (serving an index and a few files) are all it takes. If your goal is to expose data to the outside world, creating a basic server allows you to use standard software such as Safari and Firefox to retrieve files from the iPhone.

Recipe: Building a Simple Web-Based Server

A Web server provides one of the cleanest ways to serve data off your phone to another computer. You don't need special client software. Any browser can list and access Web-based files. Figure 10-3 shows an iPhone serving to a Web browser; the iPhone screenshot is superimposed over the browser screen.

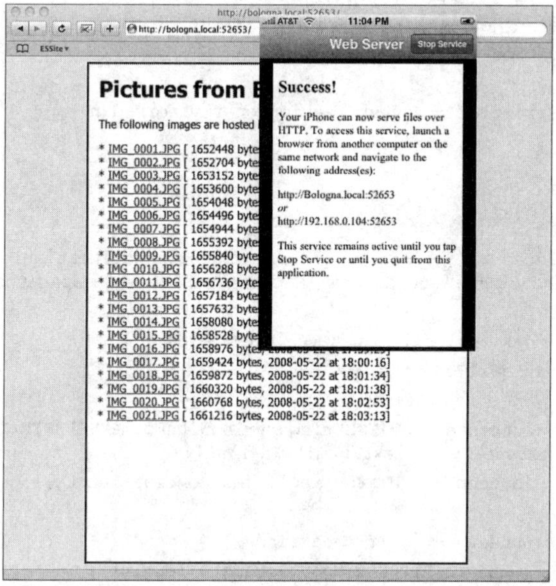

Figure 10-3   With a bit of programming, you can set up your iPhone to serve files to networked computers.

A Web server requires just a few key routines. You must establish the service, creating a loop that listens for a request (`startServer`), and then pass those requests onto a handler (`handleWebRequest:`) that responds with the requested data. One more method (`stopService`) is needed to handle service shutdown. Recipe 10-7 shows these three core methods for establishing and controlling Web service.

The loop routine uses low-level socket programming to establish a listening port and catch client requests. When the client issues a GET command, the server intercepts that request and passes it to the Web request handler. The handler decomposes it to find the name of the desired data file. It then looks up the file in its folder and, if found, reads and then serves the requested file data.

Recipe 10-7   **Serving iPhone Files Through a Web Service**

```objc
// Serve files to GET requests
- (void) handleWebRequest:(NSNumber *)fdNum
{
    NSAutoreleasePool * pool = [[NSAutoreleasePool alloc] init];
    int fd = [fdNum intValue];
    static char buffer[BUFSIZE+1];
    int len = read(fd, buffer, BUFSIZE);
    buffer[len] = '\0';

    NSArray *reqs = [[NSString stringWithCString:buffer]
➥componentsSeparatedByString:@"\n"];
    NSString *getreq = [[reqs objectAtIndex:0] substringFromIndex:4];
    NSRange range = [getreq rangeOfString:@"HTTP/"];
    if (range.location == NSNotFound)
    {
        printf("Error: GET request was improperly formed\n");
        close(fd);
        return;
    }

    NSString *filereq = [[getreq substringToIndex:range.location]
➥stringByTrimmingCharactersInSet:[NSCharacterSet whitespaceCharacterSet]];

    // Serve an index.html file to "GET /" requests
    if ([filereq isEqualToString:@"/"])
    {
        NSString *outcontent = [NSString stringWithFormat:@"HTTP/1.0 200
➥OK\r\nContent-Type: text/html\r\n\r\n"];
        write(fd, [outcontent UTF8String], [outcontent length]);

        NSString *outdata = [self createindex];
        write(fd, [outdata UTF8String], [outdata length]);
        close(fd);
        return;
    }

    // Check extensions against known MIME types
    NSString *mime = [self mimeForExt:[filereq pathExtension]];
    if (!mime)
    {
        printf("Error recovering mime type.\n");
        NSString *outcontent = [NSString stringWithFormat:@"HTTP/1.0 200
➥OK\r\nContent-Type: text/html\r\n\r\n"];
        write (fd, [outcontent UTF8String], [outcontent length]);
        outcontent = @"<p>Sorry. This file type is not supported</p>\n";
        write (fd, [outcontent UTF8String], [outcontent length]);
        close(fd);
```

```
        return;
    }


    // Read and serve the file
    NSString *outcontent = [NSString stringWithFormat:@"HTTP/1.0 200
    ➥OK\r\nContent-Type: %@\r\n\r\n", mime];
    write (fd, [outcontent UTF8String], [outcontent length]);
    filereq = [filereq
    ➥stringByReplacingPercentEscapesUsingEncoding:NSUTF8StringEncoding];
    NSString *fullpath = [PICS_FOLDER stringByAppendingString:filereq];
    NSData *data = [NSData dataWithContentsOfFile:fullpath];
    if (!data)
    {
        printf("Error: file not found.\n");
        NSString *outcontent = [NSString stringWithFormat:@"HTTP/1.0 200
        ➥OK\r\nContent-Type: text/html\r\n\r\n"];
        write (fd, [outcontent UTF8String], [outcontent length]);
        outcontent = @"<p>File was not found.</p>\n";
        write (fd, [outcontent UTF8String], [outcontent length]);
        close(fd);
        return;
    }

    printf("%d bytes read from file\n", [data length]);
    write(fd, [data bytes], [data length]);
    close(fd);

    [pool release];
}

// Begin serving data
- (void) startServer
{
    NSAutoreleasePool * pool = [[NSAutoreleasePool alloc] init];

    int socketfd;
    socklen_t length;
    static struct sockaddr_in cli_addr;
    static struct sockaddr_in serv_addr;

    // Set up socket
    if((listenfd = socket(AF_INET, SOCK_STREAM,0)) <0)
    {
        isServing = NO;
        return;
    }
```

Recipe 10-7 **Continued**

```
// Serve to a random port
serv_addr.sin_family = AF_INET;
serv_addr.sin_addr.s_addr = htonl(INADDR_ANY);
serv_addr.sin_port = 0;

// Bind
if(bind(listenfd, (struct sockaddr *)&serv_addr,sizeof(serv_addr)) <0)
{
    isServing = NO;
    return;
}

// Find out what port number was chosen.
int namelen = sizeof(serv_addr);
if (getsockname(listenfd, (struct sockaddr *)&serv_addr, (void *)
➥&namelen) < 0) {
    close(listenfd);
    isServing = NO;
    return;
}
chosenPort = ntohs(serv_addr.sin_port);

// Listen
if(listen(listenfd, 64) < 0)
{
    isServing = NO;
    return;
}

// Service has now successfully started
self.navigationItem.rightBarButtonItem = [[[UIBarButtonItem alloc]
                                    initWithTitle:@"Stop Service"
                                    style:UIBarButtonItemStylePlain
                                    target:self
                                    action:@selector(stopService)]
                                    autorelease];

// Respond to requests until the service shuts down
while (1 > 0) {
    length = sizeof(cli_addr);
    if((socketfd = accept(listenfd, (struct sockaddr *)&cli_addr, &length)) < 0)
    {
        isServing = NO;
        return;
    }
```

```
        [self handleWebRequest:[NSNumber numberWithInt:socketfd]];
    }

    [pool release];
}

// Shut down service
- (void) stopService
{
    printf("Shutting down service\n");
    isServing = NO;
    close(listenfd);
    [self stoppingService];
    self.navigationItem.rightBarButtonItem = [[[UIBarButtonItem alloc]
                                        initWithTitle:@"Start Service"
                                        style:UIBarButtonItemStylePlain
                                        target:self
                                        action:@selector(startService)]
                                        autorelease];
}
```

Push Notifications

Although Apple has announced official push notification services for the iPhone, at the time of this writing they have not been introduced. Push services allow your application to provide user notifications when new data becomes available for download at your Web server. Push notices include badges—those little red circles that appear on SpringBoard icons (see Listings 4-2 and 4-3), text-based alerts (Listing 4-1), and custom sounds (Recipe 4-11).

To add this functionality to your application, your server needs to send notifications to the iPhone's onboard push notification service. From the server end, you supply the bundle identifier for the application you want to notify, the unique device ID for the iPhone, and a node name for your service. Notifications, which must not exceed 1K in length (including all Apple DTD definitions), can specify the following:

- A short message
- A button that launches your application (normally "View")
- A badge number (a positive integer)
- An alert sound that specifies which application sound file to play (or UIDefaultSound)

No data is sent. To keep the push mechanism efficient and to respect that 1K limit, notifications offer status changes only. Your application retrieves data as needed.

From the iPhone side, your application registers with a service (thus providing the unique iPhone identifier to the service) and enables or disables notifications. When notifications for your application get pushed to a device, your application responds via a `UIApplicationDelegate` method, yet to be announced. (See Listing 10-1 to get a hint of what that method might look like, with notification handling replacing URL handling.)

The delegate method can choose to handle the notification or to ignore it. Typical methods either update an "available data" list or downloading new data. For example, if your user subscribes to a PDF-based newsletter, a push system would allow the user to know when new editions were available. The user would then launch your application to download and read those issues.

Summary

This chapter introduced a wide range network supporting technologies. You've seen how to add preferences panes, build custom URL schemes, check for network connectivity, work with keychains, and more. Here are a few thoughts to take away with you before leaving this chapter:

- Keychains provide a high level of program security, but they cannot be integrated into those easy-to-use custom settings panes. Consider carefully whether a minimal security approach of obscuring the password is enough for your program. If so, you can bypass the keychain and take advantage of one of the nicest developer integration features on the iPhone.

- Although custom URL schemes provide a limited application-to-application communication pattern, you can also launch one application from another by calling the (undocumented) `launchApplicationWithIdentifier: suspended:` method.

- Most of Apple's networking support is provided through very low-level C-based routines. If you can find a friendly Objective-C wrapper to simplify your programming work, consider using it. The only drawback occurs when you specifically need tight networking control at the most basic level of your application.

- Even when Apple provides Objective-C wrappers, as they do with `NSXMLParser`, it's not always the class you wanted or hoped for. Adapting classes is a big part of the iPhone programming experience.

11

One More Thing:
Programming Cover Flow

Although Cover Flow is not officially included in the iPhone SDK, it offers one of the most beautiful features of the iPhone experience. With Cover Flow, you can offer users a gorgeously intense visual selection that puts standard scrolling lists to shame. This chapter introduces Cover Flow and shows how you can use it in your applications. Boom!

The `UICoverFlowLayer` Class

`UICoverFlowLayer` is a standard `UIKit` class although it does not appear in the official SDK. Steve Nygard's class-dump (www.codethecode.com/projects/class-dump/) enabled me to extract the `UICoverFlowLayer` header file shown in Listing 11-1 from the `UIKit` framework. Class-dump works by generating class declarations from the Objective-C segments of Mach-O files.

Listing 11-1   The UICoverFlowLayer.h Class Header

```
/*
 *      Generated by class-dump 3.1.1.
 *
 *      class-dump is Copyright (C) 1997-1998, 2000-2001, 2004-2006 by Steve
 *Nygard.
 */


@interface UICoverFlowLayer : NSObject
{
    void *_private;
}

- (id)initWithFrame:(struct CGRect)fp8 numberOfCovers:(unsigned int)fp24;
- (void)dealloc;
- (void)setDelegate:(id)fp8;
```

Listing 11-1 **Continued**

```
- (void)setPlaceholderImage:(void *)fp8;
- (void)_prefetch:(unsigned int)fp8 atIndex:(unsigned int)fp12;
- (void)_requestBatch;
- (void)addSublayer:(id)fp8;
- (void)_requestImageAtIndex:(int)fp8 quality:(unsigned int)fp12;
- (void)_requestImageAtIndex:(int)fp8;
- (void)_notifySelectionDidChange;
- (void)startHeartbeat:(SEL) aSelector inRunLoopMode: (id)whatever2;
- (void)transitionIn:(float)fp8;
- (void)transitionOut:(float)fp8;
- (void)transition:(unsigned int)fp8 withCoverFrame:(struct CGRect)fp12;
- (void)transitionIn:(float)fp8 fromFrame:(struct CGRect)fp12;
- (void)transitionOut:(float)fp8 toFrame:(struct CGRect)fp12;
- (void)setDisplayedOrientation:(int)fp8 animate:(BOOL)fp12;
- (void)setInfoLayer:(id)fp8;
- (void)setImage:(void *)fp8 atIndex:(unsigned int)fp12 type:(unsigned int)fp16;
- (void)setImage:(void *)fp8 atIndex:(unsigned int)fp12 type:(unsigned int)fp16
➥imageSubRect:(struct _NSRect)fp20;
- (void)setImage:(void *)fp8 atIndex:(unsigned int)fp12;
- (unsigned int)indexOfSelectedCover;
- (unsigned int)_coverAtScreenPosition:(struct CGPoint)fp8;
- (void)_recycleLayer:(int)fp8 to:(int)fp12;
- (void)_setNewSelectedIndex:(int)fp8;
- (void)_updateTick;
- (void)displayTick;
- (void)dragFlow:(unsigned int)fp8 atPoint:(struct CGPoint)fp12;
- (void)selectCoverAtIndex:(unsigned int)fp8;
- (void)selectCoverAtOffset:(int)fp8;
- (unsigned int)coverIndexAtPosition:(float)fp8;
- (void)_setupFlippedCoverLayer:(id)fp8;
- (void)flipSelectedCover;
- (int)benchmarkTick;
- (void)benchmarkHeartbeatLongScrub;
- (void)benchmarkHeartbeatShortScrub;
- (void)benchmarkHeartbeatScrubAndWait;
- (void)benchmarkTightLoop;
- (void)benchmarkTightLoopScrub;
- (BOOL)benchmarkLoadScrub;
- (BOOL)benchmarkImageManager:(void *)fp8;
- (void)benchmarkSetEnv;
- (void)benchmarkMode:(int)fp8;
- (void)benchmarkTickMode:(int)fp8;
- (void)benchmarkImageMode:(int)fp8;
- (void)benchmarkPerformanceLog:(BOOL)fp8;
- (void)benchmarkTightLoopTime:(unsigned int)fp8;
```

Listing 11-1   **Continued**

```
- (void)benchmarkLongScrubSpeed:(float)fp8;
- (void)benchmarkSkipImageLoad:(BOOL)fp8;
@end
```

As this listing shows, the `UICoverFlowLayer` class defines a layer, not a view. Layers are the abstract rendering class that lies inside every `UIView` object, providing an internal canvas for those views. So if you're going to use this class, you need to wrap it in a usable view. The next section shows you how.

Building a Cover Flow View

To start working with Cover Flow, you need to insert `UICoverFlowLayer` instances into `UIViews`. Placing layers into a view brings Cover Flow technology into standard `UIKit` terms, letting you work with the `UIView` class you've seen throughout this book. To accomplish this, you do nothing more than create the view and assign the layer. Getting the view to display and work properly takes a few more steps.

Those extra steps mean customizing the way that users interact with Cover Flow. The Cover Flow view needs to respond properly when users touch, drag, and tap within the view. To do this, the view must hand off touch and drag interactions to the Cover Flow layer by sending `dragFlow: atPoint:` messages.

Double-tap handling provides a different challenge. The Cover Flow layer does not implement any standard response to double-taps. Instead, you want your application to recognize that interaction and provide some meaningful response. The way I designed this class, you can set a host that conforms to the `CoverFlowHost` protocol. When the view intercepts double-taps, it invokes the host's `doubleTapCallback` method. This enables the view controller that owns the Cover Flow view to respond when users perform a double-tap on the selected cover.

Cover flipping refers to the interaction where a Cover Flow image flips out of the way to reveal a secondary view (`flipSelectedCover`). As a rule, you can use double-tap feedback or you can use cover flipping, but do choose one or the other. By implementing both, you cause the two interaction styles to unnecessarily compete, and you may not be able to control which response gets called.

> **Note**
>
> The complete project for this chapter appears in this book's sample code. See
> http://ericasadun.com for details.

Listing 11-2   **Building a Cover Flow View**

```
#import <UIKit/UIKit.h>
#import "UICoverFlowLayer.h"
```

Listing 11-2   **Continued**

```
@protocol CoverFlowHost <NSObject>
- (void) doubleTapCallback;
@end

@interface CoverFlowView : UIView {
    id                      <CoverFlowHost> host;
    id                      info;
    UICoverFlowLayer        *cfLayer;
    UILabel                 *label;
}
- (CoverFlowView *) initWithFrame: (CGRect) aFrame andCount: (int) aCount;
- (void) tick;
- (void) setHost: (id)anObject;
- (void) flipSelectedCover;
- (UILabel *) label;
- (UICoverFlowLayer *) cfLayer;
@end
@implementation CoverFlowView

- (CoverFlowView *) initWithFrame: (CGRect) aRect andCount: (int) count
{
    self = [super initWithFrame:aRect];
    cfLayer = [[UICoverFlowLayer alloc] initWithFrame:[[UIScreen mainScreen]
    ➥bounds] numberOfCovers:count];
    [[self layer] addSublayer:cfLayer];

    // Add the placeholder (image stand-in) layer
    CGRect phrect = CGRectMake(0.0f, 0.0f, 200.0f, 200.0f);
    UIImageView *phimg = [[UIImageView alloc] initWithFrame:phrect];
    [cfLayer setPlaceholderImage: [phimg layer]];

    // Add its info (label) layer
    label = [[UILabel alloc] init];
    [label setTextAlignment:UITextAlignmentCenter];
    [label setFont:[UIFont boldSystemFontOfSize:20.0f]];
    [label setBackgroundColor:[UIColor colorWithRed:0.0f green:0.0f blue:0.0f
    ➥alpha:0.0f]];
    [label setTextColor:[UIColor colorWithRed:1.0f green:1.0f blue:1.0f
    ➥alpha:0.75f]];
    [label setNumberOfLines:2];
    [label setLineBreakMode:UILineBreakModeWordWrap];
    [cfLayer setInfoLayer:[label layer]];

    return self;
}
```

Listing 11-2   **Continued**

```
- (void) touchesBegan:(NSSet*)touches withEvent:(UIEvent*)event
{
    UITouch *touch = [touches anyObject];
    CGPoint pt = [touch locationInView:self];
    [cfLayer dragFlow:0 atPoint:pt];
}


- (void) touchesMoved:(NSSet*)touches withEvent:(UIEvent*)event
{
    UITouch *touch = [touches anyObject];
    CGPoint pt = [touch locationInView:self];
    [cfLayer dragFlow:1 atPoint:pt];
}

- (void) touchesEnded:(NSSet*)touches withEvent:(UIEvent*)event
{
    UITouch *touch = [touches anyObject];
    CGPoint pt = [touch locationInView:self];

    if ([touch tapCount] == 2)
    {
        if (host) [host doubleTapCallback];
        return;
    }

    [cfLayer dragFlow:2 atPoint:pt];
}
- (void) flipSelectedCover
{
    [cfLayer flipSelectedCover];
}


- (BOOL) ignoresMouseEvents {return NO;}
- (void) tick {[cfLayer displayTick];}
- (void) setHost: (id)anObject {host = anObject;}
- (UILabel *) label {return label;}
- (UICoverFlowLayer *) cfLayer {return cfLayer;}
@end
```

Building a Cover Flow View Controller

Once the CoverFlowView class is established, you can add that view to any view controller you like. The secret to making everything work lies in checking off several to-do boxes. The following sections show the steps you need to take to make your Cover Flow presentation work best:

- **Hide the application status bar.** Your Cover Flow application should occupy the entire screen without a distracting status bar on hand. Hide the status bar by calling `[[UIApplication sharedApplication] setStatusBarHidden:YES]`.

- **Allocate and initialize the view.** You must know in advance the number of covers you'll use. Prepare the cover art and title strings. These power the view data source. Then pass the initializer a count of the covers.

- **Start the heartbeat.** Wait until your `loadView` method to set the Cover Flow as your main view, and then start its heartbeat for the current run loop.

- **Supply delegate and data source methods.** Make sure your view controller can handle the required Cover Flow delegate and data source callbacks. Details about these required and optional methods follow in the next sections.

When you've accomplished each of these goals, you should have a working Cover Flow presentation quickly up and running. Figure 11-1 shows a Cover Flow interface built by the view controller established in Listing 11-3. In this Cover Flow, users are presented with crayon colors as a series of circular swatches. Tapping flips the swatch and reveals the six-character hex code for that color.

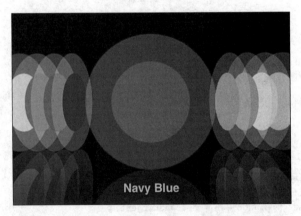

Navy Blue

Figure 11-1   The undocumented `UIKit` Cover Flow layer class allows you to build compelling image-based Cover Flow presentations in your applications.

Cover Flow Data Source Methods

For standard Cover Flow operation, your view controller supplies `UIImages` to the `coverFlow: requestImageAtIndex: quality:` method. Use the supplied index to determine which image to return. This method is required for the data source to work properly. For faster loading, use lazy image generation rather than the array I use here—create the images you need on-the-fly. You can store them into a sparse dictionary, only building those images that are used.

Flip layers are optional. They're the layers that enable your center covers to flip when a user taps them. When working with flip layers, add a `coverFlow:requestFlipLayerAtIndex:` method to your view controller. This method returns an image layer showing the back of the flipped item.

Cover Flow Delegate Methods

As with tables, Cover Flow views produce a `selectionDidChange:` callback when users pick a new cover. Use this method to update the displayed label text and to keep track of which item was most recently selected.

Another delegate method, `coverFlowFlipDidEnd:`, lets you know when any flip animation completes. This method is called for both front to back flips as well as for back to front flips, so keep track of the state; note whether the flip view is out or hidden.

Listing 11-3   **Build a Cover Flow View in a View Controller**

```
#import <UIKit/UIKit.h>
#import "CoverFlowView.h"

@interface CoverViewController : UIViewController
{
    CoverFlowView          *cfView;
    UICoverFlowLayer       *cfLayer;
    UILabel                *label;
    NSMutableArray         *covers;
    NSMutableArray         *titles;
    int                    whichItem;
    id                     target;
    SEL                    selector;

    NSMutableDictionary    *colorDict;
    UILabel                *flippedView;
    BOOL                   flipOut;
}
@end


// ********************************************
// Cover Flow View Controller
//
@implementation CoverViewController
- (CoverViewController *) init
{
    if (!(self = [super init])) return self;
```

Listing 11-3   **Continued**

```objc
// Read in the crayons and set up the arrays and dictionaries
NSArray *crayons = [[NSString stringWithContentsOfFile:[[NSBundle mainBundle]
➥pathForResource:@"crayons" ofType:@"txt"]]
➥componentsSeparatedByString:@"\n"];
covers = [[NSMutableArray alloc] init];
titles = [[NSMutableArray alloc] init];
colorDict = [[NSMutableDictionary alloc] init];

// Create the title and cover arrays
for (NSString *crayon in crayons)
{
    NSArray *theCrayon = [crayon componentsSeparatedByString:@"#"];
    if ([theCrayon count] != 2) continue;
    [titles addObject:[theCrayon objectAtIndex:0]];
    [covers addObject:createImage([theCrayon objectAtIndex:1])];
    [colorDict setObject:[theCrayon objectAtIndex:1] forKey:[theCrayon
    ➥objectAtIndex:0]];
}

// Create the flip object
CGRect fliprect = CGRectMake(0.0f, 0.0f, 480.0f, 480.0f);
flippedView = [[FlipView alloc] initWithFrame:fliprect];
[flippedView setTransform:CGAffineTransformMakeRotation(3.141592f / 2.0f)];
[flippedView setUserInteractionEnabled:YES];

// Initialize
cfView = [[CoverFlowView alloc] initWithFrame:[[UIScreen mainScreen]
➥applicationFrame] andCount:[titles count]];
[cfView setUserInteractionEnabled:YES];
[cfView setHost:self];
cfLayer = [cfView cfLayer];
label = [cfView label];

// Finish setting up the Cover Flow layer
whichItem = [titles count] / 2;
[cfLayer selectCoverAtIndex:whichItem];
[cfLayer setDelegate:self];

selector = NULL;
target = NULL;

return self;
}

// *********************************************
// Cover Flow delegate methods
//
```

Listing 11-3 **Continued**

```objc
- (void) coverFlow: (id) coverFlow selectionDidChange: (int) index
{
    whichItem = index;
    [label setText:[titles objectAtIndex:index]];
}


// Detect the end of the flip - both on reveal and hide
- (void) coverFlowFlipDidEnd: (UICoverFlowLayer *)coverFlow
{
    if (flipOut)
        [[[UIApplication sharedApplication] keyWindow] addSubview:flippedView];
    else
        [flippedView removeFromSuperview];
}
// ********************************************
// Cover Flow datasource methods
//

- (void) coverFlow:(id)coverFlow requestImageAtIndex: (int)index quality:
➥(int)quality
{
    UIImage *whichImg = [covers objectAtIndex:index];
    [coverFlow setImage:[whichImg CGImage]  atIndex:index type:quality]; // used
➥to be cfLayer
}

// Return a flip layer, one that preferably integrates into the flip presentation
➥- (id) coverFlow: (UICoverFlowLayer *)coverFlow requestFlipLayerAtIndex: (int)
➥index
{
    if (flipOut) [flippedView removeFromSuperview];
    flipOut = !flipOut;

    // Prepare the flip text
    [flippedView setText:[NSString stringWithFormat:@"%@\n%@", [titles
objectAtIndex:index], [colorDict objectForKey:[titles objectAtIndex:index]]]];

    // Flip with a simple blank square
    UIView *view = [[UIView alloc] initWithFrame:CGRectMake(0.0f, 0.0f, 140.0f,
➥140.0f)];
    [view setBackgroundColor:[UIColor clearColor]];

    return [view layer];
}


// ********************************************
```

Listing 11-3   **Continued**

```
// Utility methods
//

- (CoverFlowView *) cfView {return cfView; }
- (UICoverFlowLayer *) cfLayer {return cfLayer; }
- (int) selectedItem {return whichItem; }

- (void) start
{
    [cfView startHeartbeat: @selector(tick) inRunLoopMode:
    ➥(id)kCFRunLoopDefaultMode];
    [cfLayer transitionIn:1.0f];
}

- (void) stop
{
    [cfView stopHeartbeat: @selector(tick)];
}

- (void) loadView
{
    [super loadView];
    self.view = cfView;
    [self start];
}

// **********************************************
// Callback method for double tap
//
- (void) doubleTapCallback
{
}
@end
```

Summary

As you've seen in this chapter, and throughout this book, some of the nicest bits of
iPhone programming are included in the public iPhone frameworks but not in the SDK.
Apple's unofficial policy on this is clear: You can use these items in your programs, but
you do so at your own risk. Your code may break at each firmware release. Striking the
balance between risk and reward is up to you.

A

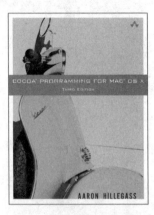

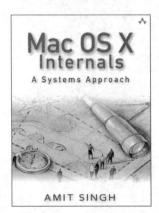

Developer's Library

ESSENTIAL REFERENCES FOR PROGRAMMING PROFESSIONALS

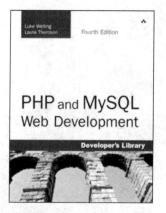

PHP & MySQL Web Development, Fourth Edition

Luke Welling and Laura Thomson

ISBN-13: 978-0-672-32916-6

Programming in Objective-C 2.0

Stephen G. Kochan

ISBN-13: 978-0-321-56615-7

Mac OS X Leopard Phrasebook

Brian Tiemann

ISBN-13: 978-0-672-32954-8

Other Developer's Library Titles

TITLE	AUTHOR	ISBN-13
MySQL, Fourth Edition	Paul DuBois	978-0-672-32938-8
Zend Studio for Eclipse Developer's Guide	Peter MacIntyre / Ian Morse	978-0-672-32940-1
Ruby Phrasebook	Jason D. Clinton	978-0-672-32897-8
Dojo: Using the Dojo JavaScript Library to Build Ajax Applications	James E. Harmon	978-0-13-235804-0

Developer's Library books are available at most retail and online bookstores. For more information or to order direct visit our online bookstore at **informit.com/store**

Online editions of all Developer's Library titles are available by subscription from Safari Books Online at **safari.informit.com**

Developer's Library

informit.com/devlibrary

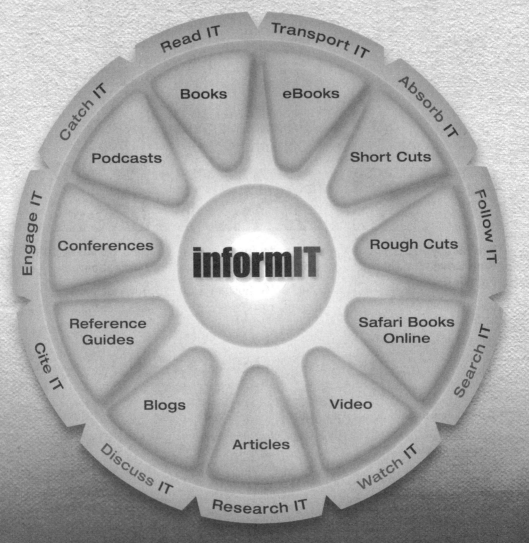

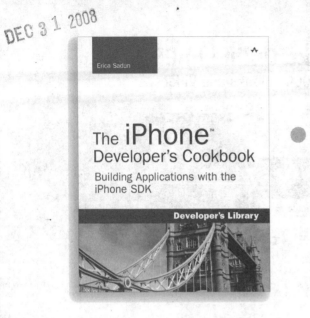